New Family Values

New Family Values

Liberty, Equality, Diversity

Karen Struening

ROWMAN & LITTLEFIELD PUBLISHERS, INC.
Lanham • Boulder • New York • Oxford

ROWMAN & LITTLEFIELD PUBLISHERS, INC.

Published in the United States of America
by Rowman & Littlefield Publishers, Inc.
4720 Boston Way, Lanham, Maryland 20706
www.rowmanlittlefield.com

12 Hid's Copse Road
Cumnor Hill, Oxford OX2 9JJ, England

British Library Cataloguing in Publication Information Available

Library of Congress Cataloging-in-Publication Data

Struening Karen, 1960–
  New family values : liberty, equality, diversity / Karen Struening.
    p. cm.
Includes bibliographical references and index
  ISBN 0-7425-1230-4 (cloth: alk. paper)—ISBN 0-7425-1231-2 (pbk. : alk. paper)
  1. Family—United States. 2. Liberty. I. Title.
HQ536 .S82 2002
306.85'0973—dc21
                                        2002001813

Printed in the United States of America

∞™ The paper used in this publication meets the minimum requirements of American National Standard for Information Sciences—Permanence of Paper for Printed Library Materials, ANSI/NISO Z39.48-1992.

Contents

Acknowledgments

I want to thank three teachers who were especially important to my education in political and social theory: Joan Cocks, Jim Schmidt, and Andy Markovits. My research and writing on the topic of family values began at Kalamazoo College. I am grateful for the encouragement I received from colleagues Chris Latiolais, Bob Stauffer, Tom Smith, and Ahmed Hussen. I owe a special debt of gratitude to Morris Kaplan, whose pathbreaking work on privacy rights is a primary source of inspiration for this book. I also want to give my heartfelt thanks to Christina di Stefano for her continued support of this project. Elmer L. Struening, Jennifer Case, Paul Davis, Jerry Mayer, Jennifer Uleman, and Marilyn Power each read early chapter drafts and I am grateful for their helpful comments. A special thanks goes to James Clarke for reading and providing advice on each chapter. I explored many of the themes developed in this book with students at Kalamazoo College, Barnard College, Eugene Lang College at New School University, and Sarah Lawrence College. Their questions and comments strengthened the arguments that appear here. I am grateful to my editor, Eve DeVaro, and the dedicated editorial and production staff at Rowman & Littlefield for their support in bringing this book to completion. For teaching me the value of family, I want to thank my sister, Aviva Struening, and my parents, Elmer L. Struening and Karen Sue Struening. And for teaching me the value of lifelong partnership, I want to thank James Clarke.

Introduction

The welfare of families is an important state interest because it is difficult for people, adults as well as children, to do well unless they receive support from others. Very few individuals are truly self-sufficient. Most adults are a paycheck, or an illness, or some other personal crisis away from needing the help of other caring adults. The very survival of children, including their development to maturity, depends on the presence of an adequate caretaker. To be isolated and alone, cut off from others, is dangerous to mental and physical health. Caring families of various forms, both traditional and nontraditional, are essential to the well-being of their members.[1] When families successfully care for and nurture their members, they make an inestimable contribution to the larger society.

Since the 1970s the two-parent family has become less common, and nontraditional forms of family have been on the rise. Married couples with children declined from 40 percent of all households in 1970 to 24 percent of all households in 2000.[2] According to the National Survey of America's Families, an ongoing study conducted by the Washington, D.C.-based Urban Institute, 64 percent of children under age eighteen live with two biological or adoptive parents.[3] A significant number of children live in lesbian or gay families. It is estimated that out of the 70.2 million children in the United States, between 6 and 14 million live with at least one lesbian or gay parent.[4] Single-parent families, most of which are headed by women, make up 31 percent of all families with children.[5] However, some of these single parents have cohabiting partners who are not the biological parents of their children. Sixteen percent of children living with single fathers and 9 percent of children living with single mothers also live with their parents' partners. Three percent of children live with two unmarried biological or adoptive parents, 8 percent live in blended families, and 4 percent live in households or institutional settings that do not include a parent.[6] These figures suggest that families in the United States take a variety of forms.

What counts as a family and what families should look like is a topic on which the citizens of the United States are deeply divided. Some parties to the debate argue that divorce, nonmarital birth, and the growth of alternative family forms pose a tremendous threat to children and to the larger society. Those who oppose family diversity argue that one form of family—the married, two-biological-parent family—is clearly superior to all nontraditional family forms such as blended families, single-parent families, cohabiting couples, families composed of grandparents and grandchildren, and lesbian and gay families. Supporters of the traditional family argue that it should be promoted by law and policy. Others, including myself, assert that all family forms should be treated equally and that nontraditional family forms should be supported with rights and resources.[7]

This is a book about progressive and feminist family values. I argue that thinking about families and family policy should consider three principles—liberty, equality, and diversity. Without personal liberty in sexuality, procreation, and intimate association, women and men are not able to be self-determining in matters of the heart. Great weight is attributed to emotional intimacy in contemporary society. Caring for others and being cared for is understood to be constitutive of whom we are. Our intimate relations with others make an important contribution to our self-development and individuality. Therefore, restricting the ability of the individual to control the nature of her or his intimate associations with others violates an important liberty. Moreover, if the state is to treat all of its citizens with equal concern and respect, it must protect their personal liberty.[8] When legislators and political officials use their political authority to promote one form of family over others, they fail to treat all of their citizens equally.

Fully embracing the principles of liberty and equality means expanding the definition of what counts as a family and recognizing single-parent, extended, blended, and lesbian and gay families as legitimate family forms. It means endorsing the idea that the defining feature of family life is the commitment to care. It also requires the state to take an affirmative role in promoting the health and well-being of all families. In some cases, this will mean providing low-income families that are struggling to survive with income supports, subsidies, and new economic opportunities.

In contrast to the position I have just outlined, supporters of more traditional family values assert that the state should take an active role in strengthening the two-biological-parent family. This book provides a feminist and progressive response to a group of scholars and authors who are opposed to family diversity and who argue that one family form is superior to all others. I am not concerned here with the arguments of right-wing activists or politicians like Pat Robertson or Pat Buchanan, nor do I take aim at leading conservative academics such as Charles Murray,[9] Lawrence Mead,[10] or James Q. Wilson.[11] Instead, this book analyzes the arguments of self-described political moderates such as William Galston,[12] Jean Bethke Elshtain,[13] Barbara Dafoe Whitehead,[14] Mary Ann Glendon,[15] David Popenoe,[16] and David Blankenhorn.[17] These authors are not likely to be considered right wing or extremely conservative in their views. In the words of sociologist David Popenoe, "Most of us are neoliberal—you know, New Democrats, affiliated with the Progressive Policy Institute. We try to keep to the middle of the road."[18] These scholars and authors work together to influence public opinion and family policy through their articles, books, forums, and conferences. Several of the authors listed above have edited books together and all of them belong to the Council on Families in America (CFA). The Institute for American Values, codirected by Blankenhorn and Whitehead, has sponsored several of their conferences and publications.

Throughout this book, I refer to the scholars and authors I discuss as "family communitarians." I do this to underscore the fact that their views on the two-parent family are embedded in a virtue-based political philosophy. A variety of political theorists have been grouped together under the rubric of communitarianism in recent years.[19] I am using the term here to refer to those authors who reject the liberal tenet that principles of justice provide a sufficient basis for a democratic society.[20] Communitarians argue that principles of justice are not enough; a well-functioning democracy requires a substantive conception of the common good or a shared set of moral values. According to communitarians, liberalism places too much emphasis on protecting personal liberty and individual rights. This emphasis on the individual and her freedom to make her own choices makes it difficult to maintain a sense of common purposes and shared moral values. But without a shared understanding of the common good, citizens become disengaged from the political process. As both Elshtain[21] and Galston[22] argue, once our sense of common purposes and values has been eroded, a vibrant democracy cannot be maintained. In order to maintain our identity as a democratic political community, we need to share more than a commitment to equal rights and liberties. We need to embrace a common vision of the good life.

I refer to the family communitarians as *communitarians* because a critique of personal liberty and individual rights is central to their account of why and how the American family is being undermined. They hold that the scope of personal liberty has become overly expansive in the last thirty years and that this has allowed men and women to disregard their family obligations. I refer to this group of scholars as *family* communitarians because they believe that the two-parent family is the primary source of moral values.[23] Without the proper moral education, young people will not become good citizens.

The goal of the family communitarians is to revive a moral culture that will support the intact, married, two-parent, heterosexual family. Strengthening the two-parent family requires opposing the social acceptance of nontraditional families, such as blended families, single-parent families, and lesbian and gay families. If nontraditional family forms lose their social stigma, the normative force of the two-parent family will decline. While moral culture is first and foremost a matter of beliefs and values that cannot be mandated by the state, family communitarians claim that law and policy have an important role to play in changing behavior. They seek to enlist the state in promoting marriage and the two-parent family. They argue that every possible public policy should be used to promote marriage and to discourage divorce, out-of-wedlock childbearing, and what they refer to as alternative lifestyles.[24]

It is important to analyze the family communitarians' position because they have been able to broaden the appeal of conservative family values beyond its traditional constituency of religious conservatives and evangelicals. Instead of taking a fiercely antifeminist and antigay stance, family communitarians have developed a softer position that appeals to those who find the angry rhetoric of more conservative family values advocates offensive. Moreover, while they frequently speak of the importance and value of religion, family communitarians do not represent any one religious perspective. And, they do not quote scripture to provide support for their arguments. Instead, they use social science research to defend their positions.[25]

However, while they have successfully toned down the angry rhetoric, the positions supported by family communitarians are often much closer to those of their conservative colleagues than they might at first appear to be. For example, family communitarians are careful to say that they support equal rights and opportunities for women. However, this statement conflicts with their support for the gender-based division of labor in the home. Scholars have shown that if women remain responsible for the vast majority of housework and childcare, they will not enjoy equal opportunities in work, school, or politics.[26] In addition, most family communitarians avoid discussing lesbian and gay rights, but consistently argue that the acceptance of "alternative lifestyles" poses a threat to the traditional family.[27] And, while some of the family communitarians assert their respect for single mothers, they consistently blame these same families for high rates of crime, drug use, teen pregnancy, and low educational achievement.[28] Unlike right-wing commentators and politicians, the family communitarians have been successful at portraying themselves as not *against* anyone or anything, but only *for* a revival of marriage and the two-parent family. But, the truth is that their position defines anyone who does not conform to the traditional family as morally deficient and as a potential threat to the greater society.

Family communitarians are not the only political moderates who have sounded an alarm concerning rising rates of divorce and nonmarital birth during the last twenty years. Throughout the 1980s and 1990s, social scientists have linked changes in family structure with the deep and persistent poverty that characterizes very low-income neighborhoods in cities and rural areas.[29] However, there is an important difference between progressive social scientists and family communitarians. Social scientists such as William Julius Wilson,[30] Christopher Jencks,[31] and Sara McLanahan[32] argue for economic reforms and social programs that would help fragile families stay together and would assist single mothers in caring for their children.[33] Instead of calling for the elimination of no-fault divorce, the restigmatization of nonmarital birth, and the removal of children from their teen mothers—ideas that are popular with the family communitarians—these scholars focus on improving education and economic opportunities, investing in low-income communities, and providing income supports and subsidies for low-wage workers.

Family communitarians are right to connect the well-being of families with the health of the greater society. If a society is to flourish, its members must be able to depend on their families for care and nurture. As Aristotle explains in the opening of *The Politics*, human beings are not self-sufficient on their own. Consequently, they need to form partnerships and associations in order to meet a wide range of needs.[34] But where both Aristotle and the family communitarians go wrong is in thinking that these partnerships and families must take one form. With the proper social and economic supports in place, a variety of different kinds of families are capable of caring for their members. The goal of family policy should not be to use every mechanism at our disposal to privilege marriage and the two-parent family. This insults and denigrates blended families, single-parent families, and lesbian and gay families. Instead, we should restructure our society so that nontraditional forms of family are not placed at a disadvantage. Policies that promote one form of family violate the principles of liberty and equality. They violate liberty by failing to respect the right of the individual to choose the nature and form of her intimate associations. They violate equality by failing to provide citizens who choose to live in nontraditional families with the same rights and resources that are enjoyed by those who choose to live in traditional families.

The response to growing family diversity advocated by the family communitarians will undermine personal liberty, stigmatize and marginalize nontraditional forms of family, and fail to alleviate or actually contribute to gender, racial, and economic inequality. In contrast, I advocate a family policy guided by three moral principles—liberty, equality, and diversity. These are not the only principles that should be considered when we think about families, but they are essential to constructing policies that are appropriate to a democratic society in which citizens regard one another as equals.

LIBERTY

Personal liberty includes sexual freedom, reproductive freedom, and the freedom to form and exit the intimate associations of one's own choosing. To employ Justice Harry Blackmun's words in his dissent to the *Bowers v. Hardwick* 478 U.S. 186 (1986) decision, personal liberty includes "the freedom to control the form and nature of our intimate associations."[35] Liberty in sexual and intimate relationships is essential to both independent identity formation, or individuality, and personal happiness. Our intimate associations are formative of "who we are and who we want to be."[36] Constraining and limiting personal liberty has grave costs for individuals. It prevents them from exercising self-determination in what is for many people the most important area of their lives. Women and men should be able to determine for themselves the meaning and value of sexuality, procreation, marriage, and parenting. When the state promotes one family form it violates the personal liberty of its citizens.

DIVERSITY

It is impossible to use law and policy to promote the traditional family without insulting nontraditional families. When the married, heterosexual, two-parent family is held up as the ideal family form, adults and children who live in nontraditional families are stigmatized for failing to conform to convention and custom. Moreover, when families are labeled as illegitimate, it becomes easier to deny them the social supports that they need. Family communitarians have not written extensively about welfare reform. However, they are among the strongest critics of single parenthood. They support the position that poverty is a consequence of irresponsible personal behavior, and they downplay the roles that racial and gender discrimination and the inadequacies of the low-wage labor market play in creating economic hardship for single-mother families.[37] Policymakers have used the argument that single motherhood causes poverty to regulate the procreative choices of, and cut public support for, low-income single mothers.[38]

In contrast, recognizing diverse forms of family protects the liberty interests of adults and benefits children living in nontraditional families by protecting their relationships with their caregivers.[39] Advocates of family uniformity argue that the family has one key purpose—raising good citizens—and that the intact, married, heterosexual, two-parent family should be promoted by the state because it is best able to fulfill this key purpose. I argue that families are multipurpose associations and that a variety of nontraditional family forms, including single-parent and lesbian and gay families, are capable of meeting the needs of their members. When the state promotes one form of family over others it discriminates against its citizens. Treating citizens with equal concern and respect requires the state to recognize and protect nontraditional family forms.

In addition, recognizing and protecting diverse forms of families makes sense if we believe that most individuals, adults as well as children, benefit from living in partnerships and associations. The argument that the state has a special interest in promoting one form of family is false. This position would reduce the number of individuals who are knit together in associations based on economic cooperation, caretaking, and mutual support. It would, for example, deny children in the foster care system loving homes provided by lesbian and gay parents. In contrast, state policies that support diverse forms of family would proliferate and increase the number of people, children and adults, whose relationships are legally protected.

EQUALITY

In the United States, economic opportunity and the ability to become economically secure are strongly influenced by race, ethnicity, and immigrant status. Our nation's history of slavery, segregation in housing, schools, and jobs, and its refusal to treat African Americans or recently arrived immigrants as legal and political equals has often resulted in the intertwining of racial status and economic status. Black men and women are much more likely than whites to grow up poor, have poor health, lack assets, live in poverty, and experience long periods of unemployment.[40] This is also true for Latinos and Native Americans. According to the National Survey of America's Families (NSAF), 27 percent of black families and 26 percent of Latino families were poor by official standards in 1998. This means that they lived at or below the poverty line, which was $16,660 for a family of four in 1998. In comparison, only 8 percent of white families were poor. Over half of black and Hispanic families are classified as low-income because their income is below 200 percent of the poverty line. In contrast, 24 percent of white families have incomes below 200 percent of the poverty line.[41]

Poverty and racism, combined and interlocking, can present parents with daunting circumstances in which to raise children. As scholars such as Dorothy Roberts and Bonnie Thornton Dill have argued, it is not just the lack of economic resources that works against low-income families of color, but also a lack of ideological and institutional support.[42] While white, middle-class babies are welcomed into the world with joy, the media and policymakers often portray low-income children of color as a potential source of crime or as a potential drain on the state.

Many white families also struggle with unemployment, underemployment, declining wages and incomes, and scant social support. A large number of these families live in rural areas that are often ignored in discussions of poverty.[43] Whatever their racial or ethnic background, low-income parents, many of whom are single mothers, find it very difficult to control the environment in which their children grow up. They cannot provide their children with suitable and warm housing, clean streets, healthy food, health care, good schools, or safe places to play. Nor can low-income parents effectively protect their children from violence, crime, and substance use. Studies have found that "children raised in low-income families score lower than children from more affluent families do on assessments of health, cognitive development, school achievement, and emotional well-being."[44] Compared to their better-off peers, children living below the poverty line also are more likely to become teen parents and, as adults, to earn less and be unemployed more frequently.[45] As individuals, low-income parents have neither the economic resources nor the political influence needed to change their communities. Moreover, there is little they can do to alter their children's sense that politicians and the general public do not care about them or their community. The parents of poor children cannot protect their children from the degrading effects of being poor in an affluent country.[46]

For the most part, family communitarians ignore the harm caused to children by income inequality and poverty. However, many social scientists claim that low income is the most important factor in determining children's achievement and ability outcomes.[47] In this book, I argue that the best way to strengthen families is to provide low-income families with greater support, services, and opportunities, and to invest public and private funds in their neighborhoods. Low-income families are often socially isolated and lack connections to the community-based and governmental organizations that could provide them with support. Families function best when they are embedded in larger associations such as neighborhood centers, religious institutions, schools, health clinics, and community-based social service agencies. Through their membership in these associations, family members can participate in the political decisions that affect their communities and neighborhoods.

While family communitarians fail to address economic and racial inequality, they launch a direct assault on gender equality. According to Popenoe, a sociologist, and Blankenhorn, the Director of the Institute for American Values, if we want to reduce the high number of fatherless families, we must recommit ourselves to traditional gender roles and reject the egalitarian model of family in which men and women share breadwinning and childcare. Both authors argue that even within dual-earner couples, men should be recognized as the primary breadwinners and women should be considered the primary caretakers. However, as I stated earlier, many feminist authors have shown that traditional gender roles undermine the effort of women to achieve equality in the labor market, civil society, and politics. In addition, conventional gender roles compel women to be economically dependent on men, and subsequently provide a material basis for male dominance in the household.[48]

I endorse the feminist critique of the gender-based division of labor and defend the egalitarian model of family in which breadwinning and child rearing are shared. The egalitarian model best realizes the goal of equal opportunities for women in the public sphere, and provides the basis for an equal partnership between men and women in the home. However, it should be recognized that men and women choose more conventional ways of dividing parenting duties for a variety of reasons, including the lack of high-quality, affordable childcare and the belief that caring for children is more important and more rewarding than making money or succeeding in a career. Under current conditions, few parents—whether they care for their children themselves or pay for their children to be cared for by others—are entirely satisfied with their childcare arrangements. All of the available methods of caring for children have costs and benefits. My purpose is not to devalue women's caretaking in the home, but to raise awareness about the costs of traditional, gender-based family roles and to argue against the view that all men and women are obligated to conform to them.

To argue, as I will, that the family communitarians' analysis of family instability and diversity is deeply flawed, is not to take the position that the changes that have altered family life in the last thirty years have been uniformly beneficial to children, adults, and the greater society. Divorce is clearly traumatic for most children.[49] It often means that they are separated from a parent, usually their father, who likely provided them with care and material support. Women who bear children while they are still in their teens are more likely to drop out of high school and to earn less than their peers who postponed childbirth.[50] Policymakers, social service providers, and the research community must respond to the consequences of family instability. But the question remains, how should they respond? The solutions offered by family communitarians are punitive and operate by stigmatizing men and women who divorce and young women who are sexually active. In contrast, it is possible to devise policies that encourage noncustodial parents to remain active in the lives of their children, and that offer poor teenagers a future so that they are more motivated to consistently use birth control; it is possible to design policies that respect the right of individuals to control the nature and form of their intimate associations, and that assist parents in meeting the needs of their children.

The chapter outline of this book is as follows: chapter 1, "Debating Family Values," examines the relationship between personal liberty and intimacy. While family communitarians argue that the expansion of personal liberty is destructive of family bonds, I counter that it is the precondition of true intimacy. In chapter 2, "Personal Liberty and the Right of Privacy," I explain why personal liberty is valuable and describe how an individuality-based conception of the right of privacy can be used to defend liberty in sexual and intimate associations. Chapter 3, "What Are Families For: An Argument for Diversity in Family Forms," provides a critical analysis of Galston's proposal for eliminating no-fault divorce and Elshtain's opposition to same-sex marriage. In response to their assertion that the family has only one purpose and should take only one form, I argue that the family has multiple purposes and can take multiple forms. Chapter 4, "Fatherless Families and the Reinstitutionalization of the Gender-Structured Family," responds to two recent books that argue that the best way to decrease fatherless families is to strengthen gender roles. I argue that gender-structured families contribute to gender inequality without fostering stronger ties between fathers and their children. Chapters 5 and 6 are slightly different from the first four chapters of this book. While these chapters continue to develop my argument for the new family values of liberty, equality and diversity, they are not written in response to family communitarians. In chapter 5, "Do Women Receiving Welfare Have a Right of Privacy? A Public/Private Paradox," I argue that welfare rules that attempt to regulate procreative choices place unjust constraints on recipients' right of privacy. The state cannot legitimately use its distributive powers to promote marriage and discourage out-of-wedlock birth. Chapter 6, "Feminist Family Policy: A Comparison of the Egalitarian and Caregiver Models," examines differences within feminism over how to realize gender equality while also valuing the caretaking traditionally performed by women. Reconciling these two goals is essential to designing a feminist and progressive family policy. In chapters 5 and 6, I also discuss the kinds of economic reforms that would benefit low-income families, particularly single-mother families and their children.

Our society, like many others, is deeply divided on the question of what constitutes a family. Given this lack of consensus, it is important that we continue to reflect on what moral principles should guide our thinking about families and intimate life. Families are vital to the emotional life, material support, and development of adults and children. Successful families operate as small mutual aid societies, in which resources are pooled, intimacy and companionship needs are met, and caretaking is performed. It is because of the centrality of familial and intimate associations to adults and children—and to the greater society—that our definition of what constitutes a family must be broadened. If we are to make good on our commitment to democracy, we must respect all of our citizens equally. This requires that the state recognize the choices its citizens make about their intimate associations. Working toward greater equality—economic equality, equality between racial and ethnic groups, equal rights for lesbians and gays, and gender equality—is perhaps the most effective way of bettering the lives of children and families. The principles of liberty, equality, and diversity provide the basis for a feminist and progressive family policy.

NOTES

1. Historians refer to the two-parent family with children as the "modern" family to indicate at what point in history it emerged. I am using the term "traditional" to suggest that the two-parent family once functioned, and for many people still does function, as the ideal model of family in the United States. In other words, the two-parent family is "traditional" because it is supported by custom and convention. Nontraditional families are less likely to be widely accepted. For a discussion of the "traditional," the "modern," and the "postmodern" family, see Judith Stacey, "Backward Toward the Postmodern Family," in *Rethinking the Family*, ed. Barrie Thorne with Marilyn Yalom (Boston: Northeastern University Press, 1992).

2. Bureau of the Census, *America's Families and Living Arrangements: Population Characteristics, 2000, P20-537,* U.S. Department of Commerce, Economics and Statistics Administration (Washington, D.C., June 2001).

3. Sharon Vandivere, Kristin Anderson Moore, and Martha Zaslow, "Children's Family Environment: Findings from the National Survey of America's Families," *Snapshots of America's Families II: 1999 Results* (Washington, D.C.: Urban Institute, 2002). http://newfederalism.urban.org/nsaf/family-environ.html (accessed 27 January 2002).

4. J. Laird, "Lesbian and Gay Families," in *Normal Family Processes*, ed. Froma Walsh (New York: Guilford Press, 1993), 282–328.

5. Bureau of the Census, *America's Families and Living Arrangements.*

6. Federal Interagency Forum on Child and Family Statistics, *America's Children 2000: Key National Indicators of Well-Being, 2000* (Washington, D.C., 2000).

7. Defenders of nontraditional family forms include Stephanie Coontz, *The Way We Never Were: American Families and the Nostalgia Trap* (New York: Basic Books, 1992); Judith Stacey, *In the Name of the Family* (Boston: Beacon Press, 1996).

8. Ronald Dworkin, *Taking Rights Seriously* (Cambridge, Mass.: Harvard University Press, 1977).

9. Charles Murray, *Losing Ground: American Social Policy, 1950–1980* (New York: Basic Books, 1984).

10. Lawrence Mead, *The New Politics of Poverty* (New York: Basic Books, 1992).

11. James Q. Wilson, *The Moral Sense* (New York: Free Press, 1993).

12. William Galston served as an advisor to President Clinton on domestic policy. He is the author of *Liberal Purposes: Goods, Virtues, and Diversity in the Liberal State* (Cambridge, England: Cambridge University Press, 1991).

13. Jean Bethke Elshtain, who serves as the cochair of the Council on Families in America, is one of the coeditors (with Steven Bayme and David Blankenhorn) of *Rebuilding the Nest: A New Commitment to the Family* (Milwaukee: Family Service America, 1990). She is also the author of *Power Trips and Other Journeys: Essays in Feminism and Civic Discourse* (Madison: University of Wisconsin Press, 1990).

14. Barbara Dafoe Whitehead, codirector of the Institute of American Values, is the author of "Dan Quayle Was Right," *The Atlantic* 271, no. 4 (1993): 47–84, and *The Divorce Culture: Rethinking Our Commitments to Marriage and Family* (New York: Vintage, 1996).

15. Mary Ann Glendon is the coeditor, with David Blankenhorn, of *Seedbeds of Virtue* (Lanham, Md.: Madison Books, 1995) and is the author of *Rights Talk: The Impoverishment of Political Discourse* (New York: Free Press, 1991).

16. David Popenoe is the cochair of the Council on Families in America and the author of *Life Without Father* (New York: Free Press, 1996).

17. David Blankenhorn is the codirector of the Institute for American Values and the author of *Fatherless America: Confronting Our Most Urgent Problem* (New York: Basic Books, 1995).

18. Judith Stacey, *In the Name of the Family* (Boston: Beacon Press, 1996), 54.

19. For an introduction to a variety of communitarian authors see Michael Sandel, *Liberalism and Its Critics* (New York: New York University Press, 1990).

20. John Rawls is the best-known proponent of the view that justice is the foundation of liberal democracy. See John Rawls, *A Theory of Justice* (Cambridge, Mass.: Harvard University Press, 1971), and John Rawls, *Political Liberalism* (Cambridge, Mass.: Harvard University Press, 1994).

21. Jean Bethke Elshtain, "A Call to Civil Society," *Social Science and Modern Society* 36, no.5 (July/August 1999): 11–19.

22. Galston, *Liberal Purposes*.

23. Elshtain, "A Call to Civil Society," 13.

24. Council on Families in America, "Marriage in America: A Report to the Nation," in *Promises to Keep: Decline and Renewal in America*, ed. David Popenoe, Jean Bethke Elshtain, and David Blankenhorn (Lanham, Md.: Rowman & Littlefield, 1996), 293–318, 307.

25. Galston makes a distinction between intrinsic and functional traditionalists and associates himself with the latter form. He explains that while intrinsic traditionalists rest their objection to divorce on the claim that it is a violation of divine law, the func-

tional traditionalist relies on social science to show that divorce harms children. See Galston, *Liberal Purposes*, 280.

26. See Daphne Spain and Suzanne M. Bianchi, *Balancing Act: Motherhood, Marriage and Employment Among American Women* (New York: Russell Sage Foundation, 1996); Susan Moller Okin, *Justice, Gender, and the Family* (New York: Basic Books, 1989); and Arlie Hochschild with Anne Machung, *The Second Shift* (New York: Avon, 1989).

27. Galston, *Liberal Purposes*, 285.

28. The Council on Families in America, "Marriage in America," 296; and William Galston, "A Liberal Case for the Two-Parent Family," in *Rights and the Common Good*, ed. Amitai Etzioni (New York: St. Martin's, 1995), 139–49, 141.

29. Janet M. Fitchen, *Endangered Spaces, Enduring Places: Change, Identity, and Survival in Rural America* (Boulder, Colo.: Westview Press, 1991), 142–46; William Julius Wilson, *When Work Disappears: The World of the New Urban Poor* (New York: Vintage Books, 1996), 87–110.

30. Wilson, *When Work Disappears*.

31. Christopher Jencks, *Rethinking Social Policy: Race, Poverty, and the Underclass* (New York: HarperPerennial, 1993).

32. Sara McLanahan and Gary Sandefur, *Growing Up with a Single Parent: What Helps, What Hurts* (Cambridge, Mass.: Harvard University Press, 1994).

33. The term "fragile families" is used to describe low-income unmarried parents and their children. Studies show that over 40 percent of never-married fathers live with their children when they are first born. However, after a period of years, many unmarried fathers move away and lose contact with their children. Policymakers and scholars would like to find ways to help these families remain together. See U.S. Department of Health and Human Services, *HHS Fact Sheet: Promoting Responsible Fatherhood, 2001*. http://www.hhs.gov/news/press/2001pres/01fsfatherhood.html (accessed 16 January 2002).

34. Aristotle, *The Politics,* ed. Stephen Everson and trans. Jonathan Barnes (Cambridge, England: Cambridge University Press, 1988), 2.

35. *Bowers v. Hardwick* 478 U.S. 186 (1986), 205. *Bowers* upheld a Georgia statute that made engaging in same-sex sexual relations a crime.

36. Jean Cohen, "Redescribing Privacy: Identity, Difference, and the Abortion Controversy," *Columbia Journal of Gender and Law* 3 (1994): 43–116, 100.

37. Galston, "A Liberal-Democratic Case," 141.

38. Dorothy Roberts, *Killing the Black Body: Race, Reproduction, and the Meaning of Liberty* (New York: Pantheon Books, 1997), 202–45.

39. Stacey, *In the Name of the Family*, 139.

40. Andrew Hacker, *Two Nations* (New York: Ballantine Books, 1995); Jennifer L. Hochschild, *Facing Up to the American Dream* (Princeton: Princeton University Press, 1995).

41. Sarah Staveteig and Alyssa Wigton, "Key Findings by Race and Ethnicity: Findings from the National Survey of Families," *Snapshots of America's Families II, 1999 Results* (Washington, D.C.: Urban Institute, 2002). http://newfederalism.urban.org/nsaf/race-ethnicity.html (accessed 28 January 2002).

42. Dorothy Roberts, *Killing the Black Body;* Bonnie Thorton Dill, "Fictive Kin, Paper Sons, and Compadrazgo: Women of Color and the Struggle for Family Survival" in *American Families: A Multicultural Reader*, ed. Stephanie Coontz with the assistance of Maya Parson and Gabrielle Raley (New York: Routledge, 1999).

43. Fitchen, *Endangered Spaces.*

44. Jeanne Brooks-Gunn, Greg J. Duncan, and Nancy Maritato, "Poor Families, Poor Outcomes: The Well-Being of Children and Youth," in *Consequences of Growing Up Poor*, ed. Jeanne Brooks-Gunn and Greg J. Duncan (New York: Russell Sage Foundation, 1997), 1.

45. Forum on Child and Family Statistics, *America's Children 2000.*

46. Jonathan Kozol, *Amazing Grace* (New York: Crown Publishers, 1995).

47. Greg J. Duncan and Jeanne Brooks-Gunn. "Income Effects Across the Life Span: Integration and Interpretation," in *Consequences of Growing Up Poor*, ed. Jeanne Brooks-Gunn and Greg J. Duncan (New York: Russell Sage Foundation, 1997), 596–610; Sara McLanahan, "The Consequences of Single Motherhood," in *Sex, Preference, and Family: Essays on Law and Nature*, ed. David M. Estlund and Martha C. Nussbaum (New York: Oxford University Press, 1997), 306–18.

48. Okin, Justice, *Gender and the Family*

49. Andrew J. Cherlin, *Marriage, Divorce, Remarriage* (Cambridge, Mass: Harvard University Press, 1992), 75.

50. Saul D. Hoffman, E. Michael Foster, and Frank F. Furstenberg, Jr., "Reevaluating the Costs of Teenage Childbearing," *Demography* 30, no. 4 (February 1993): 1–13

Chapter One

Debating Family Values

In recent years, several scholars and authors, whom I will call family communitarians, have argued that American families are in crisis. William Galston, Jean Bethke Elshtain, Barbara Dafoe Whitehead, Mary Ann Glendon, David Popenoe, and David Blankenhorn assert that high levels of divorce and nonmarital childbirth pose an enormous threat to children and to our society as a whole. According to family communitarians, the cause of family instability and diversity is a shift in cultural values that began in the 1960s and 1970s. The moral discourses that once placed marital permanence and family obligation above the self-interests of adults have steadily eroded. Consequently, the two-parent family no longer retains its normative force. Family communitarians assert that when it comes to matters of sexuality and family, Americans have too much personal liberty. Reversing the decline of the family, they argue, will require placing both cultural and legal constraints on personal liberty.

My purpose in this chapter is to challenge the claim that personal liberty has had an entirely negative effect on families and intimate relationships. I argue that the expansion of personal liberty is the result of a long-term change in the meaning of marriage and family. As greater weight has been attributed to affection, emotional support, and sexual pleasure, women and men have demanded greater freedom to make their own decisions about how they order their intimate lives. It is not, then, the expansion of personal liberty that undermines families, but the increasing importance of emotional and sexual intimacy in the daily lives of men and women that leads to the expansion of personal liberty. The demand for greater self-determination in intimate relationships is the inevitable consequence of a relatively new, affect-based conception of marriage and family. Personal liberty and emotionally intense

1

intimate relationships are highly interdependent—we cannot have one without the other. If we value intimacy and mutuality, we need to protect personal liberty.

In arguing for the value of emotionally rich relationships and the personal liberty that makes them possible, I do not make the claim that women and men never abuse their newfound liberties. It is not difficult to find examples of adults who have acted selfishly and irresponsibly. Greater choice for adults sometimes means depriving children of security and stability. Moreover, family breakup and the formation of stepfamilies is something that happens *to* children—they are forced to live with the choices that their parents and other adults have made. Nonetheless, my point in this chapter and throughout this book is that increased family instability is associated with some very good and valuable things. By portraying family instability as a consequence of moral deficiency, the family communitarians are able to downplay the interdependence of intimacy and personal liberty.

In section 1 of this chapter, "The Demise of the Package Deal," I examine how sexuality, procreation, and parenting, once united in a "package deal," became distinct activities during the 1970s. Section 2, "Personal Liberty and Family Decline," presents the family communitarians' assessment of the decline of the package deal. In section 3, "An Alternative Story: The Rise of a New Intimacy Ideal," I argue that personal liberty is the necessary precondition of authentic emotional and sexual intimacy. In section 4, "Family Innovators," I examine those family forms that the family communitarians blame for destabilizing the two-parent family norm. I argue against their position that contemporary men and women are self-centered individualists who no longer understand the nature of meaningful commitment. Instead, I suggest that some women and men are consciously dissenting from a marital and family order they find oppressive, while others are involuntarily innovating new forms of family because of harsh economic conditions and blocked opportunities. Finally, in section 5, "The Meaning of Marriage: Fixed or Mutable?" I argue against the family communitarians' position that marriage is a static institution to which individuals must conform.

I. THE DEMISE OF THE PACKAGE DEAL

Throughout most of the twentieth century, sex, marriage, parenting, and family have been part of a "package deal" in the United States. This package has been held together by five basic principles: (1) Sexual activity, but especially women's sexual activity, is legitimate only within marriage; (2) Marriage is a lifelong commitment; (3) Procreation and child rearing take place within marriage; (4) Men and women perform different but complementary roles within the family; and (5) Heterosexuality is the only natural and normal form of sexual expression. One of the most significant developments of the late twentieth century has been the demise of the package deal. Activities and institutions that were once tightly bound together have come undone. Sexual activity, procreation, and child rearing have all been detached from marriage. Divorce, which had been on the rise since mid-century, rose sharply in the 1970s. While in the 1950s one-third of all marriages ended in divorce, by the 1980s, one-half of all marriages did.[1] Since then, divorce rates have declined slightly and stabilized. Currently, about 40 percent of all marriages are predicted to end in divorce.[2] The proportion of all births to unmarried women rose from 18 percent in 1980 to 31 percent in 1998.[3] Increases in divorce and nonmarital birth have led to greater numbers of single-parent families, 86 percent of which are headed by mothers. In 1970, 13 percent of all families with children were headed by one parent. In 2000, 31 percent of all families with children were headed by an adult with no spouse present.[4] Almost one in five white children, one in three Latino children, and one half of all black children live in single-parent families.[5] The 1970s also witnessed increases in premarital sexual activity among teenagers and young adults, particularly among girls and women, since a double standard in sexual conduct had long condoned premarital sexual activity for men but prohibited it for women.[6] In the 1970s and 1980s, men and women began to marry at a later age than they had in the 1950s, although not significantly later than they had earlier in the century. Currently, the median age of marriage is twenty-seven for men and twenty-five for women. In addition, the proportion of women and men who remain unmarried into their thirties or who never marry has increased. Among thirty to thirty-four-year-olds, 21 percent of women and 30 percent of men have never married.[7]

The demise of the package deal and the rise in family diversity and instability does not have one cause or explanation. It is probably best understood within the context of a number of cultural, political, and economic changes.[8] According to historians, the sexual revolution of the 1960s and 1970s, which is often identified as the cause of the package deal's demise, was in fact the culmination of a trend toward greater sexual freedom that began at the end of the nineteenth century. After enjoying a great leap forward in the 1920s, the movement for sexual liberalization slowed down during the depression and the post–World War II years, and then experienced a renewed burst of energy in the late 1960s.[9] The political movements and countercultural lifestyles that developed at this time posed a challenge to the family arrangements and sexual culture that reigned during the 1950s. Equally important, during the early 1970s, large-scale economic changes, which effectively ended the era of the family wage and drew more and more women into the workplace, further destabilized conventional assumptions about sexuality, marriage, gender roles, and family.[10]

One reason for the demise of the package deal has been the gradual acceptance of premarital sex and sex outside of marriage. Beginning in the 1920s, with the rise of new courtship rituals and the development of new leisure and entertainment spaces such as the movie theatre and jazz club, men and women began to experiment with premarital sexuality. However, for most women, marriage remained the only legitimate social arrangement for regular sexual intercourse. It was not until the youth culture of the 1960s and 1970s that sex outside of marriage and cohabitation were openly embraced.[11] At the same time, a new conception of marriage that stressed emotional and sexual intimacy became dominant. While in previous generations marriage had been seen as a lifelong commitment, by the 1970s fewer and fewer Americans were willing to remain in unhappy unions. As this new intimacy ideal developed and more and more Americans ended their marriages, the stigma once attached to divorce decreased.[12] New sexual freedoms, the rise in cohabitation, and the postponement of marriage contributed to increasing numbers of nonmarital birth.[13]

The political movements that caught fire in the 1960s and 1970s called for an end to social hierarchies based on race, gender, and sexuality, and encouraged experimentation with gender and sexual identities, life patterns, and intimate relationships. Activists within the feminist and lesbian and gay movements argued that gender is a primary principle of social organization.[14] Power, status, opportunities, and labor are all distributed according to a gender structure that also enforces compulsory heterosexuality.[15] Feminists viewed the breadwinner/homemaker model of family that dominated during the post–World War II years as the contemporary manifestation of this gender structure. Perhaps the most radical claim made by early Second Wave feminists was that the gender structure was not natural or immutable, but a social construction that could be transformed to reflect the principle of equality. With this claim, feminists effectively called into question the gender-structured family and the naturalness of heterosexuality.[16]

Large-scale changes in the economy and the labor market begun in the early 1970s have continued to undermine the economic basis of the gender-structured family. The decline of manufacturing and heavy industry, the weakening of unions, corporate downsizing, the rise of part-time, temporary, and contingent work, and the globalization of the domestic economy have all contributed to decreased wages for working men without a college degree or specialized skills.[17] With the loss of the family wage, the gender-based division of labor established during industrialization, in which the husband provided the household income and the wife labored in the home ministering to the needs of her husband and children, was dealt a heavy blow. This made it more difficult for men to occupy their traditional role as head of the family. Underemployment and unemployment have taken a particularly high toll on African-American men, whose rates of unemployment since the 1970s have been twice as high as white men's.[18]

At the same time that men's wages declined, greater economic opportunities opened up for women. While black and Asian women had high rates of labor force participation in 1970, many white women left the labor force when they married and had children. As the service sector grew in the 1970s, married white women with children began to work outside the home in greater numbers. In 1970, 38 percent of all married women between the ages of twenty-five and thirty-four worked outside of the home. By 1998, this proportion had increased to 71 percent.[19] A large number of women found jobs in data entry, retail sails, telemarketing, financial services, and in more established areas such as secretarial work. Most of these jobs are low-paid, part-time, and do not include benefits.[20] Nonetheless, women's entry into the labor market in large numbers has made an important contribution to the demise of the package deal. While women's traditional roles as mothers and caretakers continue to disadvantage them in the labor market, many women now are able to support themselves and their children. They have fewer economic incentives to stay in abusive or loveless partnerships with men. In addition, women's performance of the traditionally male provider role has upset the gender-based division of labor in the family. Historically, religious and secular beliefs about marriage and family have held that men and women have different but complementary natures and/or capacities. Since men and women were believed to be incomplete on their own, it was thought necessary for them to form lifelong unions. Women's new economic independence, and their ability to care and provide for their children, has called this fundamental assumption into question.

The demise of the package deal raises questions about the principles that once held it together. Can marriage be considered a lifelong commitment if so many marriages end in divorce? If men and women no longer have interdependent and complementary roles in the family, are two-parent heterosexual families really necessary? If same-sex couples are a permanent and visible part of society, can we continue to think of heterosexuality as the only natural and normal form of sexual expression? If sex occurs regularly outside of marriage, are higher rates of unmarried birth inevitable? Demographers assure us that family patterns stabilized in the late 1990s. Recent reports even suggest that marriage may be on the rise among some groups and that the number of children living with single mothers has declined slightly.[21] Yet, knowing that rates of change are leveling off does not help us come to grips with what the demise of the package deal means for our society.

II. PERSONAL LIBERTY AND FAMILY INSTABILITY

Family communitarians claim that the decline of the married, two-parent family and the rise of divorce and nonmarital birth have had enormous costs for our society. This is because they believe that family structure—which refers to whether children are raised in two-parent, one-parent, or stepfamilies—determines how well children are raised. Family communitarians believe that only one kind of family—the married, heterosexual, two-biological-parent family—provides children with the proper moral upbringing. Alternative family forms, such as single-parent families and stepfamilies, "have been demonstrated to be inferior in child outcomes."[22] It is necessary, family communitarians argue, to make distinctions between families and to state clearly that some family forms are better than others, in order to uphold and strengthen the two-parent family norm.[23]

Family communitarians blame family instability on a shift in cultural values that began in the countercultural and self-realization movements of the 1960s and 1970s. It was at this time that the expressive individualism of Ralph Waldo Emerson and Henry David Thoreau experienced a renaissance. According to Galston, the central tenet of expressive individualism is that "the fullness of existence craved by each person stands in opposition to the constraints of morality and society."[24] During the 1960s and 1970s, this belief was revived by a countercultural elite and then spread to the general population. Encouraged to express themselves and find self-fulfillment, men and women began to put their own interests above their familial and civic duties. This shift in cultural values led to sexual experimentation, delayed marriage, and an increase in divorce and nonmarital birth.

Family communitarians argue that the expansion of personal liberty in the 1960s and 1970s undermined the moral discourses that held the package deal in place. According to the Council on Families in America (CFA), "Our culture has become increasingly skeptical of marriage or other institutions as well that are thought to restrict or confine adult behavior. In their place, we now put a much higher value on individualism, choice, and unrestricted personal liberty."[25] Elshtain explains that "modern subjects are enjoined to remain as untrammeled as possible in order to attain individual goals and to enjoy their 'freedom.'" As a consequence of being "located inside a wider ethos that no longer affords clear-cut moral and social supports for familial relations and responsibilities, young people, unsurprisingly, choose in growing numbers to postpone or evade their responsibilities."[26] In her famous article, "Dan Quayle Was Right," Whitehead decries the fact that "political principles of individual rights and choice shape our understanding of family commitment and solidarity. Family relationships are viewed not as permanent or binding but as voluntary and easily terminable."[27] Whitehead echoes Elshtain's assertion that an excess of personal liberty has undermined older understandings of familial obligation and commitment.

According to family communitarians, the rise of divorce and nonmarital birth can be explained, for the most part, as the result of selfish behavior on the part of adults who do not understand the true meaning of binding moral commitments. They claim that a mistaken view of what the good life consists of has come to dominate popular culture. Too great an emphasis on personal liberty has undermined the ability of men and women to understand the value of lifelong marriage. Ordinary Americans have been seduced by a "puerile understanding of personal happiness" that masks itself in the expressive language of self-fulfillment and personal growth.[28] Consequently, we have lost access to the moral discourses within which lifelong commitment once made sense.

Family communitarians claim that the expansion of personal liberty has had a devastating impact on our nation's children. According to the CFA, the "break-up of the married, mother-father child rearing unit is the principle cause of declining child well-being in our society."[29] They cite family instability as the "most important causal factor" behind a long list of social ills, including crime, poverty, substance abuse, low educational attainment, suicide, and depression.[30] Popenoe states that the "movement away from the two-natural-parent family has led to considerable social malaise among the young, not to mention social decay in general."[31] Many family communitarians, particularly Popenoe and Blankenhorn, argue that one of the most serious consequences of divorce and nonmarital birth is father absence. Blankenhorn claims that fatherlessness is "the engine driving our most urgent social problems, from crime to adolescent pregnancy to child sexual abuse to domestic violence against women."[32] The separation of fathers from families also has harmful consequences for men. According to the family communitarians, families have a "civilizing effect" on men. Marrying and having children encourages men to direct their energies toward positive social goals and rewards them for living a settled and lawful life.

Family communitarians are deeply concerned about the well-being of children. However, to view them simply as child welfare advocates would be a mistake. For the family communitarians, family instability has moral and political consequences. Speaking for The Council on Civil Society (CCS)—an association that includes Blankenhorn, Popenoe and Glendon—Elshtain argues that a flourishing democracy requires a shared understanding of the common good and a virtuous citizenry. The common good consists of a set of moral truths that are largely biblical and religious, but also are informed by the classical natural law tradition and the ideas of the Enlightenment.[33] The problem is, according to Elshtain, that while our democracy is dependent on the reproduction of these moral truths, our political institutions alone cannot reproduce them. Elshtain explains that the moral ideals that "authorize our civic creed" do not "derive from it."[34] How are these moral ideals cultivated and reproduced? Elshtain's response is that moral character and virtue are fostered through civil society, which she defines as "relationships and institutions that are neither created nor controlled by the state." Elshtain explains that the purpose of these civil associations, or "seedbeds of virtue," is "to foster competence and character in individuals, build social trust, and help children become good people and good citizens." The family, according to Elshtain, is the "first and most basic" of civil associations.[35]

It turns out, then, that the family communitarians are making two kinds of claims about the two-parent family. The first asserts that family structure determines the well-being of children. The second argues that the two-parent family is essential to the reproduction of the moral culture on which our democracy rests. The first argument makes claims about measurable outcomes such as academic achievement or behavior that can be supported or challenged through the use of social science research. The second makes philosophical claims about the nature of morality and politics that cannot be adjudicated by the social sciences. For example, social scientific research cannot determine whether sharing core moral truths is necessary to the reproduction of democratic societies. However, the family communitarians themselves do not distinguish between these two kinds of claims. They propose to use social science indicators of child well-being to prove that divorce and nonmarital birth pose serious threats to the democratic political process.

It is important to recognize that the family communitarians' position is a moral and political argument, and not a more narrowly conceived sociological argument. The claims they make are fundamentally different from those of the researchers—mostly psychologists and sociologists—that they cite. Instead of limiting themselves to the statement that children who grow up in single-parent families are at a slightly higher risk for dropping out of high school than their peers from intact families, the family communitarians also claim that children who grow up in the former are less likely to possess the virtues necessary to good citizenship. Thus, their argument assumes that the two-parent family is *morally* superior to alternative family forms. This means that single-parent families, stepfamilies, and lesbian and gay families are understood to be morally deficient. However, it is not at all clear that civic virtue can be measured using the methods of the social sciences.

What is the family communitarians' solution to the decline of the two-parent family? They argue that we must use cultural education and policy to reinvigorate the idea and practice of marital permanence. If the two-parent family is revived, moral virtue and good citizenship will be revived with it. In their twenty-page report, *Marriage in America*, the CFA asks us to commit ourselves to the following four principles: (1) reclaim the ideal of marital permanence and affirm marriage as the preeminent environment for child rearing; (2) decide unequivocally that out-of-wedlock childbearing is wrong, that our divorce rate is far too high, and that every child deserves a father; (3) resolve that the next generation will increase the proportion of children who grow up with their two married parents and decrease the proportion that do not; and (4) resolve that the next generation will increase the time that parents spend raising their children—for married couples with children at home, aim for an overall commitment to paid employment that does not exceed sixty hours per week.[36] Family communitarians acknowledge that instituting these principles will require sustained effort throughout the society. In *Marriage in America*, they provide policy advice for religious and civic leaders, educators, employers, human service professionals, marriage counselors, health care providers, family attorneys, children's advocates, philanthropists, family scholars, the media, and the entertainment industry.

Family communitarians argue that if marriage and the two-parent family are to be revived, the real change must come at the level of attitudes and culture. Individual men and women must embrace the moral discourses that give meaning to family obligations, and reject the currently dominant values of expressive individualism and free choice. Despite their emphasis on reviving the two-parent family through cultural education, the family communitarians nonetheless believe that law and policy have an important role to play in reinvigorating marriage. The CFA urges legislators to redesign the tax code as well as welfare and housing policies to favor married couples and to promote marriage, to eliminate no-fault divorce and establish a five-year waiting period for contested divorces, and to formulate vision statements that call for the strengthening of marriage and the undesirability of births to unmarried women.[37] Family communitarians acknowledge that these policies would restrict the liberty of adults, but insist that they are legitimate given the danger that family instability poses to the well-being of our children and the health of our democratic polity.[38]

The chapters that follow develop several objections to the family communitarians' position. In chapter 2, I argue that the right of privacy entitles individuals to determine the nature of their intimate relationships. In chapter 3, I argue that the family communitarians vastly overstate the harmful effects of family structure on child outcomes. I explain how the family communitarians' position will perpetuate the economic inequality of women in chapter 4.

Throughout this book, I make the case that using the state to promote one form of family and to stigmatize others is wrong. The remainder of this chapter will be devoted to a critical analysis of one part of the family communitarians' argument; in brief, I will challenge their assertion that the expansion of personal liberty has had an entirely negative effect on family life and intimate relationships.

III. AN ALTERNATIVE STORY:
THE RISE OF A NEW INTIMACY IDEAL

As we have seen, family communitarians tell a story that blames increased family diversity on the expansion of personal liberty. The central fact in their story is that personal liberty is destructive of familial ties. Men and women leave—or fail to form—marriages because they are more interested in momentary pleasures or short-term interests. However, this is not the only way to evaluate the demise of the package deal. In my counternarrative, I argue that there is a positive relationship between personal liberty and intimate relationship. The central fact in my story is the interdependence of intimacy and liberty: the more weight individuals attribute to sentiment and emotion, the more likely they are to seek self-determination in the conduct of their personal relationships. My claim is that men and women demand greater liberty in their personal lives as the significance they ascribe to intimate relationships grows. While family communitarians hold that "too much" freedom has corrupted marriage and family life, I argue that liberty and individual choice are the bases of *true* intimacy between adults.

Ever since what historian Edward Shorter calls a "revolution in sentiment" remade modern family life, women and men have increasingly claimed greater freedom in the areas of marriage, divorce, procreation, sexuality, and in recent years, sexual preference.[39] However, until relatively recently, sentiment was not the organizing principle of marriage and family. Instead, the family was a hierarchical association in which men were recognized as the natural rulers of children, women, and other subordinate household members. Marriage was not a voluntary association for men or women. Indeed, the romantic view of marriage based on mutual attraction and love that is dominant in the United States today did not become popular until the nineteenth and twentieth centuries. In the past, marriage was not so much an intimate relationship as a social institution that controlled sexuality (primarily the sexuality of women), ensured the production of legitimate offspring, placed men and women into a gender-structured division of labor, power, and status, and forged alliances between families.[40]

In his account of the classical Greek household, Aristotle explains that marriage is not a relationship based on choice. He states that "there must be a union of those who cannot exist without each other; namely, of male and female, that the race may continue, and this union which is formed, not of choice, but because, in common with other animals and with plants, mankind have a natural desire to leave behind them an image of themselves."[41] Along with asserting the imperative of reproduction, Aristotle defines a principle that was to be echoed by religious and secular authors with little dissent well into the twentieth century—man and woman are incomplete on their own; to achieve completeness they must form a union in which each contributes what the other lacks. The French philosopher Jean-Jacques Rousseau explained the principle governing relations between the sexes like this: "The social relationship of the sexes . . . produces a moral person of which the woman is the eye and the man is the arm, but they have such a dependence on one another that the woman learns from the man what must be seen and the man learns from the woman what must be done."[42] Thus, according to Aristotle and Rousseau, the lifelong union of man and woman has its basis in the need to procreate and takes the form it does because "natural" gender differences are complementary.

According to historian Lawrence Stone, early modern conceptions of marriage did not permit freedom in spouse selection. Stone writes that "romantic love and lust were strongly condemned as ephemeral and irrational grounds for marriage." Parents, particularly fathers, exercised authority over their children and determined whom they could marry. Extended kin and patronage systems played an important part in organizing social and political life. Marriages, particularly among the upper classes, were "a collective decision of family and kin, and not an individual one."[43] The primary aim of marriage was the "preservation, increase and transmission" of property and status.[44] Marriage was used to solidify ties between powerful families. Among the middle and lower classes, it was conceived primarily as an economic partnership. The gender-based division of labor divided duties between men and women and made their union an economic necessity. Husbands and wives, Stone asserts, had very low expectations of their marriages, and as a result were not disappointed if sentimental ties failed to develop. Socializing among both the upper and lower classes was highly sex-segregated, and as a result, husbands and wives were not required to spend a great deal of time with each other.[45]

Toward the end of the eighteenth century, subtle changes occurred in the understanding of marriage. The notion of the companionate marriage, in which men and women were expected to feel affection for each other, arose at this time among the middle classes, but did not become dominant among

all classes until much later. Whereas in the past wealth and social rank were
the primary criteria used by the middle and upper classes to assess a potential
marriage candidate, other qualities such as compatibility grew in importance.
As the weight attached to affect increased, arranged marriages and the authority of parents over their children decreased. Historian Carl Degler claims
that in the "half-century after the (American) Revolution the bases of marriage began to change in a decidedly modern direction. Increasingly, free
choice by the partners became the basis of family formation."[46] The demand
for liberty in spousal selection grew as greater emphasis was placed on the
quality of the marital relationship.

Companionate marriage, the marital ideal among the American middle
class in the nineteenth century, encouraged men and women to associate marriage with personal happiness. As industrialization separated the home and
the workplace, the family came to be seen as an association based on affection and selfless mutual aid, in sharp contrast to the larger society that was
based on competition and self-interest.[47] The central figure in the home was
the mother who symbolized selflessness and unconditional love. Although
women were subjected to a double standard of sexual morality and were not
guaranteed a full spectrum of rights, by the end of the nineteenth century their
status within the home was given greater importance. Husbands and fathers,
who throughout the sixteenth and seventeenth centuries were considered to be
the spiritual leaders of the household, ceded moral leadership to their wives.[48]
Middle-class women were assumed to remain morally pure because they
were not exposed to the corruption and vice of the public world. In contrast,
their husbands were required to participate in a competitive world in which
self-interested behavior was rewarded. The doctrine of separate spheres improved white women's position in society, but racism prevented nonwhite
women from being accorded moral authority.[49] This change in white, middle-
class women's status suggests that men and women found it difficult to reconcile affection and marital intimacy with the idea of women's inferiority.
Despite this shift toward a more sentimental marital bond and greater respect
for women's roles in the family, intimate relations between adult men and
women existed within a social and political context in which women were
clearly second-class citizens. Considerable tension existed between the ideal
of the affection-based marriage and the reality of severe penalties for female
sexual behavior outside of marriage, lack of legal rights and economic and
educational opportunities for women, and the absence of easily available divorce.

During the Victorian era, sexuality was viewed as a powerful and potentially dangerous drive that could only be legitimately expressed within marriage. According to sociologist Steven Seidman, the Victorians believed that

"marriage channeled the sex instinct in ways that made it serve spiritual and moral ends."[50] This view of sexuality began to change by the 1920s as sexual liberals sought to associate marital sex with pleasure and intimacy. Marital love gradually came to be seen as "anchored in mutual sexual attraction and gratification."[51] By the 1940s and 1950s, popular magazines and marriage manuals suggested that love and sexual attraction between marital partners formed the basis of marital intimacy and personal happiness.[52] As love and sexual fulfillment came to be seen as central to marriage, rates of divorce increased, as did sexual experimentation prior to marriage. In the same way that the notion of the companionate marriage had signaled the end of arranged marriages, the demand for sexual and emotional fulfillment within marriage increased agitation for divorce reform and greater freedom during the courtship period.

Seidman argues that the "sexualization of love" within marriage gave men and women permission to value sex for its multiple nonprocreative functions. Seidman explains, "As sex functioned as a medium to demonstrate, maintain and revitalize love, as the pleasurable, expressive and communicative aspects of sex were legitimate ways to show and be in love, the erotic aspects of sex were developed in a deliberate, energetic way."[53] While it once had been viewed as part of a package deal that included marriage and children, sexual activity came to be seen as valuable on its own. As the value attributed to sexual pleasure and sex as an expression of intimacy increased, men and women demanded increased liberty to engage in sexual activity without marrying.

The sexual and marital order that typified the post–World War II period contained tensions that ultimately led to the demise of the package deal in the 1960s and 1970s. During the 1940s and 1950s, the basis of marriage was understood to be intimacy, happiness, and sexual pleasure, but men and women were expected to choose a lifelong partner after a brief period of limited sexual activity. Sexual pleasure was celebrated and extolled, but limited to the marital bedroom. Men and women were urged to "find that special someone," but few consolations were offered to those men and women who found that they had chosen badly. Moreover, sexual expression was limited to heterosexual sexual activity, and same-sex sexual activity was heavily stigmatized and criminally sanctioned.[54] The sexual double standard, which punished women far more harshly than men for premarital sexual activity, was still in place.[55] This sexual and family order ultimately self-destructed because it extolled intimacy and sexual pleasure while simultaneously limiting opportunities to pursue them.

Historians claim that the so-called sexual revolution should not be understood as a sudden and abrupt break with the past. Instead, they describe a gradual process of sexual liberalization that began in the last decades of the nineteenth century and culminated in the 1970s. As intimate relationships were accorded greater value, and as more weight was attributed to emotional closeness and sexual pleasure, women and men argued for greater personal liberty. The ultimate result of this demand for greater personal liberty has been the separation of sexual activity from marriage, the near universal acceptance of the use of birth control, a decrease in the stigma attached to nonmarital birth, divorce reform and the widespread acceptance of divorce, and greater acceptance in some metropolitan areas for same-sex relationships.

During the last third of the twentieth century, a new intimacy ideal came to dominate U.S. culture. According to this ideal, intimate relationships are central to personal happiness and are founded on individual choice. Many men and women believe that finding true love is only possible after a lengthy period of sexual experimentation. As a result, marriage or committed unions are not advisable until the mid- to late-twenties or thirties. If closeness and intimacy fade away, marriages must be dissolved because love is the only legitimate basis for marriage. At the core of this new intimacy ideal is the belief that the individuals engaging in a love relationship must be free to define it in their own way. Decisions concerning intimate relationships should not be controlled by external expectations or social conventions. To do so would be to undermine the very possibility of true intimacy.

The lesbian and gay liberation and the feminist movements have made a unique contribution to the new intimacy ideal. These movements have argued that personal relationships should be not only mutually satisfying and emotionally meaningful, but that they should be based on equality. When early Second Wave feminists declared that the personal is political, many of them had in mind their own relationships with boyfriends and husbands. They argued that popular conceptions of love, marriage, and family made women dependent on men and encouraged women to sacrifice their own needs and dreams for their husbands and children. Feminists challenged the idea that all women needed a husband and children to make them happy. While some feminists rejected marriage and family, others argued for egalitarian partnerships between men and women based on mutuality and respect. Such relationships required an end to the gender-structured family. Feminists argued for a new type of marriage in which men would become more involved in caring for children and daily housework, and women would take part in earning the household income.

Several scholars have noted that same-sex relationships are more egalitarian than heterosexual relationships.[56] Lesbian and gay couples do not replicate the caretaker/provider roles found in the majority of heterosexual families. And, in most cases, they do not attribute greater status to the partner who earns more money. Instead, same-sex couples tend to share the tasks of earning income and managing the household. Because they come much closer to embodying the egalitarian partnerships that she has argued for, Susan Moller Okin suggests that "gay and lesbian family relationships may provide, in important respects, a very good model for heterosexual families to follow."[57] Similarly, Nan Hunter argues that the legalization of same-sex marriage could foster greater equality between heterosexual couples. She explains that same-sex marriage could "destabilize the cultural meaning of marriage" by creating "the model in law for an egalitarian kind of interpersonal relation."[58] Same-sex married couples could provide heterosexual couples with a powerful example of how to fuse intimacy and equality.

Feminist relationships, because they insist on equality between men and women, and same-sex relationships, because they do not involve gender inequality, establish equality and mutuality as the basis of intimacy. Although equality between men and women remains an elusive goal, and lesbians and gay men continue to face multiple forms of discrimination as they attempt to live out the new intimacy ideal, the models of family that have been created by these two social movements constitute a historic achievement for two reasons: first, they bring us closer to ordering our intimate relationships according to principles of justice, and second, equality between partners enriches and deepens intimacy and mutual emotional support.

The story that family communitarians tell to explain greater diversity and instability in family life does not explore the connection between personal liberty and intimate relationship. They do not acknowledge that much of what is good about contemporary intimate relationships—their emotional richness and mutuality—required the expansion of personal liberty. They claim that the actions of men and women who do not conform to the two-parent family are based, at best, on moral ignorance, and at worst, on selfishness and irresponsibility. Perhaps, most importantly, they do not admit that the package deal was built on the subordination of women, lesbians, and gay men.

IV. FAMILY INNOVATORS

Family communitarians confuse the decline of one form of family—the married, heterosexual, two-parent family—with the rejection of all intimate bonds and obligations to others. They fail to recognize that family innovators, who dissent from a specific form of family and the gender-based roles and expectations tied to it, are simultaneously creating new kinds of intimate association that involve new and different commitments. Nothing proves this better than the various "experiments in living" engaged in by participants in the lesbian and gay and women's movements. The rejection of the package deal by feminists, gay men, and lesbians cannot accurately be described as a move away from family obligations. It is better understood as a refusal to participate in a sexual, gender, and family order that many men and women find oppressive. Instead of being perceived as refusing to fulfill their obligations to others, gay men, feminists, and lesbians should be seen as inventors of new family forms based on an ideal of egalitarian intimacy. Lacking traditions and customs to follow, feminists, gay men, and lesbians created these new bonds with "an exceptional degree of reflection and intentionality."[59] Nonmarital love relationships and partnerships, friendship networks, housemates, countercultural communities, and political groups have given gay men, feminists, and lesbians the support and care historically provided by more traditional families. The ability of friends to take on roles historically performed by family members, including caring for the sick, has been clearly demonstrated by the AIDS crisis. However, there are a multitude of other cases in which friends share homes, economic resources, and sometimes, parenting responsibilities.[60] The gay movement also posed a challenge to the assumption that one lifelong monogamous relationship that combines sex, love, and companionship is necessarily superior to sexual experimentation combined with nonsexual lifelong friendships.[61] In recent years, lesbian and gay families with children have gained greater visibility, and the issue of parenting rights for lesbians and gay men has received increased attention. Most lesbian and gay parents have children from a former heterosexual relationship. However, during the 1980s, lesbian couples began to use artificial insemination in order to raise children together. Greater numbers of lesbian and gay couples were able to adopt children in the 1990s. Unfortunately, as I discuss at greater length in chapter 3, lesbian and gay parents are not accorded equal custody, visitation, adoption, or foster care rights. One of the biggest obstacles to equal parenting rights for lesbians and gay men is the refusal of the state to recognize same-sex marriage. However, lesbian and gay parents have been able to provide warm and safe homes for their children despite social stigma and discrimination. Lesbians and gay men who have rejected the "package deal" and departed from the traditional family should not be called self-centered individualists. Instead, they can best be described as voluntary family innovators.

The changes in family patterns that have occurred over the last thirty years are not in all cases the product of conscious innovation. Families are located in social and economic structures that both constrain and enable the actions of individuals. As I suggested in the introduction, economic and racial inequality have affected the ability of families to flourish and have influenced the forms that families take. Dill explains that from the "founding of the United States, and throughout its history, race has been a fundamental criterion determining the kind of work people do, the wages they receive, and the kind of legal, economic, political and social support provided for their families."[62] The interaction of social and economic structures with ethnic cultural traditions has caused African American families to be more variable and diverse than white families.[63] African American family forms include extended families, grandparents raising grandchildren, single-parent families, and families with nonbiological children. African Americans have a long tradition of relying on family members, in part, because racial discrimination and segregation has made it more difficult for them to gain access to assistance and resources available to white families. As a result, blacks are two times as likely as whites to live in extended families.[64] And, while commentators often point to single parenthood as evidence of the black family's instability, they ignore the strong tradition of elder care that explains why 34 percent of blacks older than sixty-five live in multigenerational homes, compared with 18 percent of whites.[65] African American families also have a long tradition of social parenthood, or what Patricia Hill Collins calls "othermothers."[66] When biological mothers have had to work long hours outside of the home, "othermothers" in the community, whether biological relatives or friends, have stepped in to care for their children. This tradition of social parenthood allows African American families to provide nonbiological children who have lost their parents with new homes.

Gender roles in African American families also have been shaped by racial inequality. Historically, many low-income families have found the traditional family ideal—consisting of the breadwinning husband, domestic wife, and their children—difficult to emulate. This has been especially true for African American families who have had to contend with the combined effects of racism and poverty. For example, while the higher wages attainable by many white men permitted white women to care for their children and manage their households full-time, most mothers in African American and immigrant families were compelled to work for pay, often in the homes of affluent white families.[67] Black women's long history of economic independence contrasts with middle-class white women's dependence on their husbands. Thus, the material basis of male domination in the family—the family wage—has not existed in many African American families. This, some black feminists argue, has led to tensions between African American men and women. African American women have been condemned for their economic independence because it violates the dominant culture's stereotype of femininity.[68]

African American families are less likely to conform to the two-parent family norm than white families. According to the family communitarians, this suggests that black men and women are self-centered individualists who are failing to fulfill their family commitments. Yet, how does such an appraisal square with African Americans' tradition of strong extended families, elder care, and social parenthood? The family communitarian analysis blames family dissolution and diversity on an expansion in personal liberty that gave men and women greater freedom to make bad choices. But variability in family form is not just a product of individual behavior. It is also the product of large-scale social and economic conditions that include racial and economic inequality. Families take shape within larger economic and political contexts. They also are the products of distinct cultural traditions and practices.

So far, I have discussed specific groups that have engaged in conscious and not-so-conscious family innovation. I now turn to forms of family innovation—divorce and nonmarital birth—which are not confined to a specific group. Divorce does not necessarily signify a conscious rejection of conventional sexual and gender patterns, but only of a particular man or woman. Families dissolved and reformed because of divorce are often quite different from the intentional families created by gay men, feminists, and lesbians. Moreover, divorce is certainly not experienced as "freely chosen" by children. It is a decision that parents make and that children are forced to live with. And, there certainly are cases of abandonment in which spouses leave marriages because they cannot or will not take responsibility for the daily care and support of family members. However, the family communitarian assertion that the primary cause of divorce is selfishness or moral ignorance goes too far. Some men and women seek divorce not to withdraw from interpersonal commitments but in the hopes of building a more emotionally rich and mutually supportive marriage. After all, three-fourths of all men and three-fifths of all women eventually remarry.[69] Making divorce more difficult, a policy advocated by most family communitarians, may or may not prevent the dissolution of marriages. Husbands and wives can live apart without obtaining a legal divorce. But divorce reform will certainly make it more difficult for men and women to form new families.

Family communitarians fail to acknowledge that marriages were less likely to dissolve in the past in part because of women's economic and social dependence on their husbands. Marriages were more stable prior to the 1970s, but their stability was founded on gender inequality.[70] It is not, as the family communitarians maintain, that women in the past had a better understanding of their moral obligations to their children and spouse, but rather that they could not afford to leave their husbands. Marriage was not sustained because women and men embraced the value of marital permanence and placed the well-being of the family above their individual interests. Marriage as an institution relied on a gender ideology and a discriminatory labor market that prevented women from achieving economic independence. Therefore, they were not able to leave their marriages. The rise in divorce rates during the 1970s is clearly linked to women's greater participation in the labor force at that time. Despite the loss of income experienced by contemporary divorced women, they are better able to support themselves and their children due to their high rates of consistent labor force participation. Divorce, in some cases, is a rejection of a marital and gender order that required the subordination of women.

What about unmarried mothers? Isn't it always selfish to bear a child or children outside of marriage? Isn't it wrong to intentionally bring a child into the world who will not have the benefit of a father, or whom the mother cannot afford? Many people who applaud egalitarian marriages, support the extension of full civil rights to lesbians and gay men, and feel comfortable with liberal divorce laws, are strongly opposed to nonmarital birth. Some people's opposition stems from their belief that nonmarital birth causes poverty, and that many women who bear children on their own are incapable of providing for their children. Others argue that "every child needs a father" and that choosing to have a child out-of-wedlock is an irresponsible act on the part of the child's mother. Finally, many people are opposed to nonmarital birth for all of the above reasons, and because they are uncomfortable with sex outside of marriage.

As I stated at the beginning of this chapter, about one-third of all births are to unmarried women. The increase in the proportion of births to unmarried women can be explained, in part, by the postponement of marriage and the increase in cohabitation. In other words, fewer women of childbearing age are married. Between 1960 and 1994, the proportion of women of childbearing age who were unmarried increased from 29 to 46 percent. About 25 percent of unmarried women ages twenty-five to forty-four were in cohabiting relationships in 1994. The proportion of unmarried births also has increased because married women are having fewer children.[71]

Nonmarital birth occurs in all educational and economic groups. However, women with less education and lower incomes are significantly more likely to have children when they are unmarried than those with a college degree or higher incomes. In 1998, 60 percent of births to women who never graduated from high school, and 38 percent of births to women who were high school graduates but had not received any college education, occurred outside of marriage. In contrast, among women with a bachelor's degree or more, only 3 percent had a child while unmarried.[72] These figures suggest that women from the most disadvantaged backgrounds and with the least promising economic opportunities are more likely than their better-advantaged peers to give birth outside of marriage. Clearly, economic hardship and blocked opportunities play a role in determining whether a woman is likely to give birth when she is unmarried. However, the family communitarians' explanation of the decline of the two-parent family focuses almost exclusively on changes in cultural values.

The traditional family is premised on the idea that men are able to provide for their families. When this is not the case, two-parent families often do not form, or if they do, they often end in separation, abandonment, or divorce.[73] Most economists recognize that the long-term changes in the structure of the economy begun in the mid-1970s have made it much harder for men without a college education or special training to support their families. Urban and rural communities, in which poor families are concentrated, experience high rates of homelessness, crime, and ill health, including mental and physical illness and substance abuse. The forms of stress and hardship that individuals living in poor communities face make it more difficult to enter into and sustain marital unions.[74] It is sometimes the case that marriages are ended or never begun because the men and women involved do not have the resources, emotional or financial, to take on a lifelong commitment to care. Loss of the provider role is so painful for some men that they have failed to form stable families. Several studies have found that high rates of joblessness, incarceration, drug use, and murder in low-income African American communities has reduced the number of men available to women who want to have children.[75] More than one in four black men and one in six Hispanic men will enter prison at least once. In comparison, one in twenty-three white men are incarcerated at some point in their lives.[76]

However, while economic hardship obviously has a large impact on the formation and continuance of marriage, changes in cultural attitudes also have contributed to the rise in nonmarital birth. For instance, sexual activity outside of marriage is now common across all income, educational, and racial/ethnic groups. The question is, Why are some women having children outside of marriage while others are not? The answer is primarily that some women have a reason to delay childbirth and others do not or believe that they do not. Women who expect to have careers themselves and to marry men with good job opportunities want to postpone starting a family until they and their husbands have begun their careers. Less advantaged women realize that waiting to have a child until their mid-twenties will not greatly increase their marriage prospects or their earning potential.[77] According to a recent study, "black teenagers who had lower expectations of completing a college education and those in urban war zones who felt that they might be killed at a young age may be more likely to consider a nonmarital birth."[78] In addition, many nonmarital births occur because women are not able to control their fertility. There are many reasons for this. Cultural and attitudinal barriers prevent the use of the cheapest and most accessible form of birth control—the condom. Birth control is still not easily accessible or affordable, particularly for teenagers. Comprehensive sex education that includes information on where to find and how to use contraceptives is not available to many young men and women. A recent study found that while sex education is widely available, "steep declines occurred between 1988 and 1999 in teacher support for coverage of birth control, abortion, information on obtaining contraceptives and sexually transmitted disease (STD) services, and sexual orientation, as well as in the proportions actually teaching those topics."[79] This is largely because of increased federal support for abstinence-only education and greater activism on the part of abstinence-only advocacy groups.[80] And finally, a significant percentage of sex between men and women, particularly young women in their teens, is nonconsensual. According to the Alan Guttmacher Institute, seven in ten women who had sex before age fourteen, and six in ten of those who had sex before age fifteen, report having had sex involuntarily.[81]

Even if young women had greater control over their fertility and disadvantaged men and women had better economic prospects, the proportion of births to unmarried mothers would still be greater today than it was in the 1950s. This is, in part, because we no longer force young men and women to marry. Marriage today is less a matter of coercion and more a matter of personal choice. While as I have already stated, current economic conditions have a large influence on the "choices" that low-income men and women make, it is also the case that some men and women have lost faith in the institution of marriage and are choosing not to marry. However, rejecting or not being able to marry has not prevented women from becoming mothers. Is this, as the family communitarians believe, an inherently selfish and irresponsible act? My answer to this question is no. As I elaborate in chapter 5, women, including economically disadvantaged women who cannot afford their children, have a right to bear children and deserve public support in raising them. Unmarried, disadvantaged women (and men) have children for the same reason that married, middle-class women (and men) have children. They want to experience a unique bond that only takes place between parents and children. This is an affirmation of family, not an effort to undermine it.

What about the rising, but still small, number of older single women with college degrees who are having children on their own? Most of these women would have liked to have children with a partner, but find themselves approaching an age at which they feel they either must have a child soon or give up their dream of becoming a mother.[82] These women are in most cases unwilling dissenters from the two-parent family who have carefully thought out their child rearing plans and have found ways to provide their children with a network of loving parental figures. And yet, family communitarians condemn even older, economically secure women who have children on their own, and argue for policies that would prevent them from gaining access to sperm banks and fertility technologies.[83] Far from rejecting family obligations, most single mothers create loving families, despite many challenges and without the benefit of male wages. To accuse these women of undermining family values is wrong. Single mothers, like lesbian and gay families, are a powerful symbol of the decline of the old sexual and gender order. However, they have not rejected the most important component of family life, which is the commitment to care for others on a daily basis.

In a very short amount of time many of the expectations and assumptions governing sexuality and family life have been shattered. As a result, individuals enjoy greater freedom in their intimate relationships and they have created several different kinds of family forms. While this greater freedom is not without its costs, it would be wrong to describe all of those who have rejected the traditional family as self-centered individuals who are unwilling to make lifelong commitments to care for others. Women and men dissent from the traditional two-parent family for a variety of reasons. Some men and women are rejecting a marital, gender, and family order that requires them to act against their deepest feelings, desires, and emotions. Others are saying no to a form of family that is based on their subordination. Some men and women aspire to be in traditional, gender-structured marriages, but find that economic conditions make this impossible. Others have chosen to end relationships that did not provide them with the emotional support and sexual intimacy that they take to be the basis of a rich and rewarding life. And finally, some men and women have abandoned their families because they were not ready for a major responsibility, or because they were not willing to work at a relationship that was sometimes difficult and not always exciting. The family communitarians are right to argue that if we do not uphold the two-parent family as an important norm, men and women will continue to leave their marriages and families for reasons that could be described as selfish or irresponsible. However, as I discuss at greater length in chapter 2, curtailing personal liberty involves serious costs. It will undermine the capacity of men and women to be self-determining in an area of life that has tremendous meaning and importance to them.

V. THE MEANING OF MARRIAGE: FIXED OR MUTABLE?

Central to the debate on family instability is the question of whether marriage is a fixed social institution or a relationship that should be open to change. In one sense, it is clearly the former. After all, marriage is a legal relationship, regulated by state law, which imposes obligations on the married couple and third parties. However, the institution of marriage has changed so much in recent years that it is no longer clear what social expectations and conventions govern it. High rates of divorce have called into question the concept of marriage as a lifelong commitment. The influx of married women into the paid labor force has undermined the assumption that marriage is based on interdependent gender roles and a gender-based division of labor. In addition, while it was once assumed that marriage was a necessary prerequisite for childbirth and child rearing, this is a difficult assertion to maintain when 31 percent of all families with children are now headed by one parent. Finally, the legalization of same-sex civil unions in Vermont and the proliferation of domestic partnership policy challenge the presumed naturalness of heterosexuality and the idea that men and women require each other in order to be complete. Given the wide variety of questions that have been raised about it, there is no longer one widely shared definition of marriage. Its meaning and the expectations that govern it are in flux.

Family communitarians argue that marriage should not be viewed as a voluntary relationship that is open to change. By this they do not mean that marriages should be arranged or even that divorce should be outlawed. Instead, their point is that the married couple should not determine the meaning of marriage. The members of the CFA complain that "marriage is now less an institution that one belongs to and more an idea that we insist on bending to our own purposes."[84] In a similar vein, Whitehead argues that "post-nuclear family ideology abandons the norm of permanence in marriage and other intimate partnerships in favor of a norm of unfettered choice."[85] The problem, according to family communitarians, is that if marriage is viewed as a voluntary arrangement it will no longer have one universal and socially sanctioned meaning. For example, permissive divorce laws allow husbands and wives to determine whether or not marriage is a lifelong commitment. Similarly, the availability of artificial insemination to single women allows unmarried women to determine whether or not children need fathers. And expanding the concept of marriage to include lesbian and gay couples allows individuals to determine whether the basis of marriage consists of complementary gender roles.

Family communitarians hold that while marriage arises out of choice, once a couple has married and had children, their relationship is no longer voluntary. Marriage transforms lovers into husbands and wives who have lifelong obligations to each other and their children. No matter how their feelings for each other change, if they are parents, they have an obligation to remain married for the sake of their children. It is only in cases of domestic violence, or when spousal conflict is frequent and potentially more damaging to children than divorce, that family communitarians acknowledge the legitimacy of marital dissolution.[86]

The idea that marriage is a contract is also rejected by family communitarians. They argue that contracts last only as long as they benefit both contracting partners. If the interests of either partner are no longer being met, the contract is dissolved. Family communitarians argue that it is almost impossible to achieve the worthy ideal of marital permanence if marriage is viewed as a vehicle for satisfying individual interests. When marriage is viewed as a voluntary relationship—one that is entered into on the basis of free choice and exited on the basis of free choice—the individual and his or her needs, desires, and interests, are placed above the well-being of the family.[87]

There are two major weaknesses with the family communitarians' position that the meaning of marriage should not be left up to its participants. The first is that in the United States, marriage is widely understood to be based on feelings, and feelings cannot be compelled. In the seventeenth century, John Locke argued in favor of religious freedom by asserting that belief cannot be compelled and that coercion is ultimately powerless against dissenting religious views.[88] What is true of religious belief is also true of love; it cannot be compelled, and is by definition, voluntary. Intimacy as we understand it today requires free choice. While earlier conceptions of marital union placed social considerations such as securing a legitimate heir or forging alliances between families above the feelings of the couple, as we have seen, this form of marriage began to lose its popularity in the United States in the early eighteenth century. Affection-based relationships are by definition based on free choice.

Family communitarians also fail to acknowledge the contribution intentionality makes to the richness and intensity of marital relationships. If marriage does not have one universal meaning, or if it is not governed entirely by social conventions and expectations, husbands and wives must take an active role in determining its meaning. When individuals share in the making of a project they often come to identify themselves with it in a particularly strong way. It has meaning for them because they helped to shape it. In addition, when relationships are voluntary they accord more fully with what each individual wants. As a result, they are often more fulfilling and provide greater opportunities for self-development. Intimate relationships between adults are most valued when they provide reciprocal opportunities for self-expression, sexual intimacy, emotional comfort and support, and mutual recognition. They must be freely chosen and engaged in voluntarily if they are to offer their participants these goods.

Family communitarians seek to hold together two principles of marriage that have been generating tension since the nineteenth century. On the one hand, they subscribe to the idea that marriage is a love- and affection-based relationship that is instrumental to the personal happiness of each marital partner. On the other hand, they seek to uphold the idea of marital permanence. These two principles are at war with each other because affection and love are not responsive to coercion. The family communitarians are willing to admit that using law and policy to increase family stability will constrain personal liberty. However, they do not view this as much of a loss because they are convinced that individuals are using their newfound freedoms to harm their families and themselves. They do not recognize that freedom is a precondition of intimacy and that constraining individual choices prevents men and women from forming and sustaining meaningful intimate bonds.

CONCLUSION

At the center of the debate on family values is the question of personal liberty. As should be clear by now, the point of disagreement between the family communitarians and myself is not whether personal liberty in sexual and family relations has expanded, but how to understand and evaluate its expansion. The family communitarians argue that too much personal liberty is destroying our most basic civil association—the two-parent family. They claim that the expansion of personal liberty in sexual and family relations has allowed for a form of individualism that emphasizes self-gratification and self-fulfillment at the expense of lifelong commitments. In contrast to this position, which assumes that liberty and the commitment to care inherently conflict, I have argued that the demand for personal liberty in intimate relations has developed in conjunction with a deeper appreciation of emotional and sexual intimacy. Instead of simply seeking freedom from the commitment to care, men and women want greater control over the form and nature of their intimate relations; their desire to be more self-determining in their sexual relationships and partnerships stems from their recognition of the value of intimacy and its centrality to the good life. Family communitarians argue that constraining personal liberty entails no great loss and promises substantial gains. I question whether the promotion of one form of family will contribute to the well-being of American families and, as I argue in chapter 2, I believe that it would involve substantial costs.

NOTES

1. Frank F. Furstenberg Jr., "Divorce and the American Family," *Annual Review of Sociology* 16 (1990): 379–403.

2. Christine Winquist Nord and Nicholas Zill, *Non-Custodial Parents' Participation in Their Children's Lives: Evidence from the Survey of Income and Program Participation, Volume II* (Washington, D.C.: U.S. Department of Health and Human Services, 2000). http://fatherhood.hhs.gov/sipp/pt2.htm (accessed 3 June 2000).

3. Bureau of the Census, *Fertility of American Women: June 1998, P20-526*, U.S. Department of Commerce, Economics and Statistics Administration (Washington, D.C., 1998).

4. Bureau of the Census, *America's Families and Living Arrangements: Population Statistics, 2000, P20-537*, U.S. Department of Commerce, Economics and Statistics Administration (Washington, D.C., June 2001).

5. Sarah Staveteig and Alyssa Wigton, "Key Findings by Race and Ethnicity: Findings from the National Survey of Families," *Snapshots of America's Family II: 1999 Results* (Washington, D.C.: Urban Institute, 2002). http://newfederalism. urban.org/nsaf/race-ethnicity.html (accessed 28 January 2002).

6. Carol A. Darling, David J. Kallen, and Joyce E. VanDusen, "Sex in Transition, 1900-1980," in *Family in Transition: Rethinking Marriage, Sexuality, Child Rearing, and Family Organization*, ed. Arlene S. Skolnick and Jerome H. Skolnick (Glenview, Ill.: Scott, Foresman and Co., 1995).

7. Bureau of the Census, *Marital Status and Living Arrangements: March 1996, P20-496*, U.S. Department of Commerce, Economics and Statistics Administration (Washington, D.C., 1998).

8. Furstenberg, "Divorce and the American Family," 381.

9. Estelle B. Freedman and John D'Elmio, *Intimate Matters: A History of Sexuality in America* (New York: Harper and Row, 1988); Steven Seidman, *Romantic Longings: Love in America, 1830–1980* (New York: Routledge, 1991).

10. Barbara R. Bergmann, *The Economic Emergence of Women* (New York: Basic Books, 1986); Daphne Spain and Suzanne M. Bianchi, *Balancing Act: Motherhood, Marriage and Employment Among American Women* (New York: Russell Sage Foundation, 1996).

11. Freedman and D'Emilio, *Intimate Matters*, 306–308.

12. Furstenberg, "Divorce and the American Family," 380–81; Cherlin, *Marriage, Divorce, Remarriage*, 45–47.

13. Annie K. Driscoll et al., "Nonmarital Childbearing Among Adult Women," *Journal of Marriage and the Family* 61, no. 1 (February 1999): 178–87.

14. For classic essays in feminist and lesbian theory, see Linda Nicholson, ed., *The Second Wave* (New York: Routledge, 1997) and Miriam Schneir, ed., *Feminism In Our Time* (New York: Vintage Books, 1994). For classic essays in lesbian and gay theory see Mark Blasius and Shane Phelan, eds., *We Are Everywhere: A Historical Sourcebook of Gay and Lesbian Politics* (New York: Routledge, 1997).

15. Gayle Rubin, "The Traffic in Women," in *The Second Wave*, 27–61.

16. Rubin, "The Traffic in Women"; Monique Wittig, "One is Not Born a Woman," in *The Second Wave*, 265–71.

17. William Julius Wilson, *When Work Disappears: The World of the New Urban Poor* (New York: Vintage Books, 1996), 25–34.

18. Wilson, *When Work Disappears*, 25–26, 145–146; Andrew Hacker, *Two Nations* (New York: Ballantine, 1995), 109.

19. Bureau of the Census, *Statistical Abstract of the United States*: 119th edition (Washington, D.C., 1999).

20. Teresa Amott, *Caught in the Crisis: Women and the U.S. Economy Today* (New York: Monthly Review Press, 1993), 49–82; Roberta M. Spalter-Ross, Heidi I. Hartmann, and Linda M. Andrews, "Mothers, Children, and Low-Wage Work: The Ability to Earn a Family Wage," in *Sociology and the Public Agenda*, ed. William Julius Wilson (London: Sage, 1993).

21. Allen Dupree and Wendell Primus, *Declining Share of Children Lived with Single Mothers in the Late 1990s*, Center on Budget and Policy Priorities (Washington, D.C., 2001). http://www.cbpp.org (accessed 15 June 2001). Using Census Bureau data, researchers at the Center on Budget and Policy Priorities report that the proportion of children living with a single mother declined from 19.9 to 18.4 percent between 1995 and 2000. In addition, the proportion of black children living with two married parents rose from 34.8 to 38.9 percent.

22. David Popenoe, "Can the Nuclear Family Be Revived?" *Social Science and Modern Society* 36, no. 5 (July/August 1999): 28–30.

23. William Galston, "A Liberal Case for the Two-Parent Family," in *Rights and the Common Good*, ed. Amitai Etzioni (New York: St. Martin's, 1995), 139–49.

24. William A. Galston, *Liberal Purposes: Goods, Virtues and Diversity in the Liberal State* (Cambridge, England: Cambridge University Press, 1991), 269.

25. The Council on Families in America, "Marriage in America: A Report to the Nation," in *Promises to Keep: Decline and Renewal in America*, ed. David Popenoe, Jean Bethke Elshtain and David Blankenhorn (Lanham, Md.: Rowman & Littlefield, 1996), 293–318.

26. Jean Bethke Elshtain, "The Family and Civic Life," in *Power Trips and Other Journeys: Essays in Feminism and Civic Discourse*, ed. Jean Bethke Elshtain (Madison: University of Wisconsin Press, 1990), 45–60.

27. Barbara Dafoe Whitehead, "Dan Quayle Was Right" *The Atlantic* 271, no. 4 (1993): 47–84.

28. David Blankenhorn, *Fatherless America* (New York: Basic Books, 1995), 4.

29. The Council on Families in America, "Marriage in America," 295.

30. The Council on Families in America, "Marriage in America," 298.

31. Popenoe, "Can the Nuclear Family Be Revived?" 28.

32. Blankenhorn, *Fatherless Families*, 1.

33. Jean Bethke Elshtain, "A Call to Civil Society," *Social Science and Modern Society* 36, no. 5 (July/August 1999): 11–19.

34. Elshtain, "A Call to Civil Society," 17.

35. Elshtain, "A Call to Civil Society," 13.

36. The Council on Families in America, "Marriage in America," 308.

37. The Council on Families in America, "Marriage in America," 309–14.

38. Galston, *Liberal Purposes,* 286.

39. Edward Shorter, *The Making of the Modern Family* (New York: Basic Books, 1977), 5.

40. Shorter, *The Making of the Modern Family,* 54–78; Lawrence Stone, *The Family, Sex and Marriage in England, 1500–1800* (New York: Harper and Row, 1979), 69–148.

41. Aristotle, *The Politics,* ed. Stephen Everson and trans. Jonathan Barnes (Cambridge, England: Cambridge University Press, 1988), 2.

42. Jean-Jacques Rousseau, *Emile or On Education,* intro. and trans. Allan Bloom (New York: Basic Books, 1979), 373.

43. Stone, *The Family, Sex and Marriage,* 70.

44. Stone, *The Family, Sex and Marriage,* 69.

45. Stone, *The Family, Sex and Marriage,* 82.

46. Carl D. Degler, *At Odds: Women and the Family in America from the Revolution to the Present* (New York: Oxford University Press, 1980), 9.

47. Jane Collier, Michelle Rosaldo, and Slyvia Yanagisako, "Is There a Family? New Anthropological Views," in *Rethinking the Family: Some Feminist Questions,* ed. Barrie Thorne with Marilyn Yalom (Boston: Northeastern University Press, 1992).

48. Degler, *At Odds,* 26.

49. Bonnie Thorton Dill, "Fictive Kin, Paper Sons, and Compadrazgo: Women of Color and the Struggle for Family Survival" in *American Families: A Multicultural Reader,* ed. Stephanie Coontz with the assistance of Maya Parson and Gabrielle Raley (New York: Routledge, 1999).

50. Steven Seidman, *Romantic Longings: Love in America, 1830–1980* (New York: Routledge, 1991), 60.

51. Seidman, *Romantic Longings,* 73.

52. Seidman, *Romantic Longings,* 79.

53. Seidman, *Romantic Longings,* 125.

54. Freedman and D'Emilio, *Intimate Matters,* 288–95.

55. Rickie Solinger chronicles public opinion toward and treatment of unmarried pregnant women before *Roe v. Wade* in *Wake Up Little Suzie: Single Pregnancy and Race Before Roe v. Wade* (New York: Routledge, 1992).

56. Susan Moller Okin, "Sexual Orientation, Gender, and Families: Dichotomizing Differences," *Hypatia: A Journal of Feminist Philosophy* 11, no. 1 (Winter 1996): 1–48; Kath Weston, *Families We Choose: Lesbians, Gays, Kinship* (New York: Columbia University, 1991); Judith Stacey, *In the Name of the Family* (Boston: Beacon Press, 1996).

57. Okin, "Sexual Orientation, Gender, and Families," 45.

58. Nan Hunter, "Marriage, Law and Gender: A Feminist Inquiry," in *Sex Wars: Sexual Dissent and Political Culture,* ed. Lisa Duggin and Nan Hunter (New York: Routledge, 1995), 107–22.

59. Judith Stacey, "Gay and Lesbian Families: Queer Like Us," in *All Our Families: New Policies for a New Century,* ed. Mary Ann Mason, Arlene Skolnick, and Stephen D. Sugarman (New York: Oxford University Press, 1998), 120.

60. For examples of how lesbians, gay men, and feminists have reinvented family, see Anndee Hochman, *Everyday Acts and Small Subversions: Woman Reinventing Family, Community and Home* (Portland, Oreg.: Eighth Mountain Press, 1994); Weston, *Families We Choose*; Esther Newton, *Cherry Grove, Fire Island: Sixty Years in America's First Gay and Lesbian Town* (Boston: Beacon Press, 1993).

61. Seidman, *Romantic Longings,* 176–89.

62. Dill, "Fictive Kin," 17.

63. Bonnie Thorton Dill, Maxine Baca Zinn, and Sandra Patton, "Feminism, Race, and the Politics of Family Values," *Philosophy and Public Policy* 13, no. 3 (Summer 1993): 13–19.

64. Robert Joseph Taylor et al., "Recent Demographic Trends in African American Family Structure," in *Family Life in Black America*, ed. Robert Joseph Taylor, James S. Jackson, and Linda Chatters (Thousand Oaks, Calif.: Sage, 1997), 14–62.

65. Sara Rimer, "Tradition of Care for the Elderly Thrives in Black Families," *New York Times*, 10 March 1998, National Edition, A9.

66. Patricia Hill Collins, *Black Feminist Thought* (New York: Routledge, 1991), 119.

67. Dill, "Fictive Kin"; Patricia Hill Collins, "Shifting the Center: Race, Class and Feminist Theorizing about Motherhood," in *American Families: A Multicultural Reader*, ed. Stephanie Coontz with Maya Parson and Gabrielle Raley (New York: Routledge, 1999).

68. Pauli Murray, "The Liberation of Black Women," in *Words of Fire: An Anthology of African-American Feminist Thought*, ed. Beverly Guy-Sheftall (New York: New Press, 1995), 186–97.

69. Furstenberg, "Divorce and the American Family," 385.

70. Judith Stacey, "The New Family Values Crusaders" *The Nation* 259, no. 44 (1994): 119–22.

71. Federal Interagency Forum on Child and Family Statistics, *America's Children 2000: Key National Indicators of Well-Being, 2000* (Washington, D.C., 2000).

72. Bureau of the Census, *Fertility of American Women: June 1998, P20-526*, U.S. Department of Commerce, Economics, and Statistics Administration (Washington, D.C., 1998).

73. Shirley Aisha Ray and Vonnie C. McLoyd, "Fathers in Hard Times: The Impact of Unemployment and Poverty on Paternal and Marital Relations," in *The Father's Role, Applied Perspectives*, ed. Michael Lamb (New York: John Wiley, 1986), 339–84.

74. Wilson, *When Work Disappears*, 87–110; Janet M. Fitchen, *Endangered Spaces, Enduring Places: Change, Identity, and Survival in Rural America* (Boulder, Colo.: Westview Press, 1991), 142–46.

75. Jill K. Kiecolt and Mark A. Fosset, "The Effects of Mate Availability on Marriage Among Black Americans," in *Family Life in Black America*, ed. Robert Joseph Taylor, James S. Jackson, and Linda Chatters (Thousand Oaks, Calif.: Sage, 1997).

76. Annie E. Casey Foundation, *Kids Count Data Book 2000* (Baltimore, Md.: Annie E. Casey Foundation, 2000).

77. Christopher Jencks and Kathryn Edin, "Do Poor Women Have the Right to Bear Children?" *The American Prospect* 20 (winter 1995): 43–52.

78. Taylor et al., "Recent Demographic Trends in African American Family Structure," 27.

79. Jacqueline E. Darroch, David J. Landry, and Susheela Singh, "Changing Emphases in Sexuality Education in U.S. Public Secondary Schools, 1988-1999," *Family Planning Perspectives* 32, no. 5 (September/October 2000): 212–19.

80. Diana Jean Schemo, "Sex Education with Just One Lesson: No Sex," *New York Times*, 28 December 2000, A1–A21; Darroch, Landry, and Singh, "Changing Emphases in Sexuality Education."

81. The Alan Guttmacher Institute, *Sex and America's Teenagers* (New York: The Alan Guttmacher Institute, 1994).

82. Melissa Ludtke, *On Our Own: Unmarried Motherhood in America* (New York: Random House, 1997), 110–13.

83. Blankenhorn, *Fatherless Families*, 233.

84. The Council on Families in America, "Marriage in America," 300.

85. Barbara Dafoe Whitehead, *The Divorce Culture: Rethinking Our Commitments to Marriage and Family* (New York: Vintage, 1996), 143.

86. William A. Galston, "Divorce American Style," *The Public Interest* 124 (Summer 1996): 12–17.

87. Whitehead, "Dan Quayle Was Right," *The Atlantic* 271, no. 4 (1993): 47–84, 82–83; Jean Bethke Elshtain, "Feminism, Family and Community, " *Dissent* 30, no. 1 (Winter 1983), 445.

88. John Locke, *A Letter Concerning Toleration*, ed. James H. Tully. (Indianapolis, Ind.: Hackett Publishing, 1983).

Chapter Two

Personal Liberty and the Right of Privacy

The defense of individual liberty has been a central tenet of liberal political thought from John Locke to Ronald Dworkin. However, it is only since 1965 that the U.S. Supreme Court has recognized a liberty interest in sexual and intimate relationships, or what I am calling personal liberty. In *Griswold v. Connecticut* 381 U.S. 479 (1965), the Supreme Court ruled that the constitutional right of privacy protects the right of married couples to use birth control. Subsequent cases extended the right of privacy to include the right to distribute birth control to unmarried persons and the right to an abortion.[1] The birth control and abortion decisions expanded the scope of sexual liberty and enhanced the individual's ability to define for herself the meaning of sexuality and intimate relationships. However, conservative court majorities have eroded the promise of the right of privacy in cases such as *Bowers v. Hardwick*, which upheld a Georgia statute criminalizing sodomy, and *Harris v. McRae* 448 U.S. 297 (1988) and *Mayer v. Roe* 432 U.S. 464 (1977), which upheld prohibitions on the use of federal and state funds to pay for abortion. Despite these significant setbacks, modern privacy jurisprudence provides one of the most important defenses of personal liberty in sexuality and intimate relationship: Justice Harry Blackmun's powerful dissent in *Bowers v. Hardwick*.

In the first section of this chapter, "Justice Blackmun's Dissent and the Freedom of Intimate Association," I examine Blackmun's claim in *Bowers v. Hardwick* that the right of privacy protects the freedom of intimate association. My reading of Blackmun's dissent highlights his claim that independent identity formation, or individuality, occurs within the context of intimate relationships. Like Blackmun, I argue that intimate relationships have a deep and lasting impact on who we are and who we will become. It is within and through these relationships that we exercise our capacities for moral independence and self-definition. Moreover, it is often through these relationships

31

that we find emotional support, care, and pleasure. For all of these reasons, individuals have a fundamental interest in exercising self-determination in their intimate and sexual relations with others.

My purpose in section 2, "What Does Privacy Protect?" is to clarify the meaning of the right of privacy at stake in *Bowers v. Hardwick* and to defend it against its critics. I begin by providing a brief sketch of three different privacy traditions that have influenced U.S. law and culture, and I then show that each tradition protects a distinct liberty interest. Only one of these three privacy traditions protects personal liberty. This form of the right of privacy—what I call the individuality-based right of privacy—is best understood as protecting the individual's interest in formulating and acting on her own conception of the good life, even if her understanding of what makes life valuable violates the majority's values and beliefs. In essence, the individuality-based right of privacy protects those individuals who dissent from, or refuse to conform to, state-sanctioned and promoted forms of sexual expression and family life.

In section 3, "Individuality and Privacy," I further develop an individuality-based right of privacy by drawing on John Stuart Mill's conception of individuality in *On Liberty*. Resting the right of privacy on individuality allows us to go beyond its traditional definition as a negative right that prohibits state intervention in certain personal decisions. Mill argues that individuality requires liberty and diversity of situations to flourish. Protecting the conditions necessary to the free development of individuality may in some cases call for positive state action.[2]

I. JUSTICE BLACKMUN'S DISSENT AND THE FREEDOM OF INTIMATE ASSOCIATION

There is, at present, no constitutional right to the freedom of intimate relationship or association. The Supreme Court recognized a constitutional right of privacy in 1965 and found that it protected the right of married couples to use birth control in *Griswold v. Connecticut*. The right to distribute birth control to unmarried couples was recognized in 1972 in *Eisenstadt v. Baird* 405 U.S. 438. The following year, in *Roe v. Wade* 394 U.S. 557 (1973), the Court held that the right of privacy includes the right of a woman in consultation with her physician to terminate a pregnancy. The Supreme Court's birth control and abortion decisions protected individual actions and decisions having a direct bearing on sexually intimate relationships from the will of the majority. In doing so, the Court legitimized the view that sex between adult heterosexuals can take place outside of marriage and for reasons others than procreation. The right of privacy, as it was applied in the birth control and abortion cases, established that the meaning and purpose of sexual activity should be determined by the individual participants and not by social conventions and institutions.

In *Bowers v. Hardwick*, the majority opinion, delivered by Justice Byron White, reversed a previous Court of Appeals decision that held that the right of privacy covered acts of sodomy committed in the home. For reasons he chose to leave obscure, Justice White restricted his opinion to same-sex sexual activity. White's opinion in *Bowers v. Hardwick* is based, in part, on the assertion that state governments have a long history of criminalizing sodomy. However, White ignored the fact that such laws were originally meant to apply to all nonprocreative sexual activity, whether heterosexual or homosexual.[3] *Bowers v. Hardwick* destroyed the hope that the right of privacy could be used to protect same-sex sexual activity. However, in his dissent to *Bowers v. Hardwick*, Justice Blackmun provides an elegant defense of the freedom of intimate association. He does this by arguing that voluntarily chosen intimate relationships are integral to independent identity formation or individuality.[4]

In his majority opinion, Justice White argues that previous privacy decisions should not be interpreted as extending protection to "any kind of private sexual conduct between consenting adults."[5] Instead, White explains, the right of privacy should be understood as protecting certain decisions regarding family, marriage, and procreation. Since, White reasons, homosexual relationships have nothing to do with family, marriage, and procreation, there is no reason to extend the right of privacy to consensual, same-sex sexual activity. White's argument suggests, as do some interpretations of *Griswold v. Connecticut*, that the purpose of the right of privacy is to protect traditional social institutions such as marriage and family.[6] White defines same-sex sexual activity as completely outside of, even opposed to, marriage and family.[7] This is an odd definition because all post–*Griswold v. Connecticut* privacy decisions have protected the freedom to engage in heterosexual sexual relations *without* being married. In suggesting that these decisions protected marital and familial autonomy, White distorts the meaning of the privacy cases.

In his dissent to the majority opinion, Justice Blackmun argues that the reason "rights associated with the family" are protected by the right of privacy is "not because they contribute, in some direct and material way to the general public welfare, but because they form so central a part of an individual's life."[8] Instead of protecting the institution of marriage or family, the right of privacy protects the individual's liberty to make her own decisions about intimate and sexual relationships. And it does so, according to Blackmun, because intimate relationships are essential to independent identity formation.

Blackmun explains that the rights to use birth control and have an abortion are protected because the decision to become a parent "alters so dramatically an individual's self-definition." Citing *Moore v. East Cleveland* 478 U.S. 186 (1986), in which the Court ruled that the state could not decide what family arrangements constitute a family for the purposes of residential zoning, Blackmun states, "we protect the family because it contributes so powerfully to the happiness of individuals."[9] The right of privacy protects not a specific ideal of family but the freedom of individuals to form the families of their choice. Individuals have a fundamental interest in controlling the nature of their intimate relationships, because it is through these relationships and because of these relationships that they are able to define and sustain themselves.

If intimate relationships are to contribute to the independent formation of identity, they must be self-chosen. According to Blackmun, "[t]he fact that individuals define themselves in a significant way through their intimate sexual relationships with others suggests, in a Nation such as ours, that there are many 'right' ways of conducting those relationships, and that much of the richness of a relationship will come from the freedom an individual has to choose the form and nature of these intensely important bonds."[10] If individuals are not given the freedom to experiment with forms of intimacy, of which the majority does not approve, a significant portion of these individuals will not be able to freely develop themselves or find satisfying relationships. Respecting individuality or independent identity formation requires public recognition and equal treatment of a variety of family forms or intimate associations.

The significance of Blackmun's opinion lies in the strong connection he establishes between individuality and self-chosen intimate relationships between peers. Initially, Blackmun appears to take the position that the right of privacy can best be understood as a right of withdrawal or the freedom to separate oneself from others. He states early in his dissent that *Bowers v. Hardwick* is about "'the most comprehensive of rights and the rights most valued by civilized men,' namely 'the right to be alone.'"[11] But Blackmun later tells us that the "'ability independently to define one's identity that is central to any concept of liberty' cannot truly be exercised in a vacuum; we all depend on the 'emotional enrichment from close ties to others.'"[12] With his second statement, Blackmun makes clear that his initial definition of the right of privacy referred to the individual's right to be free from the relationship preferences of the majority. Blackmun explains that the purpose of personal liberty in sexual and family relationships is to free individuals from conventional definitions of family and intimate relationship so that they may form the intimate associations of their choice. This is not a vulgar individualism that defines individual liberty as the absence of all obligations to others. Instead, Blackmun's point is that the dominance of heterosexual conventions should not prevent men and women from choosing same-sex love. The value of personal liberty in sexual and intimate relationships is that it allows individuals to choose the "form and nature of these intensely personal bonds."

According to Blackmun, it is within intimate relationships with others that self-definition takes place. Intimate relationships are, by definition, those in which we share those parts of ourselves that we are not willing to share with just anyone. Part of what makes a relationship intimate is our belief that the other person knows us in a way that others do not.[13] In addition, intimate relationships possess a depth and quality of care and closeness that is missing in nonintimate relationships. Intimate relationships are central to independent identity formation because it is within them that we are seen, affirmed, and emotionally and physically held. Without intimate relationships, a part of ourselves, perhaps the most important part of ourselves, would disappear because we would have no one to share it with. As important as being cared for is to self-definition, caring for others may be even more important. Many people define themselves in terms of their caring activity as mothers, fathers, lovers, siblings, friends, and adult children.

Sexual desire, which often pulls us into intimate relationships with others, is an essential component of self-definition. Our relationship to our bodies and our experiences of the powerful pleasures and feelings associated with sexual attraction and activity are most often played out in our sexual relationships. Sexual experience cannot be given a fixed meaning: for some, it is an almost purely physical pleasure; while for others, it is also a medium for expressing feelings such as love. But given the strong physical needs and emotions associated with sexual desire and activity, sexual relationships exercise a profound impact on self-definition.

It is within intimate relationships that we experience intense emotional sharing, caring, affirmation and support, and desire and sexual satisfaction. These relationships are central to our sense of self because if we feel safe within them we have a degree of safety wherever we go. If we do not feel safe within them, there is nowhere we can go where we will ever feel entirely safe. Preventing individuals from engaging in the intimate relationships of their choice prevents them from establishing and maintaining an emotional anchor. Without the freedom to form sustaining relationships with others, men and women are deprived of what is for many people the most meaningful part of their lives.

My purpose in this section was to introduce the elements of an individuality-based conception of the right of privacy through an examination of Justice Blackmun's dissent to *Bowers v. Hardwick*. In the following section, I locate

Blackmun's conception of the right of privacy in a distinct privacy tradition, and show how it differs from definitions of the right of privacy that arise out of competing privacy traditions. I then identify and describe three different privacy traditions. The first privacy tradition protects associational freedom and the freedom of contract. This form of privacy is commonly viewed as protecting economic relationships from government regulation. The second form of privacy protects the head of the household's authority over subordinate family members and prohibits the state from interfering in family matters. The third form of privacy protects personal liberty or the individual's freedom to live according to her own understanding of the good life even if her understanding of it violates values that the majority cherishes.

II. WHAT DOES PRIVACY PROTECT?

The constitutional right of privacy and the philosophical principles on which it rests are highly contested. This is, in part, because several different privacy traditions have influenced U.S. law and culture. These privacy traditions share a common purpose, which is to protect certain individual freedoms from the authority of the state. However, these traditions can be distinguished by the type of liberty they defend and the kind of interests they protect. My purpose in this section is to classify and clarify these different definitions of privacy in order to develop a clear understanding of the type of privacy that defends personal liberty in sexual and intimate relationships.[14] In addition, I will demonstrate that these three privacy traditions are not interdependent. Defending one form of privacy does not suggest a commitment to all three.

Privacy as Economic and Associational Freedom

Locke's *Two Treatises on Government* is considered by many to be the classic defense of individual liberty.[15] In his argument for constitutional government, Locke claims that the government cannot legitimately violate the individual's pre-political (or natural) rights to life, liberty, and estate. Indeed, the very definition of legitimate political authority for Locke is government recognition of the natural rights of the individual. Locke's articulation of the limits of political authority delineates a boundary between the state and civil society. Subsequent advocates of the state/civil society distinction argued that men would be good and productive if the influence of political authorities over their voluntary relations and exchanges is minimized. Truths can be discovered, business can be transacted, and souls can be saved without the assistance of government. An extreme version of this belief is captured by

Thomas Paine's comment in *Common Sense*: "Society provides many blessings, while government is a necessary evil."[16] Although not all liberal proponents of the state/civil society distinction embrace a negative characterization of government, those with libertarian leanings argue that civil associations and markets flourish without government intervention. Economic activity and activity taking place within civil associations should be spontaneous, free, and voluntary.

While it originated out of the interest individuals have in conducting a wide variety of social and civil relationships without undue government interference, the state/civil society distinction was used in the United States during the early period of industrialization to prevent the regulation of property and contracts. During the first third of the twentieth century, the Supreme Court consistently employed the due process clause of the Fourteenth Amendment to strike down laws establishing wage and hour legislation aimed at protecting the interests of workers. The Court argued that the Fourteenth Amendment protected both procedural and substantive liberties, including the freedom of contract. Facing a popular president in 1937 who was determined to use government regulation of the economy to fight the Great Depression, the Court dropped its defense of laissez-faire in *West Coast Hotel Co. v. Parish* 300 U.S. 379 (1937).

The idea that economic activity should be free from government regulation has been criticized from social democratic, egalitarian liberal, and Marxist perspectives. Social democrats such as Michael Walzer assert that large-scale economic enterprises have a direct and far-reaching impact on the lives of workers. Decisions that have such a direct bearing on the ability of individuals to be self-determining should be made democratically, and not by one individual. Ownership of capital does not give owners the authority to dictate the lives of others.[17] Egalitarian liberals, such as John Rawls, argue that unregulated capitalism causes unacceptable levels of economic inequality. Government regulation and progressive taxation is necessary to redistribute wealth and income and preserve equality of economic opportunity.[18] Marxists argue that the ideology of free and equal exchanges between capitalists and workers serves to mask the tremendous power owners of capital have over those who own only their ability to labor. In contrast to egalitarian liberals who assert that government should intervene in economic relations to correct extreme forms of economic inequality, Marxists argue that only some form of collective ownership of the means of production will bring about a just society.[19]

The state/civil society distinction is primarily concerned with social and economic (as opposed to personal) relationships. Social activity takes place in nondomestic places such as businesses, religious institutions, schools, and parks. It includes market exchanges as well as relations between colleagues, coworkers, union members, business partners, and members of voluntary associations including political clubs, movements, and parties. The state/civil society distinction protects the individual's interest in forming associations or entering into exchanges with others. However, these associations and exchanges do not generally take place in domestic spaces and are not of an intimate or personal nature. They are referred to as private activities because they are not state funded, regulated, or sponsored.

Privacy as Family Autonomy

The concept of privacy has been used to protect the husband/father's authority over subordinate household members. According to family autonomy doctrine, a man's home is his castle, and the state should refrain from interfering in the household or in relationships between family members. Beginning with Aristotle's account of household guardianship in Book One of *The Politics*, the household has been conceived as a hierarchical association ruled by a male head that is responsible for the welfare of his wife and children. As late as 1873 in *Bradwell v. State of Illinois* 83 U.S. 130 (1873), the U.S. Supreme Court affirmed common law doctrine that held that a woman has no legal existence separate from her husband who is regarded as her head and representative in the social state.[20] Prior to legal reforms initiated by the women's rights movement during the last half of the nineteenth century, husbands were accorded control over their wives' property and wages, retained custody of their children in cases of divorce and separation, and were legally empowered to physically chastise their wives.

The family autonomy-based conception of privacy rests on the assumption that the husband/father is the natural ruler of the household, and that political authorities should respect his right to rule. Relying on this doctrine, legal authorities have condoned wife abuse. A North Carolina court responded with the following words to a wife's cry for help in 1886:

> Family government is recognized by law as being complete in itself as the state government is in itself, and yet subordinate to it; . . . however great are the evils of ill temper, quarrels, and even personal conflicts inflicting only temporary pain, they are not comparable with the evils which would result from raising the curtain and exposing to public curiosity and criticism the nursery and the bed chamber.[21]

In this case, the Court used the doctrine of family autonomy to justify its refusal to protect a woman from physical abuse at the hands of her husband.

Privacy as family autonomy is easily confused with privacy as personal liberty because these forms are both concerned with relations between intimates. However, the interests protected by family autonomy are quite different than those protected by Blackmun's account of the right of privacy in *Bowers v. Hardwick*. The concept of family autonomy does not permit individual family members to have distinct interests. As the Court stated in *Bradwell v. State of Illinois*, the head of the household represents the interests of "his family" to the outside world. Privacy, in this context, means that there are few limitations on the head of the household's freedom to use and abuse subordinate family members, including his wife, as he sees fit. The liberty interest that is being protected is the head of the household's freedom to rule unimpeded by state regulation over subordinate household members.

In response to this long history of male-domination within the family, some feminists have taken the position that privacy doctrine is inimical to the interests of women. The most vocal feminist opposed to the right of privacy, Catherine MacKinnon, has stated that "women have no privacy to lose or guarantee."[22] MacKinnon explains that intimate relationships with men that take place within the private sphere are the source of women's exploitation and oppression. The right of privacy prevents efforts to redress power differences between men and women by restricting intervention in the private sphere. While she is not opposed to privacy rights herself, Francis Olsen provides an explanation for why some women are. She states, "A right to privacy analysis is . . . unappealing to women, however, insofar as women have been 'oppressed by (the) violence and sexual aggression that society (has) allow (ed) in the name of sexual freedom.'"[23] According to MacKinnon and Olsen, privacy doctrine leaves women to fend for themselves in the areas of life, sexuality, and family, in which they are most vulnerable to male power.

Feminists are right to condemn male-dominated conceptions of family and the exploitation and abuse of women in the private sphere. However, the individuality-based right of privacy should not be rejected because of the harm done to women in the name of the family autonomy-based right of privacy. While in practice they have been conflated and confused, the privacy tradition that protects the head of the household's autonomy differs greatly from the privacy tradition that protects personal liberty. The first form of privacy does bolster men's authority over women. As I discussed above, it can and has been used to justify the exploitation and abuse of women by their husbands. However, privacy as personal liberty protects the privacy of the individual and not the privacy of the family as a unit. While it is possible to see a family autonomy concept of privacy at work in the text of *Griswold v. Connecticut*, post–*Griswold v. Connecticut* decisions, beginning with *Eisenstadt v. Baird*, make quite clear that the right of privacy attaches to individuals and not to entities such as the family.[24] Most importantly, privacy as family autonomy and privacy as personal liberty protect distinct liberty interests. The first, which grows out of the tradition of the male-dominated household, protects the husband's interest in controlling his wife. The second, which grows out of a romantic tradition concerned with social conformity, protects the individual's freedom to dissent from the majority's morality.

MacKinnon's rejection of privacy doctrines rests on her conviction that women exercise very little self-determination in their personal relationships with men. She argues that the right of privacy endangers rather than empowers women, because it always benefits the more powerful person in a relationship. This position underestimates the degree of independence that women exercise in relationships with men, despite the continued existence of gender inequality. It suggests that women who seek sexual relationships with men must wait until all forms of gender inequality are abolished. In addition, the idea that privacy is of no use to women fails to recognize how an individuality-based right of privacy can be used to expand women's independence and autonomy.[25]

Privacy as Personal Liberty

The distinction between the personal and the social is the only private/public distinction that defends the personal liberty of the individual, man or woman, from political and social authority. Romantic writers who sought to preserve individual spontaneity and creativity in a society they experienced as overly conformist originally proposed this distinction.[26] According to the romantic distinction between public and private, the private sphere of the state/civil society distinction is actually part of the public sphere. In fact, it is often civil society, and its conventions and customs that the romantic nonconformist finds most oppressive. As Mill explains in *On Liberty*, the absolute monarch is no longer the greatest threat to individual liberty in the nineteenth century. The nonconformist living in a democratic republic fears his fellow citizens because of their ability to turn their stereotypes and prejudices into law.[27]

The romantic private sphere provides opportunities for dissent, experimentation, and innovation.[28] It protects moral independence and the disposition to question and criticize social conventions. It does not celebrate individualism—the individual's self-centered quest for social rewards such as wealth, fame, and power; but rather, individuality—the individual's attempt to develop her faculties and live as she chooses despite the views of a hostile majority. Individuality is erroneously understood as the opposite of community; its true opposite is conformity. Privacy as personal liberty assumes that the individual does not exist solely to serve social and political ends. I provide a more developed account of personal liberty and the principles on which it is based in section 3.

The three different privacy traditions I have described protect different liberty interests: the freedom to contract and form voluntary associations, the freedom to independently govern subordinate family members, and the freedom to dissent from socially sanctioned forms of sexual expression and family. It is the last form of liberty interest that is at stake in the *Bowers v. Hardwick* decision. Modern privacy jurisprudence arises out of the romantic distinction between the personal and the social. While there are areas of overlap among these three forms of privacy, support for one in no way implies support for all three. Indeed, privacy as family autonomy and privacy as personal liberty are in direct conflict with each other. According to the family autonomy tradition, relationships between household members are determined by conventional meanings ascribed to age and gender. In contrast, privacy as personal liberty protects the interests of individuals in forming the intimate and sexual relationships of their choice. While privacy as family autonomy upholds convention and subordinates the individual to the authority of the father and/or husband, privacy as personal liberty protects individuals from the majority's moral preferences and from traditional forms of authority.

Privacy as economic and associational liberty cannot be justified on the same grounds as personal liberty. As Dworkin has explained, there is no general or all-purpose right to individual liberty.[29] To suggest that a commitment to personal liberty implies a commitment to economic liberty is to endorse a definition of liberty as the absence of all constraints. Dworkin distinguishes between liberty as freedom from legal constraint and liberty as moral independence. Liberty as moral independence protects a person's status as an independent moral agent and an equal citizen. It does not protect the person's freedom to do whatever she would like to do. According to Dworkin, laws that "recognize and protect common interests, like laws against violence or monopoly, offer no insult to any class or individual; but laws that constrain one man, on the sole ground that he is incompetent to decide what is right for himself are profoundly insulting to him."[30] Government regulation of contracts and commerce may well have a significant impact on the ability of businessmen to run their companies as they see fit. In this sense, it places real constraints on the liberty of the individual. However, as Dworkin explains, economic regulations are not based on the idea that businessmen are unequal to or less worthy of respect than their fellow citizens. In contrast, Justice White's reluctance to extend the right of privacy to same-sex sexual activity was based on the assumption that homosexual sexual activity is deviant and perverse. This regulation is profoundly insulting to citizens who engage in same-sex sexual activity because it suggests that their sexual choices and values are less worthy of respect than those of citizens who engage in heterosexual sexual activity.

A Millian argument also can be advanced to distinguish between economic and personal liberty. According to Mill, the individual should be sovereign in affairs that do not have a direct or immediate impact on the fundamental interests or rights of others.[31] The nature of the contemporary corporate enterprise ensures that the decisions its executives make will have a direct and immediate impact on workers. Clearly, being able to earn a living and support one's family is a fundamental interest. Because of the large, direct, and immediate effects they have on the lives of workers and consumers, economic decisions cannot be considered entirely private.

The right of privacy as interpreted by Justice Blackmun is rooted in the youngest privacy tradition. Its purpose is to protect the freedom to dissent from the majority's vision of the good life. In particular, the right of privacy protects the individual's right to engage in sexual and intimate relationships that do not accord with traditional conceptions of marriage and family. In the subsection that follows, I continue to clarify what privacy protects by exploring the juridical distinction between informational and decisional privacy.

Juridical Definitions of Privacy:
Informational and Decisional Privacy

The Supreme Court currently recognizes two kinds of privacy: informational privacy and decisional privacy. Justice John Paul Stevens, writing for an unanimous Court in *Whalen v. Roe* 97 St. Ct. 869 (1977), identified both an "individual interest in avoiding disclosure of personal matters" and an "interest in independence in making certain kinds of important decisions."[32] Informational privacy is primarily concerned with restricting the access others have to information about us that is of a personal nature, such as the kind of personal facts kept in medical or credit records. It also includes cases involving unwanted observation or surveillance. Informational privacy has been most frequently used in tort law to protect the individual's interest in avoiding disclosure of personal matters. The legal history of informational privacy goes back much further than the more recent decisional privacy. The first law article to discuss the right of privacy argued for the use of civil law to protect individuals from undesired media attention. *"The Right of Privacy,"* coauthored by Samuel Warren and Louis Brandeis in 1890, grew out of Warren's indignation over sensationalist newspaper coverage of his wife.[33]

In contrast, decisional privacy cases have focused on decisions the Supreme Court has classified as personal or intimate in such areas as contraception, procreation, marriage, child rearing, and family.[34] Supreme Court decisions on family and reproduction from the first half of the twentieth century have been frequently cited as antecedents of the modern privacy cases. *Pierce v. Society of Sisters* 268 U.S. 510 (1925) and *Meyer v. Nebraska*, 262 U.S. 390 (1923) established the autonomy of parents to direct the upbringing of their children without undue state interference. In *Skinner v. Oklahoma* 316 U.S. 535 (1942), the Court ruled against the sterilization of specific categories of criminals on the basis of both the equal protection and due process clauses of the Fourteenth Amendment. However, it was not until the 1965 *Griswold v. Connecticut* decision that the Supreme Court articulated a constitutional right of privacy. *Griswold v. Connecticut* struck down a Connecticut law that prohibited the distribution and use of contraceptives. The Supreme Court ruled that the law violated a married couple's right of privacy. According to Justice William O. Douglas, the right of privacy can be found in the "penumbras and emanations" of the Bill of Rights. In a concurring opinion, Justice Arthur Goldberg relied on the Ninth Amendment, which states that the Bill of Rights does not provide a complete listing of all the rights that citizens of the United States possess, to argue that the right of privacy is an unenumerated right. Subsequent privacy decisions have placed greater emphasis on the due process clause of the Fourteenth Amendment, which forbids government from restricting individual liberty without "due process of the law." The Supreme Court subjects laws that it believes violate fundamental rights to the "strict scrutiny" test. If such laws are not based on what the Court calls a "compelling state interest," they can be overturned. The 1965 *Griswold v. Connecticut* decision and the 1973 *Roe v. Wade* decision established the right of privacy as a fundamental right.[35]

Some scholars argue that decisional privacy is a distortion of the original meaning of privacy that refers to "keeping things private" or restricting the knowledge of the general public about specific personal matters. However, this objection ignores how we employ the concept of privacy in everyday speech. Privacy clearly carries the connotation of wanting to keep things hidden from the public; however, it also suggests that being deprived of decisional autonomy on deeply personal matters constitutes a particularly grave harm. When I state that something is "my business and nobody else's," I am saying that I should be able to make decisions about it without external interference. Asserting that an issue is private suggests that it possesses a particular nature: it affects us in a special and important way. Many times, when we claim that a matter is private, we are suggesting that it has to do with our intimate or emotionally charged relationships with others. Stating that a matter is personal and should be kept private also means that it touches on our deepest beliefs and values or goes to the heart of who we are. Whether in matters of the heart or the soul, the idea that we will not be able to exercise our own independent judgment is deeply threatening to our sense of self and our well-being.

During the last half of the twentieth century, many United States citizens have come to see sexuality and intimate relationships as largely private matters. The Supreme Court's use of the terms "personal" and "intimate" suggest an attempt to identify decisions that are emotionally charged, that will have a deep and lasting impact on the individual's life, and that invoke beliefs and values about the meaning of sexuality and intimate relationship. Justice Douglas employed the term intimate to identify the kind of liberty interest at stake in *Griswold v. Connecticut*. Writing for the Court, he explained that "We do not sit as a super-legislature to determine the wisdom, need, and propriety of laws that touch economic problems, business affairs, or social conditions. This law, however, operates directly on an *intimate relation* between husband and wife and their physician's role in one aspect of that relation."[36] Justice Douglas uses "intimate" to convey the unique part the marital relationship plays in the emotional life of husband and wife. This kind of relationship, unlike the relationship between salesperson and consumer, or employer and employee, has a direct and profound effect on its participants. In addition, there is a very low probability that the choice they make about their sexual relationship will affect the fundamental interests and rights of others. It also suggests that choices about birth control invoke the individual's or the couple's understanding of the purpose of sexuality and its place in an intimate relationship. In a complex society, individuals will hold very different ideas about the meaning and purpose of sexuality. These ideas are "private" in the sense that they are essential to independent identity formation and consequently should be decided by the individual as opposed to the majority.

In subsequent privacy decisions, the Court continued to argue that the right of privacy protects decisions of a personal nature. In *Eisenstadt v. Baird*, a 1972 decision that extended the right to use contraceptives to unmarried couples, the Court declared: "If the right of privacy means anything, it is the right of the individual, married or single, to be free from unwarranted governmental intrusion into *matters so fundamentally affecting a person* as the decision to bear or beget a child."[37] In this statement, the Court identifies the enormous impact of pregnancy on the pregnant woman and to a lesser degree, her partner. Childbirth will fundamentally affect the pregnant woman because motherhood transforms a woman into a caregiver with daily responsibilities. Because it is potentially transforming and has no direct or immediate impact on the fundamental interests or rights of others, the decision to use contraceptives is a private one. It is also private because decisions about contraceptive use are based on the individual's understanding of the meaning and value of sexuality.

In *Thornburgh v. American College of Obstetricians* 476 U.S. 747 (1986), the Court struck down a Pennsylvania statute that required doctors to deliver a state-scripted lecture to women seeking an abortion, and that required abortion providers to file reports with the state on women obtaining abortions and physicians performing abortions. The Court's affirmation of *Roe v. Wade* in *Thornburgh v. American College of Obstetricians* characterized the right at risk in the following manner: "Few decisions are more *personal* and *intimate,* more properly private, or more basic to *individual dignity* and *autonomy*, than a woman's decision—with the guidance of her physician and within the limits specified in *Roe v. Wade*—whether to end her pregnancy."[38] Justice Sandra Day O'Conner used similar language to describe the interests at stake in another challenge to *Roe v. Wade*. Writing for the majority in *Casey v. Planned Parenthood* 505 U.S. 833 (1992), O'Conner states:

> These matters, involving the *most intimate* and *personal choices* a person may make in a lifetime, choices central to *personal dignity* and *autonomy*, are central to the liberty protected by the Fourteenth Amendment. *At the heart of liberty is the right to define one's own concept of existence, of meaning, of the universe, and of the mystery of human life.* Beliefs about these matters could not define the attributes of personhood were they formed under compulsion of the State.[39]

In both *Thornburgh v. American College of Obstetricians* and *Casey v. Planned Parenthood*, the Court claims that the individual's autonomy is at stake in certain deeply personal decisions. State interference in these decisions will constrain the individual's ability to act independently in an area of life that has a direct impact on her identity and well-being. In those areas of life that are commonly understood to be deeply personal, such as sexual and intimate relationships, individuals should be able to make their own determination about the nature of the good life. They should be free to decide for themselves what their relationships mean and how they fit into a broader conception of the value and meaning of life.

The right of decisional privacy, as it has been defined in the birth control and abortion cases, protects personal liberty in sexual and intimate relationships. Privacy in these cases, as well as in Justice Blackmun's dissent to *Bowers v. Hardwick*, has little to do with withholding information from the public or withdrawing from public life. Instead, it refers to the individual's ability to exercise autonomy in sexual and intimate relationships. The right of privacy is based on the idea that the individual is entitled to the freedom to make certain personal decisions even when the decisions she makes do not accord with the majority's values.

My last step in clarifying the interests that an individuality-based right of privacy protects will be to defend it against the accusation that it promotes an atomistic conception of the self. Feminist and communitarian critics of the right of privacy argue that it is based on a flawed understanding of the self. They claim that the notion of the isolated rights-bearer perpetuates an understanding of the self that is destructive of human connection and community. In the next two subsections, I examine and respond to this claim.

Feminist Criticisms of the Right of Privacy

Some feminists argue that rights discourse in general is inherently male-biased because it is based on the assumption that human beings are independent and self-sufficient. When society is portrayed as an association of self-sufficient individuals, important features of human life, such as the interdependence of human beings, are lost. While acknowledging that rights preserve "respect for certain individual freedoms," Martha Minow and Mary Lyndon Shanley claim that rights-based theories "historically lack a rich understanding of relationships, including their preconditions, their responsibilities, and their consequences."[40] Feminist advocates of the ethic of care argue that rights-based thinking fails to account for the moral imperative to care and to preserve caring relationships.[41] Other feminists argue that the portrait of the independent rights-bearer ignores the relationship between the dependent child and dependency workers, particularly mothers.[42] Moreover, if the fiction of the self-sufficient and independent rights-bearer is to be sustained, women in general and mothers in particular must be repressed.[43] The exclusion of the dependency relationship from the public world of men means that women are excluded from the political process and the public workplace.[44]

Feminist critics of rights argue that the independent and self-sufficient self should be replaced by the self-in-relation or the relational self. The self-in-relation is embedded in and sustained by relationships with others. According to feminists, recognizing the interdependence of human beings would transform gender relations by affirming women's traditional work as caregivers. In addition, if caring relationships and the moral imperative to care were recognized as central to public life, women's association with caregiving could no longer serve as the basis for their exclusion from political decision making and the public workplace.

Defenders of the right of privacy are sometimes guilty of contributing to the stereotype of the lone rights-bearer. Recall Justice Blackmun's first attempt to define the right of privacy in *Bowers v. Hardwick*. Quoting Justice Louis Brandeis, Justice Blackmun refers to the right of privacy as "the right to be left alone." However, Blackmun goes on to define the right of privacy in a way that is entirely consistent with the feminist notion of the self-in-relation. As we have seen, he argues that privacy protects relationships between individuals and that it is through these relationships that the individual's identity is shaped. Blackmun's opinion in *Bowers v. Hardwick* suggests that rights are important because they protect the individual's ability to engage in the relationships that she chooses. Privacy rights do not, then, separate us from others, but instead protect unconventional and self-chosen forms of intimacy.

Feminists are right to question those aspects of the rights-based tradition that envision political society as a collection of entirely self-sufficient individuals. And it is vital that we place the moral imperative to care at the center of our thinking about what constitutes a just society. However, it is possible to place greater emphasis on human interdependence and the obligation to care while at the same time protecting individual rights. Feminist critics of rights-based thinking fail to recognize the difference between moral independence and an extreme form of individualism, which assumes that the individual is self-sufficient. The right of privacy does not separate the rights-bearer from her intimate others. Instead, it protects her moral independence without requiring that she be emotionally or economically independent. Women are often the targets of the moral majority's efforts to regulate sexuality. Rights remain one of the key tools for protecting women's bodily and sexual autonomy. As Elizabeth Kiss explains, "The boundary-marking characteristics of liberties and immunities [are] of critical importance to society's most vulnerable members."[45] To the extent that traditional conceptions of women's procreative and domestic roles continue to dominate policy making in the areas of sexuality, procreation, marriage, and divorce, women need rights that protect their moral independence.

Communitarian Criticisms of the Right of Privacy

Communitarian critic Michael Sandel also claims that the right of privacy assumes an individualistic conception of the self. He argues in *Democracy's Discontents* that the 1965 *Griswold v. Connecticut* decision did not inaugurate a new form of privacy—decisional privacy—but was actually based on the older conception of privacy as freedom from unwanted surveillance.[46] Sandel claims that the Court's primary objection to the Connecticut law forbidding the use of birth control was that it would require officials to violate, in Justice Douglas' words, "the sacred precincts of the marital bedroom."[47] At stake in the *Griswold v. Connecticut* decision, Sandel argues, is not the freedom of the married couple to choose to use birth control, but their freedom to engage in marital intimacies without fear of surveillance. In striking down the

Connecticut contraception law, it was not the Court's intention to expand sexual liberty by providing couples with greater control over their fertility. Instead, the Court's true aim was to protect the sanctity of marriage. This interpretation is supported by Justice Goldberg's concurring opinion in which he states: "The fact that no particular provision of the Constitution explicitly forbids the State from *disrupting the traditional relation of the family—a relation as old and as fundamental as our entire civilization*—surely does not show that the Government was meant to have the power to do so."[48] Goldberg's assertion harks back to privacy as family autonomy more than it looks forward to privacy as personal liberty.

Sandel is not alone in thinking that the *Griswold v. Connecticut* decision is primarily concerned with protecting the institution of marriage. As several commentators have pointed out, it was not until the 1972 *Eisenstadt v. Baird* decision that the Supreme Court took a decisive stand in favor of individual liberty in sexual matters.[49] While *Griswold v. Connecticut* spoke of the institution of marriage and the married couple's right to be free from state surveillance, *Eisenstadt v. Baird* focused on the individual's ability to make her or his own decisions about the use of birth control. Speaking for the majority, Justice Thomas E. Brennan wrote "if the right of privacy means anything, it is the right of the individual, married or single, to be free from unwarranted governmental intrusions into matters so fundamentally affecting a person as the decision whether to bear or beget a child."[50] Justice Brennan's opinion placed special emphasis on the fact that couples, whether married or not, are composed of distinct individuals, and that the right of privacy protects the individual's freedom to make his or her own decision regarding the use of birth control.

According to Sandel, it is with *Eisenstadt v. Baird* that the Court moves from the concept of informational privacy to what it has come to call decisional privacy. Equally significant, it is also with *Eisenstadt v. Baird* that the Court shifts from protecting family autonomy to individual autonomy, or from protecting the institution of marriage to protecting individual liberty in sexual and intimate relations. Essentially, the Court had gone from upholding an institution that determines the place and meaning of sexuality in the lives of individuals to allowing individuals to make this determination themselves. Whereas the Court acted in *Griswold v. Connecticut* to promote marriage as the legitimate arena of sexual expression, in *Eisenstadt v. Baird* it affirmed the pluralistic approach to sexuality that Blackmun articulates in *Bowers*.

Sandel views this shift in philosophical and legal justification as an important step in the defeat of what he calls republican jurisprudence. He holds that republican jurisprudence, which places the affirmation of common values above individual liberty, held sway from the founding of the United States to the mid-twentieth century. *Griswold v. Connecticut* was republican in nature because it upheld a cherished institution essential to a common way of life. In contrast, *Eisenstadt v. Baird* affirmed individual desires and choices. Instead of using its authority to affirm a common moral vision, the Court legitimized a distinctly liberal and pluralist view of morality. While it may be appealing because of its emphasis on individual autonomy, Sandel warns that a jurisprudence based on liberal principles undermines both community and civic virtue. Like Elshtain and Galston, Sandel claims that an engaged and active citizenry is not possible without a shared moral culture and a legal system that upholds at least some common values.

Sandel explains that liberal jurisprudence takes as its starting point the unencumbered or voluntarist self. He contrasts the unencumbered self with the encumbered self who exists within a web of largely unchosen relationships and obligations. The encumbered self is not capable of detaching herself from the moral community that shapes her aims and values. In contrast, the unencumbered self is at the center of her world. The unencumbered self views unchosen commitments or involuntary obligations stemming from tradition or custom as impediments to free self-development. A key difference between the encumbered and unencumbered self is that the latter's relationships are voluntary and self-chosen, while those of the former are to some extent involuntary, at least in the sense that they are determined by pregiven values and traditions. Sandel does not use the term "involuntary" to refer only to those small religious communities in which marriage is literally involuntary because it is arranged without the participation of the future husband and wife. Rather, he uses the term "involuntary relationship" to suggest that the meaning our relationships have for us and the obligations they entail are shaped by the larger moral communities of which we are members. Thus, if a couple's understanding of marriage and its expectations and obligations are largely determined by their membership in a particular religion, their marital relationship could be considered involuntary. In contrast, the voluntarist or unencumbered self accepts only those obligations or forms of authority to which she has explicitly consented. In this sense, the unencumbered self rejects all forms of tradition and custom. She determines the meaning her relationship will have through discussions with her intimate other.

Sandel claims that when the Supreme Court shifted from family to individual autonomy it contributed to a dangerous form of individualism. Republican political philosophy defines individualism in terms of economic self-sufficiency and what we now call personal responsibility. This kind of individualism, because it allows for a shared moral culture, does not lead to the fragmentation of community. In contrast, liberal individualism permits each individual to make her own moral choices. Consequently, there is nothing to hold citizens together other than a shared commitment to tolerance and respecting diverse ways of life. Tolerance of diversity is not enough, Sandel warns, to inspire community or collective action. The individual's ability to develop herself according to her own wishes will come at the expense of the larger community.

Sandel casts the conflict between republican and liberal principles as one between community and individualism. The encumbered self is embedded in associations larger than herself, whereas the unencumbered self is primarily concerned with her own self-development and self-fulfillment. But this is a false dichotomy. The real difference between the encumbered and unencumbered self is not that one engages in a wide network of supportive relationships and the other stands alone. The real difference is that the relationships formed by the encumbered self are involuntary, while those formed by the unencumbered self are voluntary. Thus, we are not required to choose between membership in a community or an anomie, as Sandel suggests. The choice we face is of an entirely different nature: Should the meaning of our relationships be largely shaped by custom and tradition, or should we be actively engaged in creating their meaning?

Voluntarily chosen relationships, as Sandel suggests, are more fragile than those that he refers to as involuntary. Involuntary relationships have the backing of a larger moral community. Customs, rituals, common practices, and institutions exist to encourage and support them. Individuals are heartily praised for following convention and punished and ridiculed when they dissent from it. However, the lack of a long tradition does not mean that individuals will fail to form partnerships, associations, and communities. The relationships unencumbered individuals form may enjoy less external support than those formed by encumbered selves, but as Blackmun asserts in his dissent to *Bowers v. Hardwick*, they may mean more to their members because they are self-chosen. The fundamental difference between the encumbered and the unencumbered self is not that the former is sheltered within a larger community, while the latter is left to fend for herself; rather, the former accepts the meanings that her community of origin gives to sexuality and intimate relationship, while the latter partakes in deciding what they will mean.[51]

Morris Kaplan rejects the idea that endorsing rights requires rejecting community. Kaplan argues that viewing the struggle for lesbian and gay rights in terms of a "simple dichotomy between individual liberty and community morality" is a mistake.[52] Instead of ceding the term "community" to the communitarians and taking a stand for lesbian and gay rights on the ground of individual liberty, Kaplan urges us to rethink our notions of community and individuality. Kaplan endorses a view of the individual that he attributes to both feminists and communitarians. He argues that the individual should be conceived "as situated in concrete historical, social, and familial settings rather than as isolated and self-enclosed."[53] However, Kaplan does not think that adopting this view of the self commits one to endorsing conventional or traditional morality. Modern societies are composed of a plurality of communities, including communities that sustain and nourish lesbian and gay subjectivities. Indeed, Kaplan explains that "the legal and social recognition of the associative and communal forms of lesbian and gay life" is essential to guaranteeing a full range of civil rights for lesbians and gay men.[54] Thus, instead of viewing the struggle for lesbian and gay rights simply as a clash between community morality and individual liberty, we should instead view it as a clash between communities. The task of modern democracy, Kaplan concludes, is "to map the conditions of coexistence for disparate ethical and moral communities."[55] While I do not place as much emphasis on community as Kaplan does, I agree with his assertion that a strong defense of rights is compatible with an understanding of modern society as composed of a plurality of communities or institutional settings. The conception of the individual as a "situated self" that Kaplan endorses does not conflict with rights-based doctrine as long as the individual's ability to reflect on and dissent from the values of the communities in which she is situated is protected. Kaplan and other scholars have argued that individual moral autonomy is facilitated by the fact that modern individuals are often members of multiple communities and are therefore forced to negotiate competing ethical claims.[56]

Communitarian and feminist critics of the right of privacy share some common ground. They both claim that rights-based approaches to morality tend to isolate the rights-bearer and to separate her from a larger community. I have argued throughout this chapter that the right of privacy should in fact be seen as a tool for protecting the formation of relationships. In chapter 1, I suggested that there is an important connection between valuing intimacy and expanding personal liberty. The right of privacy protects the freedom of the individual to establish relationships based on her own conceptions of sexuality and family. Its purpose is to protect the individual's ability to think and act for herself in matters of great personal importance. In doing so, it protects those relationships that are endangered or discouraged by conventional or traditional conceptions of what constitutes a family.

My goal in this section has been to identify what interests an individuality-based right of privacy protects, and to distinguish the form of privacy that I want to defend from other privacy traditions that have influenced U.S. culture and law. In the section that follows, I provide a fuller account of the principle of individuality on which my version of the right of privacy is based. Drawing on Mill's description of individuality in *On Liberty*, I argue for an expansive conception of the right of privacy.

III. INDIVIDUALITY AND PRIVACY

Scholars defending the right of privacy have relied on the principles of autonomy just as Justice O'Conner did in *Casey v. Planned Parenthood.*[57] Dworkin argues that Supreme Court decisions on contraception and abortion are based on the principle of procreative autonomy. He explains that when a woman is denied control over her reproductive capacity, she loses her autonomy or her ability to be self-determining. Being forced to have a child will have an immediate and direct impact on her intimate relationships, her body, her life plans, and her identity. According to Dworkin, laws regulating procreation call for strict judicial scrutiny because "the moral issues they touch on are religious in the broad sense . . . touching the ultimate purpose and value of life itself."[58] In a diverse society, people will disagree on how best to respect what he calls "intrinsic values" or values concerned with the purpose and value of life. Laws prohibiting contraceptive use or abortion are wrong because they uphold one conception of the purpose and value of life. Dworkin explains that a "state may not curtail liberty, in order to protect an intrinsic value, when the effect on one group of citizens would be special and grave, when the community is seriously divided about what respect for that value requires, and when people's opinions about the nature of that value reflect essentially religious convictions that are fundamental to moral personality."[59] Dworkin claims that the First Amendment, and in particular the doctrine of freedom of religion, supplements the Court's emphasis on the due process clause of the Fourteenth Amendment. The principle of procreative autonomy holds that when citizens disagree on intrinsic moral values, such as whether abortion is morally acceptable, the decision of whether to abort should be made by the pregnant woman in consultation with a medical professional. According to Dworkin, the constitutional doctrine of religious freedom protects the individual's liberty to exercise autonomy on moral issues that are religious in nature.

In her defense of the right of privacy, Jean Cohen claims that every individual woman "is the bearer of constitutional rights that protect her moral autonomy, the inviolability of her personality, and her identity as her own."[60] She explains that "privacy rights shield the personal dimensions of one's life from undue scrutiny or interference. As such, they protect the process of self-development and self-realization that allows each individual to define herself."[61] Cohen also states that privacy rights "protect concrete fragile identities, and self-creative processes which constitute who we are and who we wish to be. When properly understood, privacy rights protect these as well as the chance for each individual to develop, revise, and pursue her own conception of the good—her identity needs."[62] Cohen argues that not only do we have an abstract interest in exercising autonomy, but we also have a more concrete interest in forging a way of life in which our particular identity needs are met. The right of privacy is based, then, on both moral autonomy, or the freedom to make our own decisions, and self-definition, or the freedom to engage in what Morris Kaplan calls "ethical self-making."[63]

In basing my account of the right of privacy on individuality, I am not rejecting the principles of autonomy and inviolate personality or personhood. Indeed, individuality is composed of and is but an alternative way of expressing these two principles. What distinguishes individuality from autonomy and personhood is that it highlights the importance of actively resisting conventional identities. In addition, by emphasizing the conditions necessary to free self-development, individuality provides us with a particularly expansive account of the right of privacy.

In *On Liberty*, Mill condemns the strong impulse toward conformity that he claims can be found in nineteenth-century democracies.[64] Like Alexis de Tocqueville in *Democracy in America*, he argues that this increased uniformity is a product of the modern movement toward greater social and political equality.[65] As democratic republics replace constitutional monarchies, status-based distinctions fade and the notion of a general public forms. Mill's fear is that unless the importance of personal liberty is recognized, the middle class will establish a monolithic and stifling moral culture. Modern democratic republics, Mill warns, are efficient instruments of uniformity in part because they are responsive to public opinion.[66] Mill asserts that public opinion is usually based on little more than an unthinking adherence to custom and convention. Custom, Mill claims, originates in sentiment and feeling as opposed to rational thought.[67] As a result, the rules of human conduct followed in a society are usually nothing more than the likings and dislikings of the majority or the dominant class.[68] The fact that their beliefs are nothing more than personal preferences does not prevent the majority or the dominant class from making them into laws that are binding on all citizens. Custom and convention also are supported because they serve the interests of powerful classes or groups. This is the case with women's legal subordination to men in marriage. According to Mill, men support customary beliefs about gender inequality because they directly benefit from these beliefs.[69]

Mill softens his elitist and dismissive stance on the value of public opinion when he explains that the majority is often right when it makes judgments concerning legislation that will have a direct impact on its own interests. Problems arise when the public decides to make policy regarding what Mill calls self-regarding action, or action that has no immediate and direct effect on the fundamental interests or rights of others. When the majority is asked to pass judgment on the self-regarding conduct of a minority, they frequently ignore "the pleasure or convenience of those whose conduct they censure and consider only their own preferences."[70] Mill also suggests that when making judgments concerning the actions of others, many people rely on "superstitions and prejudice" as well as "desires and fears."[71]

Mill's objective in distinguishing between 'self' and 'other' regarding action is to prevent prejudice or the moral preferences of the majority from serving as the basis of law. Action that is self-regarding should not be prohibited even if the majority believes it to be "foolish, perverse, or wrong."[72] Mill argues that the majority's sense of outrage, offense, disgust, or distaste at the actions of others does not provide sufficient reason for regulating personal conduct. Action is only susceptible to regulation when it causes direct and immediate harm to others.

Dworkin's distinction between external and personal preferences helps to clarify why some reasons for regulating action are not legitimate. He argues that policymaking is based on two kinds of preferences—personal and external. If I argue in favor of the regulation of smoking because I fear the effects of second-hand smoke on my own health, I am expressing a personal preference. However, if I argue for the regulation of smoking because I believe that smokers are weak-willed people engaging in a dirty habit, I am expressing an external preference. An external preference is based not on how an action will affect my welfare, but on my contempt for a specific group of people—in this case, smokers. According to Dworkin, policies based on external preferences violate the principle that the state must treat its citizens with equal concern and respect. The majority's judgment that a particular action is "foolish, perverse, or wrong" is, using Dworkin's terminology, an external preference. It denies individuals with unpopular ideas or practices the freedom to be self-determining.[73] Dworkin and Mill consider laws that regulate action on the basis of external (as opposed to personal) preferences to be illegitimate.

In chapter 3 of *On Liberty*, Mill clarifies what he thinks is at stake in the debate over personal liberty. Citing Wilhelm von Humboldt, Mill explains that without "liberty and diversity of situations" individuality will not be able to flourish. Personal liberty is valuable, then, because it is the key condition of individuality. Mill defines individuality as the free development of our faculties, capacities, desires, and impulses.[74] By "free development" he means that the opinions of the majority should not be allowed to prevent the individual from trying out different "experiments in living."[75]

Perhaps the defining feature of individuality is the individual's refusal to conform to unexamined conventions. A contemporary exponent of individuality, George Kateb, uses the term negative individuality to capture the individualist's resistance to conventional social forms. He describes negative individuality as "the disposition to disobey bad conventions and unjust laws, by oneself, and on the basis of a strict self-scrutiny."[76] Kateb goes on to explain that while the concept of autonomy captures part of the content of positive individuality, it does not exhaust it. Positive individuality includes the idea that "one's self must become a project, one must become the architect of one's soul." This is because one's "dignity resides in being, to some important degree, a person of one's own creating, making, choosing, rather than in being merely a creature or a socially manufactured, conditioned, and manipulated thing."[77] Taken together, negative and positive individuality capture the individual's abstract interest in moral autonomy and her more concrete interest in self-definition.

Individuality should not be confused with individualism. To confuse the two is to conflate moral independence with self-interest and self-sufficiency. It does not connote self-centeredness, the desire to withdraw from society, or a refusal to recognize obligations to intimate others. Indeed, self-development most frequently occurs within and through relationships. While the individualist may refuse to conform to standard forms of relationship, that does not mean that she rejects connection. In his defense of individuality in "Self-Reliance," Emerson exhorts his listeners to aim for a thoroughgoing honesty in their relationships with family and friends. He encourages them to tell their family members that they will no longer conform to conventional expectations that violate their own sense of what is morally right. However, Emerson explains that rejecting convention does not entail the refusal to recognize obligations to others. He states, "I shall endeavor to nourish my parents, to support my family, and to be the chaste husband of one wife,—but these relations I must fill after a new and unprecedented way."[78] Emerson argues for reliance on one's own conscience, and not for a kind of self-centered independence or self-sufficiency that undermines relationships.

Unlike individualism, which can be self-serving and even greedy, individuality has nothing to do with the pursuit of wealth, status, or power. The person who seeks to develop her own individuality does not seek social rewards. Seeking wealth and power usually requires conforming to the values of the majority, not dissenting from them. Individuality also implies that our personality is developed for our own enrichment and for the benefit of those who are closest to us, and not in accordance with the needs or standards of society. The concept of individuality presupposes that individuals exist to serve their own ends and not those of society.

Mill asserts that moral and intellectual independence are key components of individuality. If we are not to merely imitate the life choices made by others, we must engage in a process of independent reflection and deliberation that will allow us to arrive at our own decisions. However, Mill cautions us against reducing individuality to "independence of understanding," claiming that it includes "independence of desires and impulses."[79] Reducing individuality to independence of understanding implies a narrow conception of the important human faculties. It suggests that reflection, deliberation, and judgment are the only faculties worthy of development. Mill thought otherwise. He praises "strong impulses," "various desires and feelings," and "energetic characters."[80] Individuality requires us to do more than make our own decisions. It also requires that we explore and expand our desires and tastes. We must develop our appreciation of beauty, the capacities of our bodies and senses, and our ability to feel joy, pleasure, and love. When we admire someone because she possesses individuality we are admiring more than her capacity to act on principles upon which she has reflected. We are admiring the strength of her passions, the intensity of her feelings, and the steadfastness with which she pursues her dreams. Individuality combines "independence of understanding" and "independence of desires and impulses" to form "character."[81]

The Millian concept of individuality assumes that human beings have the potential to be both self-determining and self-creating. They make themselves through the course of piecing their lives together. By adopting one kind of life over another, they develop certain capacities and faculties and allow others to wither. Mill recognizes our self-creative powers when he states that "among the works of man which human life is rightly employed in perfecting and beautifying, the first in importance surely is man himself."[82] However, if individuals are to participate in creating their own character, the society they live in must allow them to explore their feelings, desires, and ideas. This requires different experiments in living: "To give any fair play to the nature of each, it is essential that different people be allowed to live different lives."[83] When individuality is sacrificed to social convention, more than autonomy—understood as the ability to exercise control over certain life decisions—is lost. Also at stake is the life we could have created and the person we could have become. Human beings cannot develop themselves fully if custom, convention, and the opinions of the majority restrict the kinds of lives they are allowed to lead. Individuality is only possible in a society that publicly recognizes a multiplicity of human goods and ways of life.

Holding the position that individuals can play a part in their own self-making does not commit us to the essentialist position that each individual can consciously set out to discover his or her "true self." Along with Mill we can understand the development of individuality as a process of invention rather than discovery. We may make certain choices about how we want to live our lives, but we cannot anticipate ahead of time where these choices will lead or how they will transform us. Mill does not make the strong claim that each of us possesses an essence that we must discover and to which we must be true. Instead, he makes the much weaker claim that given the multiplicity of human goods, individuals living in a society that guarantees both "freedom and a variety of situations" will tend to develop differently. If only a limited number of human goods and ways of life are publicly recognized and validated, opportunities for self-development will be dramatically decreased. Simply eradicating repressive regulation is not a sufficient condition for the cultivation of individuality. It is only when individuals are exposed to a variety of different ways of life, only when they are faced with true alternatives, that they can be self-determining. This is why public recognition of diverse ways of life and family forms is so important. When one way of life is singled out as the best or most responsible or most patriotic, experimentation, and therefore the development of individuality, is threatened. A society that fails to publicly affirm a variety of ways of life does not value individuality.

Individuality is desirable in itself, but it is also conducive to personal happiness. Fitting diverse individuals into a small number of social molds prevents them from developing the parts of themselves that they find most meaningful and pleasing. The harm caused by conforming to conventional ways of life is difficult to appreciate because it is difficult to see. It is difficult to mourn lives that haven't been lived, capacities that haven't been developed, and desires that withered because they were regularly thwarted. The power of Mill's argument in chapter 3 of *On Liberty* stems from his ability to convince us of the gravity of a loss that we often can't see. Mill writes: "Such are the differences among human beings in their sources of pleasure, their susceptibilities of pain, and the operation on them of different physical and moral agencies, that unless there is a corresponding diversity in their modes of life, they neither obtain their fair share of happiness, nor grow up to the mental, moral, and aesthetic stature of which their nature is capable."[84] A uniform moral culture prevents diverse modes of life and ways of being from ever developing. As a result, individuals who could have lived creative, rich, and fulfilling lives are dissatisfied and frustrated without, in many cases, even knowing why. In squelching experimentation, the supporters of custom and convention prevent public recognition of the full range of human goods and the ways of life that are built around them. In doing so, they cause harm to those who would flourish living an alternative way of life.

Mill appears to have had an almost aesthetic appreciation of diversity and a corresponding repulsion of uniformity. Isaiah Berlin explains: "(H)e set himself against the worship of order or tidiness, or even peace, if they were bought at the price of obliterating the variety and color of untamed human beings with unextinguished passions and untrammeled imaginations."[85] The social world is richer, fuller, more exciting and stimulating when individuals are allowed to cultivate their faculties freely. Mill claims that when individuality is allowed to assert itself, "human life becomes rich, diversified, and animating, furnishing more abundant ailment to high thoughts and elevating feelings, and strengthening the ties which bind every individual to the race, by making the race infinitely better worth belonging to."[86] Perhaps what makes diversity most appealing to Mill is the evidence it provides for the creativity of human beings. We applaud works of art both because of their beauty and power and because their existence demonstrates the creativity of human beings. After all, is not the diversity of the animal and plant kingdoms often understood as proof of God's creative power? We are delighted by diversity in tastes, ideas, and modes of life because it indicates that human beings are creators and are capable of more than what Mill called the "ape-like faculty of imitation."[87]

Basing the right of privacy on a Millian conception of individuality provides us with a broad and expansive understanding of the right of privacy. This is because the free development of individuality requires more than the negative right of freedom from state regulation. It requires positive state action to protect associational freedoms and to establish public recognition of the plurality of human goods. For example, the state will have to take both negative and positive action to guarantee the right of privacy of those individuals who engage in same-sex sexual activity. First, the state must nullify existing sodomy laws and prohibit intervention in noncommercial consensual sexual activity between adults. Second, it must pass legislation that protects lesbians and gay men from discrimination in employment and housing, and guarantees the free speech rights of lesbians and gay men. Third, it must guarantee same-sex couples the same rights that heterosexual couples enjoy—to marry, adopt, and provide foster care for children. Positive state action is necessary if lesbians and gay men are to enjoy the same opportunities for intimate association as heterosexuals.

A narrow conception of the right of privacy would limit its use to the deregulation of noncommercial and consensual sexual activity. However, if the right of privacy is to protect lesbians and gay men from the moral preferences of the majority, it must include positive state action. Individuality cannot flourish when only one form of sexuality is recognized as legitimate by the state. Allowing employers to discriminate against lesbian and gay men places a substantial burden on the free development of noncoercive and consensual forms of sexual activity and identity. The state's refusal to recognize and facilitate the formation of lesbian and gay families violates the freedom of intimate association. Providing legal protections for lesbian and gay families is one way of publicly recognizing that there is a plurality of human goods. While it may at times need to be supplemented with other constitutional rights, such as the Fourteenth Amendment's equal protection clause or the First Amendment's freedom of expression clause, the right of privacy, properly interpreted, is an important tool for establishing the civil rights of lesbians and gay men.[88]

The "don't ask, don't tell" policy regarding lesbians and gay men in the military provides a helpful case for illustrating what sort of state action would be required by an individuality-based conception of privacy. According to the "don't ask" policy, lesbian and gay military personnel who do not declare their sexual preference or their involvement in same-sex sexual activity will be allowed to stay in the military. Supporters of this policy argue that lesbians and gay men are now able to serve in the military as long as they agree to keep their private lives "private." If privacy is understood as the right to be left alone, this policy could be interpreted as protecting the right of privacy of lesbian and gay military personnel. However, the "don't ask" policy cannot meet the requirements of a Millian conception of privacy because it clearly destroys the conditions for the free development of individuality. It eviscerates personal liberty by prohibiting what Hunter calls self-identifying speech. Hunter claims that self-identifying speech "does not merely reflect or communicate one's identity; it is a major factor in constructing identity. Identity cannot exist without it."[89] In prohibiting lesbian and gay military personnel from speaking about their sexual experiences and relationships, the military commands them to live a lie and denies them the freedom to develop their faculties and desires. Most importantly, the "don't ask" policy enforces the idea that sexuality must take the form of expression that the majority endorses. Sexuality is not an activity that can be considered "one's own"; it can be colonized and made to serve the ends of the majority, or in this case, high-ranking military authorities and civilian government. From a Millian perspective, the fact that lesbian and gay military personnel who comply with the "don't tell" policy are being "left alone" cannot be considered a victory for privacy rights. The privacy of lesbian and gay military personnel will be secured only after they are protected from the moral preferences of the majority. According to an individuality-based conception of the right of privacy, the state does not exhaust its responsibility to the individual once it refrains from prohibiting conduct classified as private. Protecting the right of privacy requires guaranteeing the basic conditions necessary to the free development of individuality: liberty and diversity of situations.

CONCLUSION

I argued in chapter 1 that as greater weight has been attributed to emotional and sexual relationships, the demand for personal liberty in the areas of sexuality and intimate relationships has increased. In the United States, the right of privacy has provided some constitutional protection for personal liberty in sexual and intimate relationships. My goal in this chapter has been to clarify what interests the right of privacy protects and to develop an individuality-based conception of the right of privacy. I've argued that the right of privacy is misleadingly defined as a right to be left alone. Instead, it protects the individual's right to make choices about the nature of the good life even if her choices violate the moral values of the majority. The right of privacy is not based on an understanding of the self as self-sufficient and independent. It is compatible with the idea of the self-in-relation to others. As Justice Blackmun argues so eloquently, the right of privacy protects the individual's freedom to determine the nature and meaning of her intimate relationships.

I also have argued for an expansive and affirmative conception of the right of privacy, one that goes beyond nonintervention to include positive state action. An examination of the Millian concept of individuality helps to show why only positive state action provides full protection for personal liberty. As Mill explains, the conditions necessary to the free development of individuality include "liberty and diversity of situations." Only state recognition of multiple ways of life will protect the privacy rights of individuals who create unconventional forms of family and intimate association.

In chapter 3, I turn from the abstract philosophical debates explored in chapter 2 to more concrete policy issues like divorce reform and same-sex marriage. My goal in examining these issues is to show why the principles of liberty, equality and diversity need to be embodied in family policy. Family communitarians argue that strengthening the conventional family requires prohibiting same-sex marriage and establishing waiting periods and other barriers to divorce. I argue that both of these policies ignore individuals' privacy rights and identity needs.

NOTES

1. *Eisenstadt v. Baird* 405 U.S. 438 (1972) extended the right to use contraception to unmarried couples; *Roe v. Wade* 410 U.S. 113 (1973) established a woman's right to an abortion.

2. Several authors have argued recently that realizing the full potential of rights will in some cases necessitate positive state action. See Morris Kaplan, *Sexual Justice: Democratic Citizenship and the Politics of Desire* (New York: Routledge, 1997); Dorothy Roberts, *Killing the Black Body: Race, Reproduction, and the Meaning of Liberty* (New York: Pantheon Books, 1997); Zillah Eisenstein, "Equalizing Privacy and Specifying Equality" in *Revisioning the Political: Feminist Reconstructions of Traditional Concepts in Western Political Thought*, ed. Nancy J. Hirshmann and Christine Di Stefano (Boulder, Colo.: Westview Press, 1996).

3. Nan Hunter, "Life After Hardwick," in *Sex Wars: Sexual Dissent and Political Culture*, ed. Lisa Duggin and Nan Hunter (New York: Routledge, 1995), 85–100.

4. I am indebted to Morris Kaplan's analysis of *Bowers v. Hardwick* in *Sexual Justice*, 207–38.

5. *Bowers v. Hardwick*, 478 U.S. 186 (1986), 191.

6. Michael Sandel, *Democracy's Discontents: America in Search of a Public Philosophy* (Cambridge, Mass.: Harvard University Press, 1996).

7. Cheshire Calhoun analyzes conservative efforts to portray lesbians and gay men as outsiders to the family in "Family Outlaws: Rethinking the Connections between Feminism, Lesbianism, and the Family" in *Feminism and Families*, ed. Hilde Lindeman Nelson (New York: Routledge, 1997), 131–50.

8. *Bowers v. Hardwick*, 478 U.S. 186 (1986), 204.

9. *Bowers v. Hardwick*, 478 U.S. 186 (1986), 205.

10. *Bowers v. Hardwick*, 478 U.S. 186 (1986), 205.

11. *Bowers v. Hardwick*, 478 U.S. 186 (1986), 199.

12. *Bowers v. Hardwick*, 478 U.S. 186 (1986), 205.

13. James Rachels argues that one of the ways intimate relationships can be distinguished from non-intimate relationships is by the extent to which the participants share information about themselves. He concludes that privacy in the form of restricting others' access to information about us is necessary to intimacy. See James Rachels, "Why Privacy is Important," in *Philosophical Dimensions of Privacy*, ed. Ferdinand Schoeman (Cambridge: Cambridge University Press, 1984).

14. In section 2, I have drawn on analyses of the public/private distinction from Nancy Rosenblum, *Another Liberalism: Romanticism and the Reconstruction of Liberal Thought*, (Cambridge, Mass.: Harvard University Press, 1987) and Will Kymlicka, *Contemporary Political Philosophy: An Introduction* (Oxford: Clarendon Press, 1990).

15. John Locke, *Two Treatises of Government: A Critical Edition with an Introduction and Apparatus Criticus by Peter Laslett* (London: Cambridge University Press, 1967).

16. Thomas Paine, "Common Sense," in *Collected Writings* (New York: Literary Classics of the United States, 1995), 6.

17. Michael Walzer, *Spheres of Justice* (New York: Basic Books, 1983).

18. John Rawls, *A Theory of Justice* (Cambridge, Mass.: Harvard University Press, 1971).

19. Karl Marx, *Selected Writings*, ed. Lawrence H. Simon (Indianapolis, Ind.: Hackett, 1994).

20. *Bradwell v. State of Illinois*, 83 U.S. 130 (1873).

21. *State v. Rhodes*, 61 N.C. 453 (1886).

22. Catherine MacKinnon, *Feminism Unmodified* (Cambridge, Mass.: Harvard University Press, 1987), 100.

23. Frances E. Olsen, "Unraveling Compromise," *Harvard Law Review* 103, no.1 (1989): 105–35.

24. Jean Cohen argues that modern privacy jurisprudence attaches privacy rights to individuals, and not to entities, in "Redescribing Privacy: Identity, Difference, and

the Abortion Controversy," *Columbia Journal of Gender and Law* 3 (1994): 43–116. Martha Fineman provides a fuller account of the distinction between individual and entity privacy in *The Neutered Mother, The Sexual Family and Other Twentieth Century Tragedies* (New York: Routledge, 1996), 186–89.

25. Anita Allen argues that women need and benefit from privacy in "Privacy at Home: The Twofold Problem" in *Revisioning the Political: Feminist Reconstructions of Traditional Concepts in Western Political Thought,* ed. Nancy J. Hirshmann and Christine Di Stefano (Boulder, Colo.: Westview Press, 1996), 193–212.

26. Rosenblum, *Another Liberalism.*

27. John Stuart Mill, *On Liberty,* ed. David Spitz (New York.: Norton, 1975), 10.

28. Rosenblum, *Another Liberalism.*

29. Ronald Dworkin, "What Rights Do We Have," in *Taking Rights Seriously* (Cambridge, Mass.: Harvard University Press, 1977).

30. Dworkin, *Taking Rights Seriously,* 263.

31. Mill, *On Liberty,* 13.

32. Laurence H. Tribe cites *Whalen v. Roe* to explain the distinction between informational and decisional privacy in *American Constitutional Law* (Mineola, N.Y.: Foundation Press, 1978), 886.

33. Samuel Warren and Louis Brandeis, "The Right of Privacy," *Harvard Law Review* 4, no. 193 (1890).

34. For an account of the right of privacy's textual basis in the Constitution see Ronald Dworkin, *Life's Dominion* (New York: Knopf, 1993). For a historical account of the development of the right of privacy see David J. Garrow, *Liberty and Sexuality* (New York: Macmillan, 1994).

35. Dworkin, *Life's Dominion,* 102–17.

36. *Griswold v.* Connecticut, 381 U.S. 479 (1965), 482. Author's italics.

37. *Eisenstadt v. Baird,* 405 U.S. 438 (1972), 438. Author's italics.

38. *Thornburgh v. American College of Obstetricians,* 476 U.S. 747 (1986), 772. Author's italics.

39. *Casey v. Planned Parenthood,* 505 U.S. 833 (1992), 851. Author's italics.

40. Martha Minow and Mary Lyndon Shanley, "Relational Rights and Responsibilities: Revisioning the Family in Liberal Political Theory and Law," *Hypatia: A Journal of Feminist Philosophy* 11, no. 1 (Winter 1996): 4–29.

41. Carol Gilligan, *In a Different Voice: Psychological Theory and Women's Development.* (Cambridge, Mass.: Harvard University Press, 1982).

42. Eva Feder Kittay, "Taking Dependency Seriously: The Family and Medical Leave Act," *Hypatia: A Journal of Feminist Philosophy* 10, no. 1 (1995): 8–30.

43. Christine Di Stefano, "Autonomy in the Light of Difference" in *Revisioning the Political: Feminist Reconstructions of Traditional Concepts in Western Political Thought,* ed. Nancy J. Hirshmann and Christine Di Stefano (Boulder, Colo.: Westview Press, 1996), 95–116.

44. Carol Pateman, "Feminist Critiques of the Public/Private Dichotomy" in *Feminism and Equality,* ed. Anne Phillips (Oxford: Blackwell, 1987).

45. Elizabeth Kiss, "Alchemy or Fool's Gold?: Assessing Feminist Doubts about Rights" in *Reconstructing Political Theory from a Feminist Perspective,* ed. Mary

Lyndon Shanley and Uma Narayan (University Park, Pennsylvania: Pennsylvania State University Press, 1995), 1–24.

46. Sandel, *Democracy's Discontents*, 91–122.

47. Sandel, *Democracy's Discontents*, 93.

48. *Griswold v. Connecticut*, 381 U.S. 479 (1965), 496. Author's italics.

49. Morris Kaplan and June Aline Eichbaum argue that the *Griswold v. Connecticut* text can be read as upholding family autonomy or conventional moral values. See Kaplan, *Sexual Justice*, 211–16; and June Aline Eichbaum, "Towards an Autonomy-Based Theory of Constitutional Privacy: Beyond the Ideology of Family Privacy," *Harvard Civil Rights-Civil Liberties Law Review* 14 (1979): 360–84.

50. *Eisenstadt v. Baird*, 405 U.S. 438 (1972), 453.

51. I borrow the phrase "community of origin" from Marilyn Friedman's article, "Feminism and Modern Friendship: Dislocating the Community," in *Feminism and Political Theory*, ed. Cass R. Sunstein (Chicago: Chicago University Press, 1990), 143–58.

52. Kaplan, *Sexual Justice*, 37.

53. Kaplan, *Sexual Justice*, 38.

54. Kaplan, *Sexual Justice*, 38.

55. Kaplan, *Sexual Justice*, 39.

56. Jean Cohen discusses how the individual's involvement in multiple communities fosters individual moral autonomy in "Redescribing Privacy: Identity, Difference, and the Abortion Controversy," *Columbia Journal of Gender and Law* 3 (1994): 43–116.

57. For accounts of the right of privacy based on the moral ideas of autonomy and personhood see Tribe, *American Constitutional Law*; Jeffry H. Reiman, "Privacy, Intimacy and Personhood," *Philosophy and Public Affairs* 6, no. 1 (1976): 26–44; Eichbaum, "Towards an Autonomy-Based Theory of Constitutional Privacy," 360–84; and Joel Feinberg, "Autonomy, Sovereignty, and Privacy: Moral Ideals in the Constitution?" *The Notre Dame Law Review* 58, no. 3 (1983): 44–92.

58. Dworkin, *Life's Dominion*, 158.

59. Dworkin, *Life's Dominion*, 157.

60. Cohen, *Redescribing Privacy*, 45.

61. Cohen, *Redescribing Privacy*, 102.

62. Cohen, *Redescribing Privacy*, 101.

63. Kaplan, *Sexual Justice*, 177.

64. Mill, *On Liberty*, 6.

65. Alexis de Tocqueville, *Democracy in America* (New York: Knopf, 1994).

66. Mill, *On Liberty*, 6–7.

67. Mill, *On Liberty*, 7.

68. Mill, *On Liberty*, 8.

69. John Stuart Mill, "On the Subjection of Women," in *Essays on Sex Equality*, ed. Alice S. Rossi (Chicago: University of Chicago Press, 1970), 136.

70. Mill, *On Liberty*, 78.

71. Mill, *On Liberty*, 7–8.

72. Mill, *On Liberty*, 13.

73. Ronald Dworkin, *A Matter of Principle* (Cambridge, Mass: Harvard University Press, 1985), 197.

74. Mill, *On Liberty*, 54–5, 60.

75. Mill, *On Liberty*, 54.

76. George Kateb, *The Inner Ocean: Individualism and Democratic Culture* (New York: Cornell University Press, 1992)

77. Kateb, *The Inner Ocean*, 90.

78. Ralph Waldo Emerson, *Self-Reliance and Other Essays* (Mineola, N.Y.: Dover Publications, 1993), 31.

79. Mill, *On Liberty*, 56.

80. Mill, *On Liberty*, 57.

81. Mill, *On Liberty*, 57.

82. Mill, *On Liberty*, 89.

83. Mill, *On Liberty*, 60.

84. Mill, *On Liberty*, 65.

85. Isaiah Berlin, "John Stuart Mill and the Ends of Life," in *J. S. Mill: On Liberty in Focus*, ed. John Gray and G. W. Smith (New York: Routledge, 1991), 131–61.

86. Mill, *On Liberty*, 59.

87. Mill, *On Liberty*, 56.

88. See Nan Hunter, "Identity, Speech and Equality," in *Sex Wars: Sexual Dissent and Political Culture*, ed. Lisa Duggin and Nan Hunter (New York: Routledge, 1995), 123–41; and Morris Kaplan, *Sexual Justice*, on constitutional rights for lesbians and gay men

89. Hunter, "Identity, Speech and Equality," 140.

Chapter Three

What Are Families For? An Argument for Diversity in Family Forms

Family communitarians are disturbed by alternative forms of family, including single-parent families, blended families, and lesbian and gay families, for several reasons. First, greater family diversity undermines the ability of the two-parent family to function as the family norm that all Americans should aspire to achieve. If alternative forms of family gain greater public acceptance and the stigma attached to them is weakened, fewer Americans will remain committed to the two-parent family ideal and the values it embodies. Second, family communitarians claim that the family has one chief purpose—having and rearing children. They claim that the two-parent family fulfills this purpose better than any other form of family. Third, the existence of single mother families and lesbian and gay families challenges two ideas that have played an important role in organizing the conventional family: gender-role complementarity and male leadership in the family. In this chapter, I will examine the first two reasons family communitarians seek to promote family uniformity. Chapter 4 discusses their third reason for opposing family diversity.

Political theorists Galston and Elshtain argue in favor of policy positions that they believe will strengthen the two-parent family and discourage the formation of alternative forms of family. Galston argues that the family's chief function is to produce law-abiding and productive citizens, and that the intact two-parent family is best able to fulfill this purpose. He calls for legislation that would make divorce more difficult and thereby decrease the number of single-parent families. Galston advocates eliminating no-fault divorce laws for couples with children. Elshtain claims that the purpose of marriage is procreation and that same-sex couples are incapable of symbolizing social regenesis or intergenerationality. For this reason, she argues against the legalization of same-sex marriage. These two authors employ the same argumentative strategy composed of the following claims: (1) the family and/or marriage has but one key purpose, (2) intact two-parent families or heterosexual married couples are best able to fulfill this purpose, (3) alternative forms of family or marriage challenge the rightful hegemony of the two-parent family, and (4) single-parent or same-sex families should be discouraged by law and policy.

My overall goal in this chapter is to argue in favor of greater diversity in family forms. I do this in section 1, "Promoting Family Uniformity," by challenging Galston's case for divorce reform and Elshtain's case against same-sex marriage. Without endorsing the one-purpose definition of family provided by Galston and Elshtain, I defend the child rearing abilities of single-parent families and lesbian and gay families. In addition, drawing on my discussion of personal liberty and individuality in chapter 2, I argue that the right of privacy protects same-sex marriage and the right to divorce. In section 2, "The Multi-Purpose Family," I challenge Galston's and Elshtain's assertion that the family can be defined as an association that exists primarily for the sake of reproduction and the fostering of good citizens. I argue that today's families serve several purposes. Defining the family solely in terms of the important purpose of raising children ignores the needs of adults for intimacy and care. In the final section, "Affirming Family Diversity," I consider why the state has an interest in promoting families and what kinds of family forms it should promote. In response to Galston's and Elshtain's claims that family pluralism will endanger our collective understanding of the traditional goods and values that families embody, I argue for a reconsideration of why families are valuable to the larger society. Families benefit the larger society because they draw individuals into relationships of economic cooperation, care, and support. As a society, we should be more concerned with promoting caring relationships and less concerned with family structure. The goal of family policy should be to facilitate, protect, and support caring relationships. Conferring the rights and benefits currently enjoyed by heterosexual married couples and their children upon same-sex couples, and providing more support for low-income single parents and their children are important steps toward meeting this goal.

I. PROMOTING FAMILY UNIFORMITY

Divorce Reform

Galston argues that families serve the vital public purpose of raising children "who are prepared—intellectually, physically, morally, and emotionally—to take their place as law-abiding and independent members of their community, able to sustain themselves and their families and fulfill their duties as citizens."[1] But many families, Galston warns, are failing to adequately discharge their primary function because they do not have the proper family structure. Due to divorce and nonmarital birth, more and more children are raised in single-parent families. It is estimated that 40 percent of all marriages end in divorce[2] and that 31 percent of all births are to unmarried women.[3] Each year, 1.5 million children—nearly 2.5 percent of all U.S. children—experience the divorce of their parents.[4] In 1997, 25 percent of all children were living with a single parent.[5] Galston claims that these children will not be adequately prepared to take their place as responsible citizens.

Galston argues that family structure is a public as opposed to an exclusively private concern. He asserts that children who grow up in single-parent families do great damage to society and that, as a result, we all have an interest in fostering greater family stability. Galston states: "We all pay for systems of welfare, criminal justice, and incarceration as well as for physical and mental disability; we are all made poorer by the inability or unwillingness of young adults to become contributing members of society; we all suffer if our society is unsafe and divided."[6] Galston asserts that since the serious social problems he believes are caused by single-parent families affect all of us, public policies and laws that curtail personal freedoms—such as the freedom to exit a marriage—are legitimate. He writes: "Whenever institutions and practices have such pervasive consequences, society has the right to scrutinize them and, where possible, to reshape them in the light of collective goals."[7] The collective goal that Galston has in mind is that marriage should be presumed to be a permanent and lifelong commitment except in cases of physical abuse or high conflict. Galston views the acceptance of divorce and nonmarital birth as a threat to social stability and well-being. He warns us to "resist the easy relativism of the proposition that different family structures represent nothing more than 'alternative life-styles.'"[8] When we accept different lifestyles, Galston explains, we undermine the power of marriage as a normative ideal that all Americans should aspire to attain.

Galston claims that marriages can be strengthened and preserved by instituting waiting periods for divorce and by eliminating no-fault divorce.[9] Marital law for couples with children should undergo the following reforms:

> We should eliminate unilateral no-fault divorce—where one person can readily obtain a divorce without the other's consent—and return to an updated fault-based system, with the alternative of a five-year waiting period. And even in cases where both parties consent, there should be a suitable breaking mechanism: a mandatory pause of at least one year for reflection, counseling and mediation.[10]

While Galston admits that economic and cultural changes are the primary factors behind rising rates of divorce, he claims the adoption of no-fault divorce by all fifty states "accelerated the pace of divorce."[11] Law, Galston argues, is capable of influencing personal behavior and conduct. As a result, making divorce more difficult may keep couples together. However, in addition to making divorce a much more lengthy and involved process, reforming divorce law may also alter people's attitudes toward the morality of divorce. According to Galston, the proliferation of no-fault divorce "symbolized the spreading belief that divorce presented no particular moral problem, that there was in the moral as well as the legal sense, no fault." This encouraged what Galston calls the "destigmatization effect."[12] Galston welcomes the possibility that eliminating no-fault divorce could recreate the social stigma that was once attached to divorce.

Galston argues that no-fault divorce harms women as well as children because it punishes women who have chosen to stay at home to raise their children. After spending a majority of their lives caring for their husbands and children, these women are expected to compete in the paid labor market. While the economic consequences of divorce for women deserve careful attention, eliminating no-fault divorce will not benefit women. Many women already find it difficult to leave abusive marriages. Some are economically dependent on their husbands; others have been taught all their lives to elevate the needs of family members above their own. Many women also fear their husbands will attempt to hurt them physically or attempt to gain custody of the children if they initiate a divorce. Barbara Dafoe Whitehead, author of the *Atlantic* article "Dan Quayle was Right" and *Divorce Culture*, argues that repealing no-fault divorce will have a detrimental effect on women who are physically abused by their husbands. She comments:

> No-fault divorce provides a safety net for battered wives. Requiring marriage partners to show who is at fault before they can divorce will shred that net. Women will have to muster the time, money, and resolve to undertake what amounts to a civil prosecution of a violent crime. This is a terrifying prospect for battered wives who, for obvious reasons, want to avoid conflict with their husbands.[13]

Given contemporary power imbalances between men and women, divorce reform of the type suggested by Galston will trap some women in marriages they wish to leave. Galston claims that stay-at-home wives and their children are the true victims of no-fault divorce and that middle-aged men who selfishly end their fourteen-year marriages to marry younger women are the true culprits behind divorce. However, this is an argument that supports making the economic consequences of divorce more favorable for women and their children, not preventing it altogether. It also implies that it is men who initiate divorce when in fact women seek a disproportionate number of contemporary divorces.[14] Given that divorce often means economic hardship for women, those women who initiate divorce clearly feel that their marriage can be held together only at substantial cost to themselves.

Galston admits that for most Americans "marriage is first and foremost a means to personal happiness."[15] However, from Galston's perspective, adults' interests in emotional and sexual satisfaction should be sacrificed to the interest society has in producing law-abiding and productive citizens. According to Galston, past generations valued obligations to others, individual sacrifice, and self-restraint. In contrast, contemporary Americans value individualism, self-expression, and personal choice. This change in cultural attitudes, while advantageous, perhaps, to individuals, has caused harm to society as a whole and, in particular, to the most vulnerable members of families. As Galston states, "the past quarter century's emphasis on self-fulfillment has gone too far and we must seek a new balance between rights and responsibilities."[16] Galston concludes that using law to constrain personal freedom is legitimate if personal behavior threatens to undermine the civic order.

In assessing Galston's argument, I will first consider his claim that divorce and growing up in a single-parent home is harmful to children. Social scientists attempt to measure the effects of divorce on children by comparing children from intact and divorced families on a variety of variables, including behavioral conduct, psychological adjustment, educational achievement, idleness (e.g., youth who are neither employed nor in school), and teen pregnancy. While almost all social scientists consider divorce to be a traumatic experience for children, there is no consensus on "the magnitude, persistence and pervasiveness" of its harmful effects on children.[17] This is, in part, due to certain methodological problems that hamper the study of divorce. For example, social scientists now argue that divorce should be considered a process as opposed to an event. This raises the question of whether children's observed behavioral problems were caused by the divorce itself or by "predisruptive effects" (e.g., problems that arose prior to divorce). There is also disagreement over whether the decrease in well-being experienced by some children after divorce is caused by the divorce itself, or factors accompanying divorce, such as a drop in household income and/or the transition to a new neighborhood and school system. Finally, there are few studies that compare children from divorced families with children from unhappily married couples who have chosen to stay together for the sake of the children. Without such a comparison group, it is difficult to know whether children from divorced families are worse off, the same, or better off than children of unhappy couples who have remained married.

Divorce and the Measurement of Child Well-Being

In a 1991 meta-analysis of ninety-two studies which collectively involved over 13,000 children, Paul R. Amato and Bruce Keith measured differences between children of divorced and intact families across variables such as school achievement, conduct, social and psychological adjustment, self-concept, mother-child relations, and father-child relations.[18] Their findings "confirm that children of divorce experience a lower level of well-being than do children living in continuously intact families." However, they go on to say, "the effect sizes in this literature are weak rather than strong. The largest reliable mean effect sizes (for conduct and father-child relations) are in the order of one quarter of a standard deviation between intact and divorced groups. The mean effect sizes for psychological well-being, self-concept, and social adjustment reflect approximately one tenth of a standard deviation between groups."[19] In sum, their study shows that in terms of most variables, the differences between children who have experienced the divorce of their parents and those who have not are extremely small. Moreover, Amato and Keith state that their evidence does not support the claim that divorce has profound effects on the well-being of children.[20] Despite their own conclusions, Amato and Keith are not willing to dismiss the harmful effects of divorce. They explain that the studies they reviewed focused on children and that there is reason to think that studies of young adults will provide support for the "notion that parental divorce has lasting implications for children's life chances."[21]

Andrew Cherlin, P. Lindsay Chase-Lansdale, and Christine McRae conducted a study on the long-term effects of divorce on individuals' mental health after the transition to adulthood.[22] They examined data from the National Child Development Study (NCDS), a longitudinal study of children who were born in 1958. Parents and teachers were interviewed when the 11,759 cohort members were seven, eleven, and sixteen. At ages twenty-three and thirty-three, the cohort members themselves were interviewed. Cherlin and his associates found that at age seven, the children who would eventually experience the divorce of their parents were already experiencing more emotional problems than those who would not. Cherlin and colleagues claim that this "preexisting gap" is "consistent with the argument that divorce occurs in families that are already troubled."[23] This indicates that in some cases it is not the event of the divorce itself but the problems that accompany the divorce, such as persistent parental conflict or genetic dispositions, which cause emotional problems in children from divorced families. Cherlin states that "studies that do not take into account the preexisting differences of children and their families overstate the effects of growing up in a single-parent family."[24] However, Cherlin and his colleagues also found that the gap in mental health between young people from divorced and intact families continued to grow after the divorce itself. This indicates that the divorce itself can have a negative effect on mental health. At the age of twenty-three, women who had experienced the divorce of their parents and those who had not were asked to fill out a twenty-four-question index of mental health. Cherlin and his associates made two findings based on the results of the survey: (1) relatively few individuals in either group had mental health problems, and (2) the risk of experiencing mental health problems was 31 percent higher in the divorce group. These findings demonstrate that while divorce does not have serious and long-lasting effects on the mental health of most individuals, it does increase the risk that some individuals will experience long-term emotional problems.

Sara McLanahan and Gary Sandefur conducted one of the most widely referred to studies on family structure.[25] The data presented by McLanahan and Sandefur on the risks associated with growing up in a single-parent home are at first quite alarming. In the very first pages of their book they announce that controlling for education and race, "adolescents who have lived apart from one of their parents during some period of childhood are twice as likely to drop out of high school, twice as likely to have a child before age twenty, and are one and a half times as likely to be 'idle'—out of school and out of work—in their late teens and early twenties."[26] These figures refer to single-parent families formed through both nonmarital birth and divorce. Of those children who lived in a single-parent family in 1996, 37 percent lived with a divorced parent, 23 percent lived with a parent who was separated, 4 percent lived with a parent who was widowed, and 36 percent lived with a parent who had never married.[27] Divorced mothers are usually better educated, older, and have higher incomes than never married mothers.[28] However, because McLanahan and Sandefur have controlled for education, much of the advantage divorced mothers have over never married mothers is cancelled out.

Employing a range of data sets, including the National Longitudinal Survey of Youth (NLSY) and the Panel Study of Income Dynamics (PSID), McLanahan and Sandefur report that children from single-parent families have a 25–29 percent chance of dropping out of high school in comparison to children from intact two-parent families, who have a 13–15 percent chance of dropping out of school.[29] However, these comparisons do not consider the drop in income that almost always accompanies a divorce. Once income differences are taken into account, the dropout rate for children in single-parent families is only three percentage points higher than the dropout rate for children living in two-parent families. Similarly, the rate at which children from single-parent homes become teen mothers is four percentage points higher than children from intact families, and the rate at which boys and men become idle is seven percentage points higher than their peers from intact families.[30] McLanahan and Sandefur state that "differences in income account for as much as half of the difference in school achievement and early childbearing in children in single-parent and two-parent homes."[31] This finding indicates that a very large part of the detrimental effects associated with growing up in a single-parent home are a result of the lack of economic resources available to single-parent families. In addition, we should keep in mind that divorce is just one of many factors that increase a child's likelihood of engaging in risky behavior. Numerous risk factors and the interaction between them make children and young adults vulnerable to emotional problems and self-destructive behavior. McLanahan and Sandefur report that having a mother with less than a high school education presents children with the same risk of dropping out of school as growing up in a single-parent home does.[32]

The economic insecurity of mother-only families is an issue of national importance. In 1998, almost half of all households headed by divorced, separated, widowed, or never-married mothers lived below the poverty line. Black and Hispanic single-mother families are more likely to be poor than white single-mother families. According to a *Research Brief* prepared by Child Trends, in 1998, 55 percent of black, 60 percent of Hispanic, and 40 percent of white female-headed families were poor.[33] Divorce has a large negative impact on the economic status of women and their children. The household income of white children whose parents divorce drops on average by 40 percent. In black families, household income drops by 32 percent.[34] As we saw in chapter 1, women continue to earn substantially less money than men do. When a marriage dissolves, women almost always receive custody of, and most of the economic responsibility for, the children. Men become nonresidential parents and often, over time, contribute less and less to the support of their children.[35] As a result of diminished household income, children of divorce are more likely to grow up with limited economic resources, and as a result, to live in low-income neighborhoods, attend poor-quality schools, and have less access to the social contacts that often provide future job opportunities.[36]

Not surprisingly, Galston and other family communitarians propose to solve single mothers' poverty by promoting marriage. Galston claims that "the best antipoverty program for children is a stable intact family."[37] However, this so-called "program" sidesteps the fact that if women earned comparable wages to men, they would be able to support themselves and their children without access to a male wage. Women who work full-time should not need a man's income to lift them and their children out of poverty. In reality, the reason single-mother families are so often poor is that women do not have the same economic opportunities that men do. In addition, the U.S. economy does not provide wages to low-skilled workers that will allow one parent, particularly if she is female, to support a family.[38] In the past, marriage was a woman's only route to economic security. Women were forced to stay in marriages because they had few decent job opportunities. However, a society committed to gender justice should not tolerate the fact that a woman with children, but without a college education, marketable skills, or a husband, is condemned to a life of acute poverty. If we believe in equal economic opportunities for women we cannot be satisfied with an "anti-poverty program" that requires women's economic dependence on men.[39]

Many single mothers, particularly mothers who were unmarried or under twenty-five at the birth of their child, were raised in economically disadvantaged communities. In other words, they were poor before they became single parents. This is particularly true for African American women and Latinas. There are no simple solutions to the difficulties faced by low-income mother-headed families, or by low-income two-parent families whose children are often also at risk. Individuals who have grown up in poor families and poor neighborhoods face multiple obstacles to obtaining economic security ranging from lack of education, job opportunities, assets, housing, transportation, and health care, to the presence of physical and mental illness and drug addiction. A marriage certificate will not make these problems go away. When we pretend that it can, we avoid facing the inadequacies of the low-wage labor market and our nation's refusal to invest in low-income rural and urban communities. It is wrong to say, as Galston does, that growing up in a single-parent family harms children when, in fact, the greatest threat to the well-being of children is poverty. Referring to children who grow up in single-parent families, McLanahan explains: "Low income is the single most important factor in accounting for the lower achievement of these children. Raising income, therefore, should be a major priority."[40] The most promising policies for addressing the needs of children and families are multifaceted programs that require substantial public funding. I address this issue at greater length in chapters 5 and 6.

Income loss goes a long way in explaining why some children who grow up in single-parent families are worse off than their peers in intact families. However, it does not explain all of the differences between these two groups. In their assessment of how divorce affects children, Andrew Cherlin and Frank F. Furstenberg Jr., claim that custodial parents, usually mothers, often experience acute stress immediately following their divorce. Overwhelmed by raising children on their own and emotionally upset by the dissolution of their marriage, newly divorced mothers are often not in a good position to give their children the additional emotional support and the consistent daily routine that they need.[41] However, Cherlin and Furstenberg report that "within two or three years [of the divorce] most single-parents and their children recover substantially from the trauma of the crisis period."[42] McLanahan and Sandefur believe that children living in single-parent families caused by divorce or a failure on the part of parents to marry suffer from a deficit in "social capital."[43] They miss out on the additional emotional support and parental guidance that they would have received if the family had remained intact or their parents had formed one household. As is frequently the case, losing contact with their noncustodial parent (usually the father) and his relatives and friends, deprives children and young adults of resources, including information about jobs, and weakens their ability to trust others.[44] According to McLanahan and Sandefur, deficits in social capital explain why children in single-parent families do less well than their peers in intact families once income differences are taken into account.

The research that I have reviewed places the claims made by Galston and other family communitarians in perspective. Divorce and growing up in a single-parent family does increase the risk that some children will do less well than their peers from intact families on a range of outcomes. The harmful effects of divorce should not be ignored or downplayed. However, family communitarians greatly exaggerate the relationship between family structure and child well-being. In the following statement, Cherlin summarizes the evidence on divorce and its effects:

> Whether a child grows up with two biological parents, I conclude, makes a difference in his or her life; it is not merely an epiphenomenon. Not having two parents at home sometimes leads to short- and long-term problems, but not all the differences we see in outcomes are the results of family structure. Some of the differences would have occurred anyway. Moreover, parental divorce or being born to unmarried parents does not automatically lead to problems. Many (perhaps most) children who grow up in single-parent families or stepfamilies will not be harmed seriously in the long term.[45]

These conclusions do not support the family communitarian assertion that the decline of the two-parent family is the cause of our gravest social problems.

Furstenberg argues that if family structure determined child well-being, we could expect to see the same pattern of decline across all indicators. But this is not the case. Some indicators of child well-being have improved recently (educational achievement), others have fluctuated (drug use and crime), and some indicate a decline in well-being (increases in suicide).[46] In a 1988 study on adolescent well-being, Furstenberg and Gretchen A. Condran found that "the dependent variables selected as measures of the well-being of youth (SAT scores, suicide, drug and alcohol use, automobile death rates, teen pregnancy) do not consistently vary when changes occur in the presumed explanations of the behavior—divorce and mothers' labor force participation."[47] McLanahan, who as we have seen, does claim that single parenthood elevates the risk that young people will experience problems, rejects the claim that it is the root cause of all social problems. She states, "The evidence, however, does not show that family disruption is the principal cause of high school failure, poverty, and delinquency. . . . The story is basically the same for the other measures of child well-being. If all children lived in two-parent families, teen motherhood and idleness would be less common, but the bulk of these problems would remain."[48] In their analysis of thirteen studies that compared the effects of family income, maternal education, and family structure on child outcomes, Greg J. Duncan and Jeanne Brooks-Gunn found that family income is "usually a stronger predictor of ability and achievement outcomes than are measures of parental schooling or family structure."[49] Family structure simply does not have the clear, direct, and large effects on child well-being that would justify placing significant obstacles in the way of dissolving a marriage.

Galston and other family communitarians argue that two-parent families are morally superior to other family forms because they are best able to produce citizens with the proper virtues and moral character. However, the differential outcomes reviewed here are not large enough to support the assertion that single-parent families produce children who lack civic virtue. Moreover, it is not clear that moral character can be measured by outcomes such as teen pregnancy, educational achievement, or employment. It is unlikely that the social scientists who designed these indicators intended them to be used as measures of moral character.

Finally, we must consider whether the question we are asking—Do single-mother families do as well as intact families on a range of child outcomes?—is the right one. Historically, men have been considered the heads of households and the primary providers for their families. Only recently have we evolved a family pattern in which women are household heads. It should come as no surprise if this new family form does not produce the exact same outcomes as the traditional family. After all, this new family form exists in an economic, social, and political structure that was built to support the male-headed, father-provider, mother-caretaker family. Studies that compare two-parent and single-parent families do not look at how the larger society supports the former and disadvantages the latter. Both kinds of families are studied in isolation from the larger economic, social, and political structures. We do not ask, how well would single-parent families do if women earned the same weekly income as men? Nor do we ask, how well would single-parent families do if high quality childcare were available to all children? It is disingenuous to compare two-parent and single-parent families until the larger society has been restructured so that it provides greater support for the latter.

So far, like many critics of divorce reform, I have focused on whether the event of divorce causes the serious consequences ascribed to it by advocates of family uniformity.[50] However, evaluating divorce reform solely in terms of how it will affect children ignores the impact that it will have on adults. An important liberty interest is at stake in the decision to make divorce more difficult. When state legislators vote to impose long waiting periods on married couples—one or both of whom would like to divorce— they are placing a substantial constraint on the freedom of intimate association. The freedom of intimate association includes the right to enter or exit a marital relationship. Restricting access to divorce not only prevents the termination of a relationship; it also makes forming a new relationship more difficult.

Personal Liberty

What kind of liberty interest is at stake in the effort to make divorce more difficult, and why is it important? As I have already suggested, the freedom to exit a relationship is valuable to those individuals who are experiencing physical or mental harm at the hands of their spouse. However, the right to exit a relationship is important for other reasons as well. Placing restrictions on divorce makes it more difficult for individuals to determine the meaning of their marriage for themselves. Whether marriage is understood as permanent or terminable is part of a larger conception of the meanings of intimacy, sexuality, and commitment. For men and women who hold what I will call the romantic view, marriage is based on sexual and emotional intimacy. According to this view, husbands and wives are lovers as well as parents and household and economic partners. If women and men who hold the romantic view are not able to sustain some level of intimacy over time, their marriage seems false and dishonest to them. Consequently, they may decide to divorce.

Other men and women hold that while love is the original basis of the marital bond, once a marital commitment has been made, a lack of sexual and emotional intimacy is not sufficient reason to sunder it, especially if children are involved. Once husbands and wives have become parents, their relationship as lovers must come second. Marriage cannot be reduced to a love or sexual relationship. It is, first and foremost, the proper framework for having and rearing children. Providing a stable home for their children should be the primary consideration for parents. Men and women who hold what I will call the institutional view understand marriage to be a lifelong commitment that only can be legitimately terminated in extreme cases.

According to family communitarians, the institutional view correctly captures the correct meaning of marriage. The romantic view is a perversion because it denies that marriage is a permanent bond that exists for the sake of the children. While the former is child-centered and puts the interests of children first, the latter prioritizes the interests of adults. However, the family communitarians fail to appreciate that the real difference between these two understandings of marriage is the role that emotional intimacy plays in their respective conceptions of the good life. Parents who dissolve their marriage because it no longer provides them with an emotional home are not less devoted to their children than parents who hold the institutional view. Instead, in choosing divorce, they are modeling for their children a particular understanding of what makes life valuable. They are saying to their children: the relationship between husband and wife should be emotionally rich and meaningful. I have accepted no less and neither should you.

In truth, there are probably only a relatively small number of women and men that self-consciously hold either the institutional view or the romantic view of marriage. Many, if not most, individuals hold these two opposing views of marriage at the same time. It is only when individuals contemplate divorce that they are forced to address the conflict between the romantic and the institutional views. The elimination of no-fault divorce would effectively prevent men and women from determining for themselves the nature and meaning of the marital bond. While divorce reform does not eliminate divorce, it does impose the institutional view of marriage on all married couples. It says to married couples that they are not capable of determining the meaning of their marital relationship for themselves. They may believe that a loveless marriage is not a true or authentic marriage, but the state has determined that they are wrong, and that lack of love is an insufficient reason for terminating a marriage. In considering divorce reform, we should keep in mind that retaining no-fault divorce does not prevent men and women who hold the institutional view from acting on their belief that marriage is a lifelong commitment only to be broken under extraordinary circumstances. However, eliminating no-fault divorce will prevent men and women from acting on their belief in the romantic view.

Galston's divorce reform is a violation of the individuality-based conception of the right of privacy that I described in chapter 2. The right of privacy protects our ability to make deeply personal decisions. State officials should leave determining the meaning of marriage up to the two individuals that compose the marital couple. Marriage provides many individuals with their emotional home. Preventing individuals from shaping this most intimate of relationships in terms of their own values and moral preferences is a direct assault on their ability to exercise moral independence and self-determination.

Opposition to Same-Sex Marriage

In her argument against legalizing same-sex marriage, Elshtain asserts that some of the purposes that marriages serve are more important than others. Indeed, she claims that marriage can be reduced to one purpose—procreation. Elshtain writes, "But marriage is not, and never has been, primarily about two people—it is and always has been about the possibility of generativity."[51] She explains that although not all heterosexuals can or choose to have children, the heterosexual couple symbolizes what Elshtain refers to as social regenesis, and as a result should be elevated above other family forms. Like Galston, Elshtain believes that not all forms of intimate relationship and association are equal. Although same-sex couples should be given the option of registering as domestic partners, the intergenerational family with a married heterosexual couple at its center should remain the ideal family model. Elshtain suggests that this form of family embodies values that other kinds of families are not able to express. She explains: "The intergenerational family, as symbolism of social regenesis, as tough and compelling reality, as defining moral norm, remains central and critical in nurturing recognition of human frailty, mortality, and finitude, and in inculcating moral limits and constraints."[52] If we fail to uphold the heterosexual family norm we run the risk of not being able to distinguish between the truly important and the utterly trivial aspects of life. Elshtain explains: "We should be cautious about going too far in the direction of a wholly untrammeled pluralism lest we become so vapid that we are no longer capable of distinguishing between the moral weightiness of, say, polishing one's Porsche and sitting up all night with a sick child."[53] Elshtain apparently believes that if we give unions she believes to be inherently nonprocreative the same moral and social significance as those she considers to be inherently procreative, we will produce a moral culture in which caring for and raising children is no longer given its proper value. She suggests that childless families (and it will be recalled that for Elshtain, lesbian and gay families are by definition childless) are inherently materialistic and aim at nothing higher than the pooling of incomes. There is, however, no reason to think that parents are immune to the temptations of a materialistic and consumer culture.

Elshtain's assumption that lesbian and gay relationships are inherently childless can be easily challenged. While some heterosexual marriages are nonprocreative, many lesbian and gay male couples are raising children together. Estimates of how many children have a lesbian or gay parent range from six to fourteen million.[54] While the majority of these children are from one partner's previous heterosexual marriage or relationship, during the 1980s many lesbians bore children with the help of gay and straight male friends, progressive physicians, and home-grown methods of artificial insemination. It is perhaps with artificial insemination in mind that Elshtain opens her article on lesbian and gay marriage with an attack on what she views as intrusive interventions in human reproduction and the "technologizing of birth." According to Elshtain, "[o]ne finds more and more the demand that babies can and must be made whenever the want is there." This demand transforms human procreation into a technical operation. Elshtain claims the technologizing of birth is antiregenerative because it is "linked to a refusal to accept natural limits."[55] While Elshtain never comes right out and accuses lesbian mothers who have used artificial insemination of "refusing to accept limits," this would appear to be the link between her complaints against the "technologizing of birth" and her opposition to same-sex marriage. Indeed, her position may be that although same-sex couples raise children together, they can never symbolize social regenesis because *as a couple* they are not independently capable of creating a child the "natural way." Of course, this is equally the case with a growing number of heterosexual couples who have made use of new fertility technologies. According to Elshtain, all methods of procreation that do not involve copulation and unassisted fertilization between one man and one woman are somehow unnatural, and hence suspect. The consequence of this argument is that no matter how many children are raised in lesbian and gay families, same-sex couples can never symbolize regenesis because they are incapable of giving birth without what Elshtain would consider "outside help." Indeed, Elshtain's preference for nontechnological birth would seem to suggest that families created through adoption or the use of fertility technology are also not able to embody the value of social regenesis.

If Elshtain's goal is to foster a moral culture that values caring for and rearing children, her attempt to define lesbian and gay families as inherently nonprocreative cannot be justified. How will preventing the parents of between six and fourteen million children from marrying create a better environment for raising children? As Judith Stacey has stated, "only through a massive denial of the fact that millions of children living in gay and lesbian families are here and here to stay, can anyone genuinely concerned with the best interests of children deny their parents the right to marry.[56] In addition, how will the privileging of so-called natural conception improve the lives of children living in stepfamilies or families formed through adoption? If we want to make sure that more children grow up in families we should be celebrating and encouraging social parenthood. The privileging of biological parenthood serves to marginalize many family forms including stepfamilies, lesbian and gay families, and families formed through adoption.

The fact that lesbian and gay families with children exist and are increasing is unlikely to deter Elshtain from arguing against same-sex marriage. Given her focus on nonassisted biological conception, a married heterosexual couple *without* children would more closely approximate the true meaning of marriage to Elshtain than a lesbian or gay couple *with* children. However, there is no evidence that suggests heterosexuals make better parents than lesbians or gay men. Studies measuring variables such as school achievement, social adjustment, mental health, gender identity, and sexual orientation report no significant differences between children raised in lesbian and gay families and those raised in heterosexual families.[57] According to the American Psychological Association, "not a single study has found children of lesbian or gay parents to be disadvantaged in any significant respect relative to children of heterosexual parents. Indeed, the evidence to date suggests that home environments provided by lesbian and gay parents are as likely as those provided by heterosexual parents to support and enable children's psychosocial growth."[58] Lesbian and gay parents are as capable of raising happy, healthy children as heterosexual parents. Why, then, should their unions be defined as incapable of symbolizing social regenesis and intergenerationality?

Elshtain's argument also ignores the fact that one of the reasons that some lesbians and gay men seek state-sanctioned marriage is that it would protect the rights and enforce the responsibilities of the nonbiological partner. When a lesbian or gay partnership dissolves or the biological parent dies, the nonbiological parent has no secure legal standing in a court of law. This means that a nonbiological parent who has helped to raise a child for many years can lose custody of the child to grandparents or an aunt, and that an estranged partner can deny visitation rights to a nonbiological parent. Legalizing same-sex marriage would be a big step toward protecting nonbiological parents and their children. It also would make it easier for lesbian and gay couples to jointly adopt children.

If the right of privacy is interpreted to include positive state action, as I argue that it should be in chapter 2, it guarantees the right of same-sex couples to marry. Denial of the right to marry legitimizes the moral preferences of the majority and prevents individuals from controlling the nature and form of their intimate associations. In effect, individuals are stripped of their moral independence in an area of great importance to their identity and personal happiness. As I explain at greater length in section 3 of this chapter, state recognition of partnership or union enables a couple to interact with third parties as a unit for certain purposes. In this way, officially recognizing a partnership or union helps to maintain it. By failing to extend the same rights and responsibilities to gay and lesbian couples as it does to straight couples, the state is effectively undermining their caring relationship. Moreover, such inaction says to lesbians and gay men that the larger society refuses to respect their decisions regarding whom they have chosen to love.

Both Elshtain and Galston attempt to establish a connection between the purpose they claim to be definitive of families and family structure in order to justify the promotion of the two-parent family. I have argued that neither author is able to establish such a connection because family structure does not play the all-important role that Galston and Elshtain claim it does. The greatest problem single-mother families face is the inadequacies of the low-wage labor market. The best way to help them is to reform the low-wage labor market and to provide a better publicly funded support system including universal health care, income supports, subsidized housing, and childcare. Lesbian and gay families with children are as capable of embodying the value of the intergenerational family as heterosexual families with children. A child-centered family policy would officially recognize same-sex marriage and would provide public support for poor single-parent families.

Elshtain's and Galston's strategies for promoting family uniformity require us to belittle our relatively newfound freedom to seek personal fulfillment through love. Emotional and sexual intimacies are goods of great value to most contemporary individuals. And yet, both authors refuse to face up to the enormous loss of liberty involved in constraining the freedom of individuals to enter into and exit the intimate relationships of their choice. As I argued in chapter 1, our new freedom in intimate relationships has given us something more than rising rates of divorce and nonmarital birth. It has brought with it the possibility of freely chosen, egalitarian, and emotionally rich forms of adult intimacy. This is a historically unprecedented opportunity and it should not be closed off in a fruitless attempt to prevent divorce or preserve the preeminence of heterosexuality.

If freely chosen and egalitarian models of marriage and family are to develop, personal liberty in intimate relations must be maintained and expanded. Intimacy between peers requires that relationships be freely chosen and voluntary. In particular, individuals should have (1) the freedom to marry a member of her or his own sex, and (2) the freedom to exit a loveless marriage. Making divorce more difficult, as Galston recommends, is a direct assault on the intimacy needs of adults. Divorce reform prevents individuals from leaving loveless relationships and entering into relationships with individuals they do love. Restricting marriage to heterosexual couples, as Elshtain would like to do, limits the ability of same-sex couples to protect and preserve their intimate relationships.

In section 1, my goal was to challenge the proposition that one form of family is best able to raise good citizens. In section 2, I reconsider the question of what purposes the family exists to serve. It is not my intention to undervalue the centrality of caring for children to modern conceptions of family, but to insist that the family serves more than one purpose. The argumentative strategy pursued by Galston and Elshtain ignores the fact that marriage and family must serve the interests and needs of adults if they are to meet the needs of children. Arguing that marriage and family have no other purpose than procreation and child rearing pushes emotional and sexual intimacy outside of marriage and family. This, I argue, will not promote strong marriages and families.

II. THE MULTIPURPOSE FAMILY

In constructing my account of familial purposes, I turn to two political thinkers, Aristotle and Rousseau, who have had an important influence on how the Western philosophical tradition views the family. While I reject their strong support for gender roles, women's subordination, and the control of women's sexuality, Aristotle and Rousseau each capture features of family life that are necessary to providing a complete understanding of the purposes that families serve today. Aristotle defines the family as a mutual aid society; an association dedicated to meeting the daily material needs of its members. Rousseau reconstructs the family as an affect-based and emotionally intense association. The goal of my account of family purposes is both to show that families are multipurpose associations and that the purposes they serve have changed over time.

Any attempt to identify familial purposes immediately confronts the problem that even if we limit ourselves to Europe and North America, "family" is not a transhistorical concept. According to historian Jean-Louis Flandrin, "[t]he concept of the family, as it is most commonly defined today, has only existed in our western culture since a comparatively recent date."[59] Prior to the eighteenth century, the kin-based family as we know it in contemporary, post-industrial Western societies did not exist. Instead, members of households, kin and nonkin, shared a common authority—the head of the household—and a common residence. Households contained the limited kin groups we recognize as nuclear families (e.g., a married couple with children), but they also included servants, slaves, and apprentices.[60] Despite these significant historical differences, sufficient continuity exists between the households of the past and today's families to warrant an examination of Aristotle's account of the classical household, or *oikos*.

The classical *oikos*, described by Aristotle in *The Politics*, was an economic association, the site of both production and consumption. It included land and the means of production, such as tools, animals, and enslaved human beings, which provided for the needs of the head of household, his wife, and children. According to Aristotle, the household exists to serve three purposes: procreation, meeting the daily needs of members, and the moral education of children and women. Aristotle claims that a natural imperative brings men and

women together so "that the race may continue." An equally natural imperative lies behind the union of master and slave. Aristotle explains that slaves
exist to assist their master in the meeting of daily needs. He sums up the purpose of the *oikos* as follows: "The family is the association established by nature for the supply of men's everyday wants, and the members of it are called
by Charondas, 'companions of the cupboard', and by Epimenides the Cretan,
'companions of the manager'."[61] Aristotle's emphasis on material needs does
not mean that the household should be conceived narrowly as the site of mere
biological survival. Although book one of *The Politics* covers the economic
dimension of household life in great detail, Aristotle concludes his account by
claiming that the head of the household's most important task is the moral education of subordinate household members.[62] Aristotle's household was a hi-
erarchically ordered association in which status, power, and privilege were
determined by gender, age, and whether one was free or a slave. Women, who
were excluded from any role in the public sphere, were legally, politically,
and socially subordinated to their husbands and fathers.

The appeal of Aristotle's definition of the household is that it reminds us
that individuals form families because they lack self-sufficiency, and therefore need each other. Aristotle asserts that the origin of the household is need,
or the isolated individual's inability to provide for him or herself. We can condemn Aristotle's defense of slavery and gender inequality and his concomi-
tant assertion that different kinds of people (e.g., men or women, slaves or
free people) are suited to different tasks, without rejecting his understanding
of the household as a mutual aid society that aims at satisfying the daily needs
of its members. While this definition may seem best suited to historical periods in which the household was a productive unit, it captures the part that
families play in providing and distributing resources to their members. It reminds us that families have a strong economic dimension and that the household is the site of productive and repetitive labor, such as cooking and cleaning, which is necessary to the well-being of its members.

By the end of the eighteenth century, the idea of the family as a limited kin
group composed of parents and children began to replace the idea of the
household as an economic association composed of a household head and
subordinate household members, including children, apprentices, a wife, and
servants. According to Stone

> The four key features of the modern family—intensified affective bonding of
> the nuclear core at the expense of neighbors and kin; a strong sense of individ-
> ual autonomy and the right to personal freedom in the pursuit of happiness; a
> weakening of the association of sexual pleasure with sin and guilt; and a grow-
> ing desire for physical privacy—were all well established by 1750 in the key
> middle and upper sectors of English society.[63]

While families continued to work collectively to meet daily needs, greater emphasis was placed on emotionally intense bonds between husband and wife and parents and children. Shorter explains that while families in the sixteenth and seventeenth centuries were primarily reproductive and productive units, during the eighteenth century a "revolution in sentiment" transformed the family into an emotional unit.[64]

The concept of the sentimental family whose members are bound together by ties of love and affection was popularized in *Emile or On Education* by Jean-Jacques Rousseau, which was first published in 1764. In *Emile*, Rousseau depicts the ideal family as a small society of intimates, distinct from other household members such as servants, apprentices, and boarders, as well as extended kin, neighbors, and the larger community. The rise of the nuclear family required a new understanding of the boundaries between public and private. Members of the household who were not linked to the head of the household by blood or marriage were no longer considered a part of the family. The sentimental family is characterized by greater concern for the upbringing and care of children. This is demonstrated by Rousseau's attack in *Emile* on urban upper-class parents who paid intermediaries to perform the gender-specific roles of nurse and tutor that Rousseau felt could be carried out adequately only by the parents themselves.[65] In addition to elevating the importance attached to caring for and rearing children, Rousseau's portrayal of the sentimental family emphasized the sexual and emotional nature of the husband-wife relationship. The narrator of *Emile*, Emile's tutor, advises Emile and his beloved Sophie that although they began their marriage as lovers they will eventually lose their sexual desire for each other. However, he tells them not to worry because by the time this happens they will have become transformed into friends and companions. Another indication of Rousseau's support for marriage based on love was his opposition to arranged marriages. He criticized upper-class marriages, based on forging alliances between powerful families and transferring wealth from one generation to the next, because they produced families whose members were distant and cold. According to Rousseau, it is affection and love that both holds families together and makes them effective instruments of moral instruction.

Rousseau celebrated women's roles as mother, wife, and moral authority within the household. However, he argued in favor of rigid gender roles and the wife's subordination to her husband, the exclusion of women from the public sphere, and a punishing code of sexual conduct for women. Like Aristotle's household, Rousseau's sentimental family distributed power and status according to gender and regulated women's sexuality much more restrictively than men's. However, if we put to one side his insistence on rigid gender roles, what we can take from Rousseau is his conception of the family as an emotionally rich association based on care and affection.

Rousseau's portrait of the family in *Emile* foreshadowed changes in family life brought on, in part, by industrialization. As industrial economies developed, the household became more of a residence or home and less of a site of production. With the separation of home and workplace, the development of wage-labor, and the exclusion of nonkin from the family unit, the family was no longer viewed primarily as an economic association. Of course, changes in the economy and the sentimentalization of family ties did not mean that the family ceased to provide for the material needs of its members. It did mean that the middle-class family ideal of the nineteenth century was often defined in opposition to the world of work. While the public world of work was portrayed as dirty, corrupt, and competitive, the private sphere was idealized as a sanctuary of care and comfort. Consequently, Aristotle's small mutual aid society became a society of intimates devoted to both material and emotional sustenance. Intimacy, love, affection, and even sexual pleasure between husband and wife, became important familial purposes.

Families were transformed once again by the emergence of a more positive attitude toward sexuality by the end of the nineteenth century. Evidence for sexual liberalization is based on an increase in rates of premarital sex, as well as the evaluation of literature on sexual matters, such as articles in popular magazines and marriage manuals. During this time marriage manuals began to suggest that pleasure, and not just procreation, could be considered a legitimate reason for married couples to engage in sexual relations. By the 1940s and 1950s, experts claimed that mutual sexual satisfaction was essential to a healthy marriage. The sexualization of marriage placed greater emphasis on the marital relationship and the intimacy needs of adults. Although Rousseau's portrayal of the sentimental family had included sexual pleasure and marital companionship, this new discourse on sexuality suggested that sexual union now provided the dominant paradigm for marital intimacy. Sexual as well as emotional intimacy became one of the major purposes of marriage and family.[66]

Today's families are multipurpose associations. They perform a variety of functions such as meeting the daily material needs of their members, caring for and raising children, caring for dependent and independent adults, and meeting the intimacy needs of adults. There is, without question, a potential for conflict between adults' need for intimacy and children's need for stability. Contemporary families are unstable in part because today's adults want their marital relationship to be emotionally and sexually satisfying. This expectation has introduced a high degree of fragility into the marital relationship. Adults who are disappointed in their marriages often seek to dissolve them in order to find relationships that are meaningful and rewarding. However, the tension between the familial purposes of rearing children and providing adults with emotional and sexual intimacy cannot be resolved by ignoring the latter, as Galston and other family communitarians do. The belief that marriage is based on love and sexual attraction is too strong.

Prior to the eighteenth century, romantic love was not considered a part of marriage, but was instead associated with extramarital relationships. While the idea of romantic love was celebrated in song and poetry, actual practice favored arranged marriages aimed at producing advantageous family alliances, providing a legitimate heir, or establishing an economic partnership between husband and wife. As Stone explains:

> [In] the sixteenth and early seventeenth centuries, there had been two parallel archetypes of sexual conduct in existence: one being conjugal, primarily for the procreation of a male heir; and the other being extra-marital, exclusively for love, companionship, and sexual pleasure. What happened in the eighteenth century was that the two archetypes became increasingly fused into one.[67]

The result of this fusion is that women and men now associate not just procreation and the rearing of children, but love, companionship, and pleasure with marriage. While these associations may make marriage less stable, they also make it infinitely more valuable to its participants.

It is unclear what the family communitarians hope to achieve by denying that adults have legitimate needs for emotional and sexual intimacy. While it is difficult to believe that family communitarians want to take the romance out of marriage, this is the logical outcome of their one-purpose definition of marriage and family and their refusal to admit that lack of love is a legitimate reason for ending a marriage. The one-purpose definition of marriage and family places no value on the emotional and sexual connection between husband and wife. Indeed, the one-purpose definition of family views marriage as exclusively a state-sanctioned social arrangement for having and rearing children.

Family communitarians describe men and women who choose to dissolve their marriages as individualists who fail to understand the true value of commitment to others, and who selfishly place their own desires for self-fulfillment over their obligations to their spouses and children. While this may be an accurate description of some divorcing individuals, it is equally the case that men and women seeking divorce place a high value on fulfilling emotional bonds with others. Disappointed in their marriage, they seek to dissolve it so that they can form a richer relationship with someone else. High rates of remarriage contradict the claim that men and women who divorce are fleeing entangling commitments. It is not commitment that they fear, but squandering their one life on a marriage that does not offer them a deep and lasting companionship.

Marriage and family are more than state-sanctioned social arrangements for having and rearing children. Love and sexual desire are most often the feelings that draw two people together and motivate them to have children. Marriage and family should be viewed, then, as multipurpose associations that aim at meeting the daily needs of their members, raising young children, and meeting the intimacy needs of adults. Viewing adults' intimacy needs as legitimate does not mean that they always take precedence over creating a stable home for children or that unhappy couples should in all cases dissolve their marriage. It is, instead, to recognize and honor the value of emotional and sexual intimacy between adults.

Affirming Family Diversity

I have argued that the state should not promote family uniformity. What, then, should be the goal of family policy? To answer this question, we must first consider another: Why are families valuable to the larger society and why should the state take an interest in preserving them? Families are valuable to the larger society because as Aristotle claims, individuals, both adults and children, lack self-sufficiency. Families and intimate partnerships and associations that are not currently recognized as families provide their members with physical, material, and emotional care. A well-functioning society must provide for its needy and dependent members. Historically, the family has been the chief provider of care.

A rich and growing body of feminist thought analyzes the centrality of care to a well-functioning society.[68] Feminist thinkers define care as a social practice that is essential to the maintenance and reproduction of society. Eva Feder Kittay explains that "given the immutable facts of human development, disease, and decline, no culture that endures beyond one generation can secure itself against the claims of human dependence."[69] Concerned to correct the emphasis they claim Western political theory has placed on independence and self-sufficiency, feminists point to the prevalence of relationships of dependence between care-receivers and caregivers. The very young, the very old, and the sick and disabled, live in varying states of dependency and require the daily care of others. However, even adult human beings capable of meeting their own physical and material needs depend on others for companionship as well as emotional and sexual intimacy. Moreover, adults move quickly from states of relative self-sufficiency to dependency. The loss of a job or housing, illness, accident, or the birth of a child can make an adult dependent on others.

Caring work is for the most part ignored or taken for granted because it is often performed by women, it is often unpaid, and it takes place in the private sphere of the family. The value of caring work to the larger society is often obscured because it is enmeshed in intimate relationships between friends, long-term partners, mothers and children, adult children and aging parents, or siblings. By theorizing care as socially necessary labor and drawing it out of the domain of the purely personal, feminists have heightened our understanding of the importance of caring work.

Families are valuable to the larger society because when they are functioning well they consist in relationships of care between adults and children and between adults and adults. Given the ubiquity of human need and dependence, and the centrality of care to human survival and well-being, the state has a strong interest in encouraging and preserving relationships of care. However, it is not only families in the traditional sense that care for dependents and function as small mutual aid societies. All individuals who form long-term commitments and agree to care for and support each other through times of need contribute to the well-being of the greater society. Raising children is an especially demanding and rewarding form of caretaking. It is a unique responsibility, like no other, because it involves caring for someone when they are most dependent and because it involves the shaping of the child's character and values. But even though rearing children is of inestimable value to our society, it is not the only reason that individuals form and live in families. Families are formed when people come together to care for one another. I propose that all partnerships or associations that involve economic cooperation and a strong and long-term commitment to care should be recognized by the state as families.

In stating that the commitment to care should be central to how we define families, I am not replacing the one-purpose definition of family advocated by the family communitarians with my own. Families perform functions other than caretaking. They also pool resources and provide sexual pleasure, emotional support, intimacy, companionship, and moral education. My point is that it is the commitment to care (as opposed to family structure and composition) that should be the basis for how we decide what counts as family. Since the end of the eighteenth century, the family has been pictured as a man and a woman, joined in marriage, and their biological offspring. Up until very recently, the family was organized according to a gender-based division of labor and authority. The definition of family that I am proposing focuses more on what families do and the quality of relationships between family members, and less on structure, gender, sexual preference, and biological ties. My definition would recognize couples, gay or straight, with or without children, as families. It would allow friends who have a long-term commitment to care and who share economic resources to count as families. It also would include single parents and their children, extended families, blended families, families formed through adoption, single parents living with both their children and their mothers or parents, and adult children living with their parents.

Many of these family forms are already considered families by the state. However, family communitarians advocate laws and policies that would confer specific benefits and privileges onto the married two-parent family, and penalize or stigmatize other forms of family. Their goal is to create a two-tiered definition of families. Intact, married, two-parent families will occupy the first tier, while stepfamilies and single-parent families would make up the second tier. Lesbian and gay couples and their children would not be recognized as families, and neither would cohabiting couples or cohabiting friends. My intention is to challenge this exclusive and two-tiered definition of family by offering one that de-emphasizes structure and composition, and that defines families by the commitment to care. I advocate the legalization of same-sex marriage, and full parenting rights, including adoption and foster care rights, for lesbians and gay men, unmarried heterosexual couples, and nonromantic couples who wish to coparent.

The exclusive and two-tiered definition of family supported by the family communitarians would discourage the formation of, and fail to support the preservation of, some caring relationships. Definitions of family that exclude lesbians and gay men place obstacles in the way of individuals who are committed to relationships of mutual caring and want to raise children together. Restricting marriage and adoption to heterosexual couples is detrimental to the interests of the state because it actively discourages the formation of small mutual aid societies. In short, when law and policy prevent same-sex marriage and adoption by lesbian and gay couples, adults are discouraged from taking care of each other and from taking care of children. Allowing same-sex couples to legally marry and receive the same rights and benefits enjoyed by married heterosexual couples would help to preserve lesbian and gay relationships.[70] Securing the right of lesbian and gay couples to adopt children would increase the number of children brought up in families.

The rights of lesbian and gay parents, including custody, visitation, and adoption rights, have improved in recent years, but remain highly insecure. Laws and precedents regarding the rights of lesbian and gay parents differ from state to state. In many states, family law allows individual judges the discretion to determine who is a fit parent. Sexual preference is still used as a reason to deny custody, visitation, or adoption rights to lesbians and gay men. Currently, twenty-two states have allowed lesbians and gay men to adopt children from state or private agencies.[71] Writing for the majority in a New York state courts decision, Judge Judith K. Kaye explained that expanding "the universe of who can legally be recognized as a parent could ensure that more children secure 'the best possible home.'"[72] As the result of a 1997 agreement worked out by the New Jersey Court, state welfare officials, and the Lesbian and Gay Rights project of the American Civil Liberties Union (ACLU), New Jersey became the first state to establish a policy that explicitly agrees to treat gay and unmarried heterosexual couples seeking to adopt the same as married couples.[73] However, while there have been victories for lesbian and gay parents in some states, others (e.g., Florida, Utah, and Mississippi) expressly forbid adoption by lesbian and gay couples or unmarried couples. Many other states are likely to view same-sex sexual preference as sufficient reason to declare an individual unfit to adopt a child. Lesbian and gay parents also face difficulties securing second-parent adoptions. The term second-parent adoption refers to the action by a lesbian or a gay man to legally adopt the children (either biological or adoptive) of her or his partner, as might a stepmother or stepfather in a heterosexual family. Second-parent adoption entitles the nonbiological parent to the right to make decisions about a child's health, education, and well-being, and obligates the nonbiological parent to support the child. If a nonbiological parent is not allowed to adopt his or her partner's child, the child can be taken away from the nonbiological parent in cases when the biological parent dies or separates from the nonbiological parent.[74] Twenty-one states have allowed second-parent adoption and a few states have begun to award visitation rights to nonbiological parents in the case of separation. In a recent case, the New Jersey Supreme Court awarded visitation rights to a non-biological parent who had helped to raise five-year-old twins since their birth. The Court's decision declared that the nonbiological parent should be considered a "psychological parent."[75] Decisions such as these expand the definition of what counts as family by refusing to privilege biology when determining who can legally be considered a parent. Providing better protection for lesbian and gay parenting rights will preserve the caring relationships between nonbiological parents and children and expand the number of children who have secure, loving homes.

I have argued so far that the goal of family policy should be to encourage and support diverse forms of family. What can the state do to preserve all intimate relationships based on the commitment to care? First, state policy must refrain from privileging some forms of family over others. This would mean *not* using tax, housing, or welfare policies to privilege married couples over single-parent families or cohabiting couples. Second, it would mean state recognition of lesbian and gay marriage, equal rights for lesbian and gay parents, and greater protection for nonbiological parents. Official recognition of intimate relationships contributes to their formation and preservation. When individuals are legally recognized as family members they are able to present themselves as an economic and emotional unit to a wide variety of third parties such as school teachers, state agencies, landlords, banks, physicians, and employers. They are able to qualify for workplace leave to care for sick and dependent family members and to receive bereavement leave.[76] And they can act as intermediaries between dependent family members and medical and educational professionals. Recognition as a family makes it easier for couples to jointly manage their finances and to inherit property. However, while many rights, benefits, and responsibilities should be attached to family membership in order to preserve and strengthen families, health insurance should not be. All of the citizens and residents of the United States are entitled to adequate health care. Our current system, which allows only the spouses and dependents of employees to receive employment-related health care, makes an important universal right contingent upon marital status (and employment). A universal system of health care would detach this essential right from employment, marital status, or family membership.

Supporting diverse forms of family will require the state to go beyond a policy of equal recognition and equal rights for all family forms. As we have seen, single-mother families are in dire need of greater public support. They are not alone. As I explore at greater length in chapters 5 and 6, the idea that families are self-sufficient entities capable of caring for their members on their own is a dangerous myth. Many low-income families, particularly single-mother families, need help if they are to meet the needs of their families for housing, food, and health care. In addition, as feminist theorists of care have argued, a variety of social, economic, and demographic changes have made it impossible for caring relationships to remain purely private. Women's entrance into the workforce in large numbers means that children, the elderly, the disabled, and the sick cannot be cared for exclusively in the private home. Consequently, the state must take a greater role in supplementing the caring work that families, particularly women, have performed in the past. I discuss policies that would benefit all families, but especially single-parent families, in chapter 6.

CONCLUSION

Advocates of family uniformity argue that the family has one key purpose—having and raising children—and that the intact, married, heterosexual two-parent family should be promoted by the state because it is best able to fulfill this key purpose. I have argued, in response, that families are multipurpose associations and that a variety of unconventional family forms, including single-parent and lesbian and gay families are capable of raising healthy children. Using law and policy to foster one form of family unjustly penalizes individuals engaged in unconventional family forms, and discourages individuals from forming small mutual aid societies. Moreover, in the last section, I suggested that we rethink what it is about families that we really value. I've argued that the state has an interest in promoting all relationships that involve economic cooperation, support, and care. Expanding the definition of family would encourage and protect these kinds of relationships.

In this chapter, my primary focus has been on defending the new family values of diversity and personal liberty. In chapter 4, I examine the topic of gender equality. Two family communitarians, Popenoe and Blankenhorn, have recently written books on father absence. The reinstitutionalization of the gender-structured family is central to each author's prescription for how father absence can be decreased. I argue that Popenoe and Blankenhorn's plan is fundamentally unfair to women. Rigid gender roles in the family undermine women's ability to participate equally in the economy, civil society, and politics. In addition, I also argue that the reassertion of gender-based parenting will not realize Popenoe and Blankenhorn's goal of strengthening ties between fathers and their children.

NOTES

This chapter is based on an expanded version of an article by the author entitled "Familial Purposes: An Argument against the Promotion of Family Uniformity" that originally appeared in *Policy Studies Journal* 27, no. 3 (1999): 477–93

1. William A. Galston, *Liberal Purposes: Goods, Virtues and Diversity in the Liberal State* (Cambridge, England: Cambridge University Press, 1991), 285.

2. Christine Winquist Nord and Nicholas Zill, *Non-Custodial Parents' Participation in Their Children's Lives: Evidence from the Survey of Income and Program Participation, Volume II,* Washington, D.C.: U.S. Department of Health and Human Services, 2000, http://fatherhood.hhs.gov/sipp/pt2.htm (accessed 28 June 2000).

3. Bureau of the Census, *Fertility of American Women, June 1998, P20-526,* U.S. Department of Commerce, Economics and Statistics Administration (Washington, D.C., 1998).

4. Nord and Zill, *Non-Custodial Parents' Participation in Their Children's Lives.*

5. Sharon Vandivere, Kristin Anderson Moore, and Martha Zaslow, "Children's Family Environment: Findings from the National Survey of America's Families," *Snapshots of America's Families II: 1999* (Washington, D.C.: Urban Institute, 2000). http://newfederalism.urban.org/nsaf/family-environ.html (accessed 28 January 2002).

6. Galston, *Liberal Purposes*, 286.

7. Galston, *Liberal Purposes*, 286.

8. Galston, *Liberal Purposes*, 286.

9. Legislation repealing no-fault divorce has been introduced in Georgia, Idaho, Illinois, Iowa, Michigan, Minnesota, Pennsylvania, Virginia, and Washington. To date, no-fault divorce remains on the books in all fifty states. The Louisiana legisla-

ture passed legislation in 1997 approving a new and more binding form of marriage called covenant marriage, but left couples the option of opting for a regular marriage. Covenant marriage allows for divorce only after the couple has separated for at least two years, or with proof that one spouse has committed adultery, been sentenced to prison for a felony, abandoned the matrimonial home for at least one year, or physically or sexually abused the other spouse or child. Arizona is the only other state to have passed a covenant marriage law. See Kevin Sack, "Louisiana Approves Measure to Tighten Marriage Bonds," *New York Times*, 24 June 1997; Dana Milbank, "Blame Game: No-Fault Divorce Law is Assailed in Michigan and Debate Heats Up," *Wall Street Journal*, 5 January 1996, A1; Charles S. Clark, "Marriage and Divorce," *CQ Researcher* 6, no. 18 (May 1996): 409–32; Associated Press, "Laws Discouraging Divorce Spreading Slowly if at All," *Los Angeles Times*, 11 February 2001, A41.

10. William A. Galston, "Needed: A Not-So-Fast Divorce Law," *New York Times*, 27 December 1995, Op-Ed.

11. William A. Galston, "Divorce American Style," *The Public Interest* 124 (Summer 1996): 12–26.

12. Galston, "Divorce American Style," 18.

13. Barbara Dafoe Whitehead, "The Divorce Trap," *New York Times*, 13 January 1997, Op-Ed.

14. Frank F. Furstenberg Jr. and Andrew J. Cherlin, *Divided Families: What Happens to Children When Parents Part* (Cambridge, MA: Harvard University Press, 1991), 22.

15. Galston, "Divorce American Style," 17.

16. Galston, "Divorce American Style," 22.

17. Frank F. Furstenberg Jr., "Is the Modern Family a Threat to Children's Health?" *Social Science and Modern Society* 36, no. 5 (July/August 1999): 31–37.

18. Paul R. Amato and Bruce Keith, "Parental Divorce and the Well-Being of Children: A Meta-Analysis," *Psychological Bulletin* 110, no. 1 (1991): 26–46.

19. Amato and Keith, "Parental Divorce and the Well-Being of Children," 30.

20. Amato and Keith, "Parental Divorce and the Well-Being of Children," 30.

21. Amato and Keith, "Parental Divorce and the Well-Being of Children," 40.

22. Andrew J. Cherlin, P. Lindsay Chase-Lansdale and Christine MacRae, "Effects of Parental Divorce on Mental Health Throughout the Life Course," *American Sociological Review* 63, no. 2 (April 1998): 239–49.

23. Cherlin, Chase-Lansdale, and MacRae, "Effects of Parental Divorce," 425.

24. Cherlin, Chase-Lansdale, and MacRae, "Effects of Parental Divorce," 425.

25. Sara McLanahan and Gary Sandefur, *Growing Up with a Single Parent: What Helps, What Hurts* (Cambridge, Mass.: Harvard University Press, 1994).

26. McLanahan and Sandefur, *Growing Up with a Single Parent*, 2.

27. Bureau of the Census, *Marital Status and Living Arrangements: March 1996, P20-496*, U.S. Department of Commerce, Economics, and Statistics Administration (Washington, D.C., 1998).

28. Stephen D. Sugarman, "Single-Parent Families," in *All Our Families*, ed. Mary Ann Mason, Arlene Skolnick, and Stephen D. Sugarman (Oxford: Oxford University Press, 1998), 20.

29. McLanahan and Sandefur, *Growing Up with a Single Parent*, 40–43.

30. McLanahan and Sandefur, *Growing Up with a Single Parent*, 88–94.

31. McLanahan and Sandefur, *Growing Up with a Single Parent*, 91.

32. McLanahan and Sandefur, *Growing Up with a Single Parent*, 43.

33. Child Trends, "Poverty, Welfare and Children." *Research Brief*, Washington, D.C.: Child Trends, 1999. http://www.childtrends.org (accessed 3 December 2000).

34. Sara McLanahan, "The Consequences of Single Motherhood," in *Sex, Preference, and Family: Essays on Law and Nature*, ed. David M. Estlund and Martha C. Nussbaum (New York: Oxford University Press, 1997), 306–18.

35. Frank F. Furstenberg Jr., and Andrew J. Cherlin, *Divided Families: What Happens to Children When Parents Part* (Cambridge, Mass.: Harvard University Press, 1991), 45–61.

36. Frank F. Furstenberg Jr., "Divorce and the American Family," *Annual Review of Sociology* 16, 1990: 379–403.

37. Galston, *Liberal Purposes*, 284.

38. Roberta M. Spalter-Roth, Heidi I. Hartmann, and Linda M. Andrews, "Mothers, Children, and Low-Wage Work: The Ability to Earn a Family Wage," in *Sociology and the Public Agenda*, ed. William Julius Wilson (London: Sage, 1993).

39. Iris Marion Young identifies a contradiction in Galston's position on marriage in "Mothers, Citizenship, and Independence: A Critique of Pure Family Values," *Ethics* 105 (April 1995), 535–56. Galston calls for the promotion of the two-parent family because he believes it is best able to produce independent citizens. Young points out that the two-parent family is built on a division of labor that makes women dependent on men. She concludes that if we follow Galston, women must be dependent so that citizens can be independent. This, of course, limits citizenship to men.

40. McLanahan, "The Consequences of Single Motherhood," 317.

41. Furstenberg and Cherlin, *Divided Families*, 66.

42. Furstenberg and Cherlin, *Divided Families*, 68.

43. McLanahan and Sandefur, *Growing Up with a Single Parent*, 2.

44. McLanahan and Sandefur, *Growing Up with a Single Parent*, 19–38.

45. Andrew J. Cherlin, "Going to Extremes: Family Structure, Children's Well-Being, and Social Science," *Demography* 36, no. 4 (November 1999): 421–28.

46. Furstenberg, "Is the Modern Family," 36.

47. Frank F. Furstenberg Jr., and Gretchen A. Condran, "Family Change and Adolescent Well-Being: A Re-examination of U.S. Trends," in *The Changing American Family and Public Policy*, ed. Andrew J. Cherlin (Washington, D.C.: The Urban Institute Press, 1988), 125.

48. McLanahan, "The Consequences of Single Motherhood," 308.

49. Greg J. Duncan and Jeanne Brooks-Gunn, "Income Effects Across the Life Span: Integration and Interpretation," in *Consequences of Growing Up Poor*, ed. Jeanne Brooks-Gunn and Greg J. Duncan (New York: Russell Sage Foundation, 1997), 597.

50. For critics of divorce reform see Stephanie Coontz, *The Way We Are Now* (New York: Basic Books, 1997), 97–108; Stephen D. Sugarman, "Single-Parent Families,"

in *All Our Families*, ed. Mary Ann Mason, Arlene Skolnick, and Stephen D. Sugarman (Oxford: Oxford University Press, 1998), 28–30; Judith Stacey, *In the Name of the Family* (Boston: Beacon Press, 1996), 67–68; and Furstenberg and Cherlin, *Divided Families*, 97–105.

51. Jean Bethke Elshtain, "Accepting Limits," *Commonweal* 18 (November 22 1991): 685–86.

52. Elshtain, "Accepting Limits," 686.

53. Elshtain, "Accepting Limits," 686.

54. J. Laird, "Lesbian and Gay Families," in *Normal Family Processes*, ed. Froma Walsh (New York: The Guilford Press, 1993), 282–328.

55. Elshtain, "Accepting Limits," 686.

56. Stacey, *In the Name of the Family*, 128.

57. Laird, "Lesbian and Gay Families"; M. Allen and N. Burrell, "Comparing the Impact of Homosexual and Heterosexual Parents on Children: Meta-Analysis of Existing Research," *Journal of Homosexuality* 32, (1996): 19–35.

58. American Psychological Association, *Lesbian and Gay Parenting: A Resource for Psychologists* (Washington, D.C.: American Psychological Association, 1995). http://apa.org/pi/parent.html (accessed 1 December 2000).

59. Jean-Louis Flandrin, *Families in Former Times: Kinship, Household, and Sexuality* (Cambridge: Cambridge University Press, 1979), 9.

60. Flandrin explains that as late as the mid-eighteenth century in both England and France, family was understood to mean "those who live in the same household" or "all those who live in the same house, under the same head." He states that "the father-mother-children triad acquired an ever-increasing independence with respect to the *lignage* and to the servants, until in the nineteenth century it became the fundamental nucleus of our society." See Flandrin, *Families in Former Times*, 5 and 9.

61. Aristotle, *The Politics*, ed. Stephen Everson and trans. Jonathan Barnes (Cambridge, England: Cambridge University Press, 1988), 2.

62. Aristotle, *The Politics*, 18.

63. Lawrence Stone, *The Family, Sex, and Marriage in England, 1500–1800* (New York: Harper and Row, 1979), 22.

64. Edward Shorter, *The Making of the Modern Family* (New York: Basic Books, 1977), 5.

65. Jean-Jacques Rousseau, *Emile or On Education,* intro. and trans. Allan Bloom (New York: Basic Books, 1979), 44–51.

66. Steven Seidman. *Romantic Longings: Love in America, 1830–1980* (New York: Routledge, 1991), 81–91.

67. Stone, *The Family, Sex, and Marriage*, 327.

68. See Carol Gilligan, *In a Different Voice: Psychological Theory and Women's Development* (Cambridge, Mass.: Harvard University Press, 1982); Joan C. Tronto, *Moral Boundaries: A Political Argument for an Ethics of Care* (New York: Routledge, 1993); and Eva Feder Kittay, "Taking Dependency Seriously: The Family and Medical Leave Act," *Hypatia: A Journal of Feminist Philosophy* 10, no. 1 (1995): 8–30.

69. Kittay, "Taking Dependency Seriously," 9.

70. In April of 2000, Vermont became the first state to adopt civil union legislation. The Vermont law provides same-sex couples with more than 300 legal rights previously guaranteed only to heterosexual married couples. See Carey Goldberg, "Vermont Gives Final Approval to Same-Sex Unions," *New York Times*, 26 April 2000, A14.

71. American Civil Liberties Union, *ACLU Fact Sheet: Overview of Lesbian and Gay Parenting, Adoption and Foster Care*, 6 April 1999. http://www.aclu.org/issues/gay/parent.html (accessed 1 December 2000).

72. James Dao, "Ruling Lets Unwed Couples Adopt," *New York Times*, 3 November 1995, B16.

73. Ronald Smothers, "Accord Lets Gay Couples Adopt Jointly," *New York Times*, 18 December 1997, B4.

74. Lambda Legal Defense and Education Fund, *Adoption by Lesbians and Gay Men: An Overview of the Law in the 50 States*, 1997. http://www.lambdalegal.org/sextions/library/adoption.pdf (accessed 28 January 2002).

75. American Civil Liberties Union, *New Jersey Supreme Court Grants Visitation Rights to Former Partner of Lesbian Mom, Establishes "Psychological Parenthood,"* 6 April 2000 http://www.aclu.org/news/2000/n040600a.html (accessed 1 December 2000). Mary Lyndon Shanley analyzes a case in which a New York court denied standing to a lesbian comother who was seeking visitation rights with a child after she and the child's biological mother separated. The court argued that the plaintiff, who had planned the pregnancy with her partner and acted as a parent to the child for five years, could not be considered a parent under state law. See Mary Lyndon Shanley, "Lesbian Families: Dilemmas in Grounding Legal Recognition of Parenthood," in *Mother Troubles: Rethinking Contemporary Maternal Dilemmas*, ed. Julie E. Hanigsberg and Sara Ruddick (Boston: Beacon Press, 1999). This case is also discussed by Nancy Polikoff in "This Child Does Have Two Mothers: Redefining Parenthood to Meet the Needs of Children in Lesbian-Mother and Other Nontraditional Families," *Georgetown Law Review* 78, no. 3 (1990): 459–575. Both articles make suggestions for how the rights of nonbiological lesbian mothers can be strengthened.

76. The Family and Medical Leave Act, an important first step toward recognizing caretaking as a public responsibility, is based on an overly narrow definition of family. See Kittay, "Taking Dependency Seriously."

Chapter Four

Fatherless Families and the Reassertion of the Gender-Structured Family

Over the last decade increased attention has been paid to the growing number of children who will spend some or all of their childhood without a father present. Researchers have estimated that approximately half of all children will live in a single-parent home for at least some time before they turn eighteen. Following divorce or separation, many noncustodial parents do not maintain regular contact with their children. According to the National Survey of Families and Households, nearly a third of children had seen their nonresidential parent only once in the past year or not at all. However, 25 percent averaged once a week or better.[1] According to one study, fathers who have never been married to the mothers of their children typically visit frequently or live with their children when they are very young. However, by the time their children are adolescents, over half of fathers have little or no contact with their children.[2] Many divorced, separated, or nevermarried nonresidential fathers do not provide financially for their children. In 1997, 42 percent of previously married women and 18 percent of nevermarried women received child support.[3]

Increased concern over fatherless families has led researchers to turn their attention to the role that fathers perform in the family and to the consequences of father absence on children. Under the Clinton administration, several federal agencies launched the *Fatherhood Initiative* in order to collect data and promote research on father absence.[4] Part of the impetus behind this new research was to find ways to strengthen the relationship between nonresidential fathers and their children. Studies show that men who see their children on a regular basis are more likely to pay child support than those who do not, and policymakers are eager to increase the amount of child support that nonresidential fathers pay.[5]

In the majority of cases, strengthening ties between children and their non-residential fathers is an important goal. However, there are some situations in which efforts should *not* be made to unite fathers and children. For example, it is often not advisable in cases in which the father has a history of violence toward his partner and children and has not sought treatment for his behavior. It is also possible that when serious conflict exists between parents, uniting nonresidential fathers and children may be detrimental to the well-being of children.[6] In addition, men who agreed to relinquish their paternity rights as part of sperm donation agreements with lesbian couples or single mothers should not be accorded paternity rights or responsibilities. While some studies do not show a strong positive relationship between child development and the amount of contact between nonresidential parents and their children, it nonetheless stands to reason that children benefit from having supportive adults in their lives.[7] Moreover, most children express a desire to continue their relationship with the nonresidential parent.[8] Research also shows that men benefit from a continued relationship with their children.[9] Finally, in those cases in which men can afford to pay child support, it is important that they do, and that the state strongly enforces child support orders. As we have seen throughout this book, single-parent families are highly likely to experience poverty. And even though child support payments will not eliminate child poverty, they can make a significant contribution to the income of single-parent households.[10]

While policy efforts to strengthen ties between children and nonresidential fathers should be applauded, two recent responses to father absence—Blankenhorn's *Fatherless America* and Popenoe's *Life Without Father*—call for policies that would undermine gender equality.[11] Both authors argue that policymakers and the public have failed to recognize the devastating social consequences of fatherless families. Popenoe warns that the "massive erosion of fatherhood contributes mightily to many of the major social problems of our time."[12] Blankenhorn takes a similar position: "Fatherlessness is the most harmful demographic trend of this generation. It is the leading cause of declining child well-being in our society."[13] Like other family communitarians, Popenoe and Blankenhorn argue that the best response to fatherless families is a renewed commitment to the institution of marriage. However, Popenoe and Blankenhorn place greater emphasis on reasserting gender roles and the gender-based division of labor in the home than other family communitarians do.

Popenoe and Blankenhorn's central aim is to reorient cultural norms and values. They claim that reducing father absence and providing the best parenting arrangement for children requires the reinstitutionalization of the gender-structured family and the rejection of the feminist vision of egalitarian shared parenting. While Popenoe and Blankenhorn are not in complete agreement regarding why gender-based differences in parenting are necessary, each author supports a somewhat modified version of the traditional gender-based division of labor. Although they recognize that in the vast majority of two-parent families, both mother and father will contribute to the household income through paid work, Popenoe and Blankenhorn insist that men should specialize in breadwinning and women should specialize in caretaking. Moreover, they subscribe to the idea that men and women have fundamentally different natures, and that women are best suited for caring for infants and children.

Why do Popenoe and Blankenhorn argue so strongly for the traditional gender-based division of labor at a time when 75 percent of mothers are in the paid workforce? Popenoe and Blankenhorn's commitment to gender roles and gender-based parenting is based on their belief that families without fathers are inherently deficient. Proving that fathers, *as men*, are necessary to families requires them to show that men and women make gender-specific contributions to child development. Popenoe and Blankenhorn argue that a child needs a mother and a father because each sex has parenting skills and capacities that the other does not. Popenoe explains that we must disavow the notions that "mommies can make good daddies," and that "daddies can make good mommies."[14] Since they base their argument for the necessity of fathers on the distinctly masculine contribution to childhood development, it is necessary for them to insist that men and women are very different and that they perform different roles in the family. Egalitarian shared parenting, in which the tasks of caretaker and breadwinner are not divided along gender lines, opens up the possibility that single women (or single men or a lesbian or gay couple) can fulfill both stereotypically male and female parenting roles. If this is the case, families without fathers cannot be viewed as inherently deficient.

Additionally, both authors suggest that men have become alienated from the family because of the new expectations placed on them by feminists and family experts. Stripped of the power they once wielded in the family when they were the sole breadwinners, men feel further diminished by being asked to perform tasks that have been historically assigned to women, such as the care of children. Blankenhorn warns that men will not return to the family if their former status as head of the household is not restored. He argues that men should not be expected to share caretaking and domestic work equally with women and that, despite women's involvement in paid work, men should be recognized as the primary breadwinners in the family. While men may at times "help out" in the traditionally female sphere, women should retain their traditional responsibility for child rearing and housework.

The model of family that Popenoe and Blankenhorn advocate is fundamentally unfair to women. Gender-based parenting arrangements, and the ideas about gender differences on which they are based, have a direct effect on women's ability to succeed in the paid labor market. While women's participation in the workforce has increased greatly over the last thirty years, for the most part women earn substantially less than men and do not occupy positions of leadership and power in the private or public sectors. In 1992, women engaged in year-round, full-time work earned 71 percent of what men earned.[15] These inequities are due in part because the revolution in women's labor force participation has not been accompanied by a revolution in parenting arrangements.[16] Since the 1970s, the gender-based organization of social life has changed enough to allow women to participate more actively in the labor market, but the gender-based structure of the household changed only slightly. As a result, while evidence of women's increased education and workplace participation indicates progress for women, this progress is not as solid as it first appears. Neither our institutions (schools, work, childcare) nor the division of labor in the family currently provides women with the support they need to succeed in the workplace. Popenoe and Blankenhorn's strategy of reducing father absence by reinstitutionalizing the traditional division of labor clearly comes at the expense of women.

Shared parenting is not the optimal parenting arrangement for all families. Many women want to be full-time caretakers and find staying at home with their children much more rewarding than earning money. While relatively few families can afford to have women leave the labor force for an extended period of time, for those that can, gender-based parenting may be desirable. In other families, dividing the responsibilities of breadwinning and caretaking may be the most financially rational choice because the husband makes more money than the wife does. In still other cases, women choose to be full-time caretakers because accessible, affordable, and high-quality childcare is hard to come by. When parents make choices about how to care for their children they face a variety of constraints. While it should be recognized that the traditional model has costs for women as a group, the aim of public policy should not be to impose one model of parenting on all families. Instead, it should be to give families real choices about how they arrange parenting by guaranteeing women equal pay and equality of opportunity in the workforce, and making accessible, affordable, and high-quality childcare available to all families.

In addition to perpetuating gender inequality, Popenoe and Blankenhorn's support for gender-based parenting is bound to undermine their stated goal of strengthening ties between fathers and children. Research suggests that the best way to foster strong ties between fathers and children is to encourage the father's involvement in infant and child care.[17] Men who are involved in the daily physical care of their children, and who develop close, nurturing ties to them, are less likely to become absent fathers even if their marital or sexual alliance with the mother of their children dissolves. The notion, advocated by Popenoe and Blankenhorn, that mothers and fathers should perform distinct functions in their children's lives and that infant care is a gender-specific responsibility may be the surest way to sabotage strong ties between fathers and children. Strengthening the gender-based division of labor in the home will foreclose opportunities for men to develop ties to their children through providing them with daily and routine care.

Finally, it is also the case that Popenoe and Blankenhorn, like most family communitarians, ignore the number one obstacle to family formation and family stability. They do not discuss how unemployment and poverty can undermine relationships between fathers and children. Research shows that the shame and low self-esteem that so often accompanies unemployment for men has a negative impact on father-child ties. Men who cannot provide for their families often feel like failures and this sense of failure drives them away from their children emotionally and physically. Because they lay most of the blame for father absence on the weakness of contemporary marriage and the feminist vision of shared parenting, Popenoe and Blankenhorn fail to recognize that there may be other sources of father absence. Consequently, they do not advocate economic policies that could reduce the multiple economic-derived stresses faced by low-income families.

The debate over father absence and how to strengthen ties between fathers and children has just begun. Basic research is still being done on how fathers influence child development, and policies designed to strengthen father-child ties are still being formulated. It is essential that the theoretical frameworks that inform public policy not be based on traditional gender roles. Building strong ties between fathers and children is a worthy goal, but it need not be pursued at the expense of women. The aim of this chapter is to show that gender-based parenting will undermine gender equality without improving father-child relationships. It is divided into two main sections: The first, "The Case for Gender-Based Specialization Parenting," provides a critical examination of Popenoe and Blankenhorn's response to father absence. The second, "Gender Norms as Obstacles to Father Involvement," shows how traditional conceptions of fatherhood and masculinity fail to promote strong relationships between fathers and children.

I. THE CASE FOR GENDER-BASED
SPECIALIZATION IN PARENTING

According to Popenoe and Blankenhorn, we know fathers are necessary to families because we know that men and women are different. Each sex has something distinct to contribute to parenting, and so children who are denied access to either mother or father will suffer. However, while they both argue in favor of gender-based parenting, Popenoe and Blankenhorn do not defend this assertion in the same way. Popenoe, who I will examine first, bases his claims on the fields of evolutionary anthropology and evolutionary psychology. He believes that men and women have different heritable dispositions, and that women are best suited to child rearing and men are best suited to breadwinning. Blankenhorn's argument is quite different. He asserts that social androgyny (or shared parenting) severs fatherhood from masculinity. Deprived of an image of fatherhood that is distinctly masculine, men are not able to identify with paternal responsibilities. In effect, Blankenhorn asserts that the failure to keep the tasks of mothers and fathers separate drives men away from the family.

Popenoe On Gender-Based Parenting

Popenoe claims that men and women possess different "inborn predispositions," and that these differences show up in the ways that they parent.[18] Universal sex differences are based on how men and women adapted to environmental pressures in the course of evolution. The most crucial period in human evolution, Popenoe explains, took place thousands of years ago on the African savannah. This period is referred to as the environment of evolutionary adaptedness. During the early hunter-gatherer societies, a division of labor existed in which "males were protectors and females were nurturers, males were hunters and females were gatherers, and both focused on the feeding of juveniles." The development of a sexual division of labor during the environment of evolutionary adaptedness has "left its mark on the biological endowment of each sex."[19] For example, women are "biologically more attuned to infant care."[20] Men, in contrast, are biologically inclined to play the roles of "protector, provider, teacher, and authority figure."[21]

According to Popenoe, the differing reproductive strategies of men and women have had a strong influence on their sex-specific behavior patterns. Because the number of offspring that women can have is biologically limited, they are strongly motivated to ensure that the children they bear are able to survive and mature. They therefore seek reliable monogamous mates to help them raise their children. Men, in contrast, are torn between two competing drives. On the one hand, if they are guaranteed paternal certitude, they may form a temporary or permanent monogamous bond with the mother of their children and assist her in the raising of their children. In this case, the man is motivated to ensure that the children he knows belong to him reach maturity. On the other hand, men also have the option of impregnating as many women as possible in hopes that at least some of their children will reach maturity. In short, men benefit from a reproductive strategy based on promiscuity, but are capable of participating in monogamous relationships if they are guaranteed paternal certitude. Women, in contrast, clearly benefit from a reproductive strategy based on monogamy.

Sex-based differences in reproductive strategy explain why men must be encouraged or even coerced into forming monogamous unions with their mates and assisting in the raising of their children. As Popenoe claims, "It is because of the greater range and flexibility in the male than in the female reproductive strategy that the male strategy can be, and is, so heavily shaped by culture."[22] According to Popenoe, marriage and the regulation of female sexuality are two social mechanisms that have in the past successfully curbed male promiscuity and motivated male investment in children. The control of female sexuality is necessary for two reasons: (1) men will only marry if they are *unable* to obtain sexual relations with women outside of marriage, and (2) men will only invest in children they know to be their own offspring. Popenoe claims that a society that fails to enforce marriage or control female sexuality will find it difficult to get men to support their children.

Popenoe concludes that even in modern societies, "men and women are different to the core."[23] He holds that "they think differently and act differently" and that these differences have a strong influence on their different, but complementary, parenting styles. According to Popenoe, studies show that fathers encourage independence, competitiveness, and risk-taking in their children and are more successful than mothers in exacting obedience, particularly from boys. While fathers push their children to excel and achieve, mothers tend to provide comfort and reassurance. Popenoe explains that "[p]sychosocial maturity and competence among humans consists of the integration of two factors: communion, or the need to be included, connected and related; and agency, or the drive for independence, individuality, and self-fulfillment."[24] Popenoe suggests that mothers' distinctly feminine parenting style develops their children's capacity for communion, while fathers' distinctly masculine style develops their children's capacity for agency. While Popenoe admits "significant overlap can exist among males and females in the range of gender-differentiated traits they express," he concludes that "gender-differentiated parenting occurs naturally in most mother-father families."[25]

Popenoe's bioevolutionary theory boils down to the age-old claim that men and women are essentially and naturally different. No better response has been made to this assertion than that given by Mill over 100 years ago.[26] Mill argued in *On the Subjection of Women* that we will never know the extent of the so-called natural differences between men and women until we live in a society in which men and women are treated the same. There is no way to

know if evolutionary theory is accurate as long as men and women are assigned different positions in the social structure. Given that men and women
are currently penalized for straying from gender-specific behavior, it is fruitless to rely on observations of the men and women around us for evidence of
inherent or natural gender differences. We continue to live in a world in which
institutions, everyday practices, and norms encourage men and women to be-
have differently and to develop different capacities. While the penalties for
violating gender norms are not as harsh as they were in the past, men and
women who fail to obey them still face ostracism, stigma, and discrimination.
There is simply no way to prove whether stereotypically male or female patterns of behavior are a product of heritable adaptations or sustained social
pressure.[27]

There is also a great deal of scholarly research on child development that
conflicts with Popenoe's assertion that fathers have a distinctly masculine
style of parenting. Based on a review of the literature on paternal influences
on child development, Michael Lamb asserts that as far as influence on children is concerned, "very little about the gender of the parent seems to be distinctly important. The characteristics of the father as a parent rather than the
characteristics of the father as a man appear to influence child development."[28] An examination of paternal influence on achievement in sons found
that the best predictor of "competent and achievement orientated sons" is not
the father's masculine characteristics but the warmth and closeness of the
bond between father and child. This is also the case with psychosocial adjustment. According to Lamb, "Paternal warmth or closeness is advantageous, whereas paternal masculinity is irrelevant."[29] In contrast to Popenoe,
this research suggests that it is the father's ability to exhibit *stereotypically*
feminine qualities such as warmth and care that most benefit his sons.

Even if, for the sake of argument, we were to accept Popenoe's assertions
about evolved sex-based differences, we would still have to resolve the question of whether social policy should encourage these dispositions if they lead
to unjust social arrangements. What, we must ask, are the consequences for
social policy of the findings of evolutionary psychology? Simply because a
trait is heritable or natural does not make it more desirable in one sex than in
the other—or desirable at all. If evolved dispositions violate moral principles
of liberty and justice, should they be encouraged or subject to change? Requiring men and women to conform to stereotypical norms of masculinity and
femininity prevents either sex from developing a full range of human competencies and capacities. Indeed, it conflicts with Popenoe's own portrait of psychosocial maturity, which involves the integration of communion and agency.
Popenoe's portrait of gender-differentiated parenting shows us human beings
who are stunted in terms of their emotional range and competencies. He as-

sumes that a parent cannot both comfort a child when she or he needs it, and exhort them to try their hardest when they are pursuing a goal. A fully developed, emotionally mature human being of either sex should be able to do both effectively.

We live in a pluralistic society in which different social contexts and spheres of action require different skills and styles of communication. Expecting men to specialize in goal-driven, purposive action, and women to specialize in nurturing and cooperative action, disadvantages men in some social contexts and women in others. Ideally, human beings should develop a broad range of competencies and capacities, and they should be able to make judgments about the kinds of behavior and styles of communication that are appropriate in a particular social context. It is dangerous to bring up young women who don't know how to be assertive or to stand up for themselves when they are being harassed or exploited. While assertiveness and independence are valuable traits, it is desirable that boys and men be able to establish bonds with others based on empathy and care.

Even Popenoe makes some significant concessions to both current economic realities and the feminist vision of egalitarian shared parenting. He argues in favor of a middle ground between the reassertion of strict 1950s style gender roles and what he calls parental androgyny. Popenoe recognizes that it is time to redefine the role of father. He claims that although men are best suited to playing the roles to which they are evolutionarily adapted—protector, provider, teacher, and authority figure—modern societies need and require them to be directly involved in the care and nurturing of their children.[30] Moreover, he acknowledges that it is important for women to enter the labor force early and remain in it consistently.[31] He even suggests that it is desirable for men to take part in the care of their young children and urges them to assist their wives "in every way possible to the degree that time permits, in day-to-day child-care activities."[32] But on the fundamental point of whether men are capable of caring for their infants and young children, Popenoe refuses to budge. He claims, "In light of all that we now know about child development, women as a general rule should be the primary caretakers of infants during at least the first year to eighteen months of life."[33] Women, Popenoe explains, are evolutionarily adapted to be more sensitive to an infant's needs. Popenoe admits that men can be *taught* to respond to an infant's needs, but dismisses this possibility quickly because "with all the other unresolved problems in the world it is resolutely silly to think of embarking on a mass reeducation campaign just so that men can do halfheartedly what women can do better."[34]

Popenoe's argument is based on the highly questionable assumption that women "just know" how to care for children, while men require "a massive reeducation campaign." As I explain in more detail in section 2, most family experts believe that men are just as capable of caring for newborns, infants, and young children as women.[35] More importantly, Popenoe's position on fathers and infant care undercuts what he himself seeks to achieve: close bonds between fathers and their children. As Popenoe himself admits, men who spend time with their young children and who are involved in their direct care are much more likely to develop a warm and close bond with them. However, by insisting that women be the primary giver of infant care, he sets in motion a parenting arrangement that ensures that women will see themselves, and be seen by their children and the father of their children, as the person most responsible for and responsive to their children's everyday needs. Given that Popenoe's goal is to connect fathers to their children, it is hard to understand why he insists on relegating men to the position of "helpers" when it comes to early childcare. There appears to be significant tension between Popenoe's commitment to gender-based parenting, on the one hand, and his portrait of employed mothers and involved fathers on the other.

Blankenhorn on Gender-Based Parenting

While Popenoe devotes one chapter to defending the assertion that men and women are naturally different, Blankenhorn's entire book is a critique of what he calls androgynous parenting or social androgyny. Blankenhorn explains that his book is not just about father absence, but is instead about the loss of the idea of fatherhood.[36] By this he means that a feminized "new father"—a father that is nurturing and who takes equal responsibility for the daily physical care of his young children—is replacing a more traditional and distinctly masculine conception of fatherhood. Blankenhorn objects to the new father because the role he plays in the family is not clearly distinguished from the mother's role, and because this new paternal ideal threatens to detach fatherhood from masculinity.

Like Popenoe, Blankenhorn believes that men are prone to sexual promiscuity and are less reliable parents than women are. Consequently, social institutions and cultural norms must be designed to pressure men into investing in their children. He explains that "cultures must mobilize to devise and enforce the father role for men, coaxing and guiding them into fatherhood through a set of legal and extralegal pressures that require them to maintain a close alliance with their children's mother and to invest in their children."[37] Blankenhorn argues that convincing men to father requires the celebration of cultural ideals that make fatherhood intrinsic to masculinity.

Blankenhorn admits that the model of the new father is attractive in some respects. However, he insists that it will contribute to father absence. Without an ideal of fatherhood that is specifically masculine or that builds on and valorizes specifically male qualities, we cannot expect men to take up or stick with their familial duties. There is a direct link, according to Blankenhorn, between the creation of a cultural ideal that feminizes fathers by asking them to carry out traditionally female tasks and the rise of fatherless families. Blankenhorn believes that men are not willing to take responsibility for childcare and housework and that asking them to do so will create a serious disincentive to fatherhood.

Both Blankenhorn and Popenoe appear to fear that shared parenting will somehow diminish men. This can be seen in Popenoe's assertion that *respecting* the institution of fatherhood requires recognizing that "[f]athers are not merely would-be mothers."[38] Blankenhorn is even more explicit about the humiliation involved in what he calls the cultural annihilation of fatherhood. He compares the "imperative of role convergence" to "the sexual equivalent of what some political scientists term 'the end of history.'" This is an apt comparison, Blankenhorn explains, because the end of history signals the end of all struggle, and "the losing side not only loses but also seeks to emulate the winning side." In the case of androgynous parenting, "the losing side is aggression, instrumentalism, competition, toughness, and other historically masculine norms. The winning side is nurture, cooperation, empathy, and other historically feminine norms."[39] Blankenhorn seems to fear that if men change one too many diapers they will lose what it is that makes them men. Sharing the work of parenting with women will unman men and lower them to the level of women.

Blankenhorn's assertion that men require a cultural definition of fatherhood rooted in conceptions of masculinity has merit. The public meaning of fatherhood (like motherhood) has varied greatly over time and is currently in considerable flux.[40] However, masculinity, like fatherhood, is shaped by cultural norms and practices.[41] At present, the idea of what it means to be a man is highly contested. Considering the different ways that manhood is currently conceptualized and practiced, Blankenhorn's notion of masculinity seems overly narrow and rigid, reminiscent of the dyadic gender norms of the 1950s. While culturally dominant conceptions of gender continue to structure our social order, many men do not identify with what Blankenhorn considers the defining male attributes, such as aggression, instrumentalism, competition, and toughness. Nor do they see manhood as incompatible with sensitivity, gentleness, cooperation, empathy, and the ability to nurture. In addition, a commitment to shared parenting does not involve the elimination of stereotypically male attributes. Men do have to be tough and aggressive sometimes, but so do women. The trick is to be able to read a social context and to be able to judge when a particular type of response is warranted. As I stated earlier, in a complex and pluralistic world, both men and women require a full range of what have been idealized as male and female qualities.

What is it, according to Blankenhorn, that makes fathers different from mothers? What roles do men play that women cannot or should not play? Blankenhorn answers this question by embracing the nineteenth-century idea that men and women have different spheres of authority. He argues that men should be the primary breadwinners in the family. According to Blankenhorn, "the breadwinning role matches quite well with core aspects of masculine identity" because it is an "instrumental, goal-driven activity in which success derives, at least in part, from aggression" and "permits men to serve their families through competition with other men."[42] Blankenhorn adds that fathers also perform the roles of protector, spiritual leader, and teacher. Women, Blankenhorn explains, hold authority in the domestic sphere—they are household managers and caretakers. While women assist men with breadwinning, and men assist women with child rearing and household labor, clarity must be maintained concerning who leads in each sphere. Blankenhorn explains that "men supplement and complement the strength of their wives, who are the conductors, the emotional quarterbacks, the primary day-to-day overseers of the children's well-being."[43] Like Popenoe, Blankenhorn subscribes to the idea that men and women bring different, but complementary capacities to parenting, and that they work best as a team, each parent leading in his or her sphere of authority.

It is not clear that the nineteenth-century ideology of separate spheres can be adapted to fit the needs of the twenty-first century. There is already abundant evidence that women are capable of performing effectively in the traditionally male sphere, and there is growing evidence that men are capable of carrying out traditionally female tasks. If 39.3 percent of married mothers are engaged in full-time, year-round work, on what basis do their husbands earn the title of primary breadwinner or leader in the sphere of paid work?[44] Is it because in many cases men make more money than women? Is it legitimate to base men's claim to the title of primary breadwinner on gender-based discrimination in the labor market? And what about the fathers that Blankenhorn praises for helping out in the home? If these fathers are such good helpers, what prevents them from doing their fair share of the housework and childcare? The ideology of separate spheres cannot be upheld if women are actively pursuing paid work and men are caring for children and cooking dinner. Once men participate in domestic work and women participate in paid work, the idea that women can't perform men's duties and men can't perform women's duties is definitively undermined. After all, if either men or women "help out" too much they eventually become competent in the other gender's sphere.

Ultimately, the reinstitutionalization of the gender-structured family has a great deal to do with the retention of male privilege, status, and power. Popenoe and Blankenhorn both believe that the natural parenting drive is weaker in men than it is in women. Popenoe explains that "fatherhood—unlike motherhood—is not something societies have been able to take for granted."[45] Popenoe and Blankenhorn argue that men will not agree to fulfill their parental responsibilities unless they are given special rewards. If we want men to parent, Popenoe and Blankenhorn assert, we must allow them to retain their traditional authority in the family. The authority men historically have exercised in the family, Popenoe and Blankenhorn explain, is based on their ability to protect and provide. In modern societies, however, both of these masculine roles have been challenged. The meaning of the protector role is ambiguous. Since so many women live on their own for at least a portion of their lives, the idea that women need a male protector is not convincing. And, as I have already discussed, many husbands share the provider role with their wives. However, while there is no longer a need for men to fulfill the role of protector as they once did, and even though many men now share the task of provider with their wives, Popenoe and Blankenhorn believe it will benefit the family if men retain their traditional authority. In a society that seems reluctant to enforce the cultural mechanisms that once guaranteed men's fidelity to their families (e.g., lifelong marriage and the control of female sexuality), Popenoe and Blankenhorn argue that rewarding men with status and power may help families stay together.

Fundamentally Unfair

Popenoe argues that it is possible to support gender equality in the workplace and gender-based parenting in the household. He states: "Social androgyny undoubtedly has been successful in the workplace. No longer are men and women thought of as so different that they should play different work roles. Yet unlike the workplace, family organization is necessarily based to some extent on incontestable biological differences between the sexes."[46] The obvious objection to Popenoe's position is that it is impossible to bring about gender equality in the workplace without promoting shared parenting in the family. Women's ability to engage fully in public life and to participate in the decisions that shape both public and private life depends on and requires equality between men and women in the household.

Even though Popenoe and Blankenhorn make some modifications to the traditional gender-structured family, the model of family they defend remains fundamentally unfair to women. There is no way to reconcile their version of what it will take to decrease father absence with justice for women. The idea that men should be the primary breadwinners and women should be the primary caretakers cannot be endorsed without simultaneously endorsing one or both of the following two views: (1) it is acceptable to relegate women to low-paying and low-status occupations in the labor market, and/or (2) women who desire success in the paid labor market should not have children. Blankenhorn and Popenoe ask us to affirm the age-old assertion that men can be fathers and have high-powered careers or demanding and lucrative jobs, but women must choose either children or careers. If women are the sex best suited to infant care, as Blankenhorn and Popenoe insist, than *they* must take time off from work to care for their children while their husbands continue to work. If women are the leaders in the domestic sphere, than *they* will have to cut back on the number of hours they work once they have children. However, their husbands will work the same hours or even increase the time they spend at work after a child is born. As long as we continue to believe that women are the primary caretakers, it will be women, and not men, who forgo career enhancing training and education. Women will not be able to put in the extra hours that are needed to obtain a raise or a promotion. Consequently, women will get fewer raises and promotions and their pay will slip behind that of their childless and male peers. This is not just a problem for women with professional careers. Women in nonprofessional jobs who would like to work full-time or overtime or seek additional training are not able to do so because they, and not their husbands, are the domestic leaders. The gender-structured family is one of the reasons that women make less money, on average as much as 29 percent less, than men do. Popenoe and Blankenhorn's call for the reassertion of traditional gender roles will perpetuate women's disadvantaged position in the paid labor market.

The harm caused to women by the assumption that they will be the primary caretakers in the family begins when they are quite young. Girls' motivation to succeed in school is undermined by what Okin has called the "anticipation of marriage."[47] Expecting to marry and to devote a large portion of their adult life to the rearing of children, girls do not take the courses that are linked to more demanding careers. Even worse, because they anticipate becoming wives and mothers, some girls leave high school early and fail to earn a high school degree. According to the study "Latinos in School," published by the American Association of University Women, young Latinas drop out earlier than young Latinos, African Americans of either sex, and whites of either sex.[48] They also are the least likely group to return to school and obtain a degree. The high (26 percent) and early dropout rate of Latinas is due to a range of factors, including growing up in low-income neighborhoods, and language barriers. However, a number of experts and young Latinas themselves interviewed for an article in the *New York Times* suggest that traditional ideas about women's role in the family influence girls' decisions to leave school early. According to Raul Gonzalez, a former teacher who is now an education policy analyst for the National Council of La Raza, "[w]e may be inadvertently sending off signals that their education is not as important as becoming a wife or mother." Rosa Talavera, a seventeen year old who dropped out when she was a sophomore, explains that she receives conflicting messages from her mother and grandmother. While her mother tells her to focus on finding a career, she is also told: "You should get married, you should have children and know how to cook for your man."[49] Given the low wages earned by men without a college education or specialized training, and the high rates of divorce, marriage and dependence on a husband is not a reliable path to an economically secure future. The perpetuation of traditional gender roles has real costs for girls like Rosa.

Gender-based parenting arrangements harm women by making them vulnerable to a sudden drop in income. Women who treat their careers and jobs as secondary to those of their husbands, or who do not work in the paid labor market often face severe economic difficulties if they divorce. As I mentioned in chapter 3, the household income of divorced women and their children drops by at least 30 percent following the divorce. Approximately 40 percent of marriages dissolve and only 50 percent of men pay all or even a portion of their child support orders. Perpetuating the idea that women and men have different areas of specialization, and that women are better suited to childcare, discourages women from investing in training and education and obtaining the job experience that will provide them with the ability to earn a decent wage.

There are more subtle costs associated with maintaining a rigidly bifurcated conception of gender capacities. When the ability to nurture and the ability to lead are defined as irreconcilable opposites, and the first is assigned to women and the second is assigned to men, women and men experience unnecessary anxiety when they attempt to exercise both capabilities. The problem is not simply that one ability is defined as feminine and the other is defined as masculine. It is also a mistake to see these two capabilities as so different and incompatible that one person cannot possess both. When leadership and nurturing are understood as opposites, women who are ambitious and assertive may refrain from having children and men who have similar qualities may refrain from becoming actively involved in the daily care of their young children. They may mistakenly believe that their ambition and assertiveness disqualifies them for the role of engaged caretaker. Women and men are both harmed when qualities and capacities that can be integrated into one personality are portrayed as opposites in order to give the gender-based division of labor ideological support.

Women who work in the paid labor force part- or full-time do not need husbands who will "be flexible" and "help out" with domestic chores and childcare. They need husbands who will do their fair share of the domestic chores and childcare. In 1998, 64 percent of married women with children under six worked, and 77 percent of married women with children between six and seventeen were in the paid labor force. Of married women who had infants, 39.3 percent worked full-time.[50] In those dual-earner families in which women work full-time, men should do half of the total amount of housework and childcare. However, research done in the 1980s and 1990s indicates that men in dual-earner households do more housework than they did in the past, but that women continue to do a much greater proportion of the housework and childcare than men. According to a literature review conducted by Scott Coltrane, by the late 1980s men performed 20 percent of indoor housework. Men spend about five to eight hours a week on indoor chores, while women spend twenty to thirty hours. In dual-earning couples, men perform 30 percent of the childcare, shopping, and meal preparation, 15 to 30 percent of the meal clean-up and cleaning, and 10 to 25 percent of the laundry.[51] That means that women do 70 percent of the childcare, shopping, and meal preparation, 85 to 70 percent of meal clean-up and cleaning, and 90 to 75 percent of the laundry. According to Coltrane, studies show that women continue to bear the responsibility for managing the household, planning their children's schedule, and arranging to meet their needs. In addition, women are likely to perform the least pleasant household duties, such as cleaning the toilet, themselves. As these studies show, women who work in the paid market continue to do a majority of all kinds of housework and childcare. Unless men take on greater responsibility for childcare and housework, women's opportunities outside of the household will be restricted by their duties inside of it. Popenoe and Blankenhorn's vision of the gender-structured family excuses men from pulling their weight in the domestic sphere.

While Blankenhorn and Popenoe seem to fear that social androgyny is likely to become a popular trend, the truth is that very few couples are able to practice shared parenting, or as Barbara Risman and Danette Johnson-Sumerford call it, "postgender" parenting. Risman and Johnson-Sumerford interviewed fifteen couples who have effectively "decoupled breadwinning from masculinity and nurturing from notions of femininity."[52] Risman and Johnson-Sumerford hypothesize that "changes in women's wage work are a precondition to changes in domestic arrangements."[53] The men and women who made up the couples in their study either earned the same amount of money, or the women earned more. Parity in earning capacity appears to be a likely precondition of postgender parenting, but in itself it does not guarantee that men and women will share household duties equally. Coltrane agrees that "differential earning capacity, along with differential investment in careers, helps to determine who works more and who is most often home to do housework and child care."[54] Risman and Johnson-Sumerford and Coltrane found that there are several different paths to postgender parenting. In some couples, both husband and wife were equally committed to career growth and postgender parenting, which allowed the wife to continue her career. In other couples, both parents were child-centered and wanted to spend substantial time with their children. Ideological commitment to shared parenting alone does not predict a postgender parenting arrangement. Work and financial constraints can push many men and women who would like to share parenting into more traditional arrangements.

Researchers found that postgender parenting offers several benefits. Coltrane explains that when fathers and mothers share childcare and household duties, it can "promote mutual understanding and enhance marital solidarity."[55] In Risman and Johnson-Sumerford's study, all fifteen couples reported a strong emotional bond and a "deep friendship." Risman and Johnson-Sumerford also studied power relationships in postgender couples, and found that neither "partner appeared to have more bargaining strength or the ability to overcome the other's resistance more often."[56] While postgender couples are still a rarity, they are likely to increase as more women obtain rewarding careers that they do not want to give up. The very existence of postgender parenting suggests that gender-based parenting is not inevitable.

Popenoe and Blankenhorn's assertion that gender-based parenting arrangements are natural and/or best for children is closely tied to their argument for why fathers are essential to families. If men and women possess fundamentally different parenting capacities, then children need both fathers and mothers. However, if men and women possess the same capacities, families without fathers will not lack parenting capacities necessary to successful child development. In this section, I argued that rigid conceptions of gender and gender roles in the home perpetuate gender inequalities. In the section that follows, I argue that gender norms are detrimental to the father-son bond. Maintaining gender-based parenting arrangements is more likely to undermine father-child bonds than it is to foster them. I also respond to the assertion that fathers *as men* are necessary to families.

II. GENDER NORMS AS OBSTACLES
TO FATHER INVOLVEMENT

Natural Mothers, Invented Fathers

Popenoe and Blankenhorn both subscribe to the traditional view that a strong, natural bond exists between mother and child. Women are expected to stay with and care for their children. They are, in this sense, unproblematic parents. However, while the mother-child bond is based on a strong and reliable natural drive, the relationship between father and child is not. Blankenhorn explains that "fatherhood, much more than motherhood, is a cultural invention."[57] He also writes: "Compared to mothers, fathers are less born than made. As a social role, fatherhood is less the inelastic result of sexual embodiment than the fragile creation of cultural norms."[58] Men have to be induced to be fathers, while women are naturally inclined to be mothers. As we saw in section 1, Popenoe believes that the existence of a strong maternal drive and the absence of a strong paternal drive can be explained by differences in male and female reproductive strategies. Popenoe and Blankenhorn argue that external pressure in the form of cultural norms and social institutions must be employed if men are to be turned into fathers.

The absence of an internal motivation to father means that the relationship between fathers and children takes an indirect route through the mother. This was the opinion of eighteenth-century French philosopher Rousseau. Speaking of the mother, he wrote, "[s]he serves as the link between [her children] and their father, she alone makes him love them and gives him the confidence to call them his own."[59] Popenoe echoes this when he says that for men, "marriage and fatherhood are very closely linked, and the amount and quality of his fathering that a man is willing to provide is highly dependent on the quality of his spousal relationship."[60] The idea that the relationship between father and child is established through the sexual alliance between mates or spouses is an unavoidable consequence of the belief that motherhood is natural, while fatherhood is a cultural invention. Since the father's bond with his children is not internally motivated, it must be grafted onto a relationship that already is. Men are able to establish a direct sexual relationship with the mother of their children, but the father's relationship with his children is in a sense dependent upon his relationship with the children's mother.

Current research on divorce confirms the belief that mothers mediate the relationship between fathers and children. Furstenberg and Cherlin claim that some men appear to understand marriage and fatherhood as a "package deal." As they explain,

[M]ost fathers, whether absent or present, relate to their children primarily through their wives. . . . Their ties to their children, and their feelings of responsibility for their children, depend on their ties to their wives. It is as though men only know how to be fathers indirectly, through the actions of their wives, who do most of the child rearing. If the marriage breaks up, the indirect ties between fathers and children are also broken.[61]

As described in the introduction to this chapter, upon divorce, many fathers spend less and less time with their children and in many cases eventually withdraw from their children's lives altogether. Furstenberg and Cherlin suggest that the reason for this is that mothers do most of the work of child rearing. When fathers are present, they do not take responsibility for the care of the children; when they no longer reside with their children, they find it difficult to take up a task that they did not do when they lived with their children.

But the fact that many fathers relate to their children through their wives does not mean that they should. This indirect or mediated relationship is a direct by-product of the expectation that women should be the primary caretakers of children. Popenoe and Blankenhorn's model of the gender-structured family perpetuates the indirect link between father and child. Indeed, by insisting that women, not men, are responsible for childcare, Popenoe and Blankenhorn place a major obstacle in the way of fathers developing direct and unmediated relationships with their children. Indirect and mediated relationships are by definition weaker than direct and unmediated ones. Developing strong ties between fathers and children requires that men take on child rearing responsibilities. If they do this when they live with their children, there is good reason to think that the direct and unmediated relationship they establish with their children will be sustained even if a divorce or breakup occurs.

Marriage should not be touted as the only or the best way of maintaining an active paternal presence in the lives of children. We have ample evidence for doubting the stability of marriage or sexual alliances between men and women. Even as strong a supporter of the institution of marriage as Popenoe urges men and women to wait until their mid- to late-twenties to marry because marriages at an early age have a poor prognosis. Moreover, the conviction that marriage is the best way to keep fathers and children together rests on the highly questionable assumption that the maternal bond is natural, while the paternal bond is cultural. If this assumption is rejected, we can no longer take for granted that the only or even the best way to connect fathers to their children is through their wives. It may be beneficial to the father-child relationship if we begin to think of it as distinct from the sexual or marital alliance. After all, we are already familiar with the idea that the mother-child bond persists despite divorce or the absence of marriage. Can the father-child bond be conceived so that it is not dependent on the marital relationship?

Rethinking the father-child bond requires rejecting the idea that motherhood is natural, while fatherhood is a cultural invention. Instead, we have to think about how the bond between child and parent develops. If motherhood is understood as an activity composed of daily acts of caring, the bond between mother and child can be seen as a product of this activity. However, our language often represents motherhood as a passive state and not as an activity. Indeed, we often say that a pregnant woman is "carrying" a fetus, as if being pregnant entails nothing more than transporting a small piece of luggage. This depiction of pregnancy as a passive state ignores the bodily and emotional transformations that a pregnant woman experiences. It ignores how she must change her daily life in order to facilitate the growth of the fetus. When a woman is pregnant, all her acts of self-care are also acts of caring for the fetus. After a child is born, the bond between mother and child continues to develop through daily acts of care, such as holding and comforting the infant, feeding and cleaning the infant, and in general, attending to the needs of the infant. It is through these acts of nurturing and caregiving that the so-called natural bond between child and mother comes into existence.

The perception that mothers and children have a natural bond can be understood as a consequence of the gender-based division of labor that assigns newborn and infant care exclusively to women. Because women take care of children, and develop the capacity to understand and anticipate their needs, they are perceived as having a natural bond with their children. As parenting expert Ron Taffel comments, "Children talk in the midst of doing other things, when someone is giving them a bath. The one who does more of that is the one who finds more out. It's not inborn; it just happens to be that women happen to do more of that."[62] Sociological and psychological research suggests that men are just as capable of caring for babies as women. According to Lamb, "Contrary to the notion of maternal instinct, parenting skills are usually acquired 'on the job' by both mothers and fathers."[63] Research also reveals that the vast majority of fathers found caring for their newborn deeply rewarding. These same studies reveal that fathers who take responsibility for infant care are likely to continue caring for their children as they grow older. According to researchers, "Early and extensive involvement in infant care can raise the father's confidence in his abilities to nurture his children and may also increase his commitment to be actively involved in infant care."[64] Such results suggest that the father-child bond arises out of the activity of caring and that the best way to establish strong ties between fathers and their children is to encourage men to take responsibility for the care of infants.

Interestingly, research on fathers who had planned on being actively involved in the daily care of their newborns, and research on fathers who had not planned on being actively involved but who had to unexpectedly step in to relieve their wives, came to the same positive conclusions about men as infant caregivers. Unplanned caregivers, such as fathers of cesarean-delivered babies who were required to perform baby care because of their partners' need for rest, were found to be competent caregivers and to develop strong ties with their child. Psychologists found that fathers of cesarean-delivered infants "tend to show more soothing behaviors toward infants and to participate in infant care on a more equal basis than those in natural birth comparison groups." These fathers "tend to develop competence and continue taking care of the infant even after the mothers have fully recovered."[65] According to research on fathers who care for toddlers and older children, "If fathers spent substantial time alone with children, they became central emotional figures to them. Substantial 'on-duty' time also contributed to the image of fathers as competent nurturing caregivers."[66] In studies of non-traditional families, in which the father is the primary caretaker or shares childcare equally with the mother, fathers have reported "enhanced self-esteem, self-confidence, or satisfaction with their parent role."[67] Researchers explain that when men take on significant childcare responsibilities they understand their children better and are more sensitive to them. Fathers who were interviewed argued that becoming competent caretakers required "spending time alone with their children and taking sole responsibility for them on a continuous day to day basis."[68] Finally, in studies that have compared single mothers and single fathers, researchers have found "few differences in either parental satisfaction or child development based on the sex of the parent"[69] Most researchers argue, then, that parenting is more a matter of learned behavior than inborn gender-based dispositions.

The research on fathers who take responsibility for the care of their infants and children challenges several of the claims made by Popenoe and Blankenhorn. First, it suggests that the bond between mother and child is not the product of a mysterious and inherent maternal drive. Instead, the relationship between mother and child and the relationship between father and child is established in the exact same way—through the *activity* of caregiving. Men develop bonds to their children by taking care of them and by playing the same role in their children's lives that mothers do. Second, it shows that men can become competent caregivers. As the study of cesarean-delivered babies indicates, even men who had not initially desired to care for their newborns developed the abilities and skills to do so.

By perpetuating the myth that motherhood is natural and fatherhood is a cultural invention, and by excluding fathers from infant care, Popenoe and Blankenhorn place an enormous obstacle in the way of achieving their goal of establishing and maintaining the father-child relationship. Contrary to what Popenoe and Blankenhorn advise, fostering strong ties between fathers and their children may require rejecting the idea that the relationship between father and child is a by-product of the relationship between husband and wife. If we want fathers and children to stay together when husbands and wives split up or when sexual partners fail to establish a long-term tie, we will have to rethink the relationship between the sexual alliance and the parenting relationship. Given high rates of divorce and nonmarital birth, keeping fathers and children together would seem to require recognizing the sexual/spousal relationship and the parenting relationship as two distinct and potentially separate relationships. Divorce and nonmarital birth are now quite common. However, we have yet to develop social institutions, legal arrangements, and cultural norms for how divorced and nonresidential fathers should relate to their children. If we reject the assumption that the father-child relationship is dependent on the sexual/spousal relationship, we need not accept that divorce or the breakup of a couple means that fathers will disappear from the lives of their children. Instead, we can devote ourselves to finding ways to maintain connections between nonresidential fathers and their children.

Developing and maintaining strong ties between fathers and children will require encouraging men to get directly involved in the physical care of their children and to do so when their children are infants. It is unlikely that fathers who have taken responsibility for the care of their infants and children, and developed strong bonds with them, would abandon them when their marital or sexual relationship to their children's mother has ended. Studies of child support payments found that fathers who were highly involved with their children prior to divorce were more likely to make the specified payment.[70] However, encouraging fathers to take on greater responsibility for childcare means rejecting Popenoe and Blankenhorn's advice about gender-specific parenting. Instead, we will have to create cultural norms and ideals that identify fatherhood with nurturing and infant care. We will have to imagine a kind of masculinity that is not diminished by holding and comforting babies, feeding them, cleaning them, and rocking them to sleep.

Absent Jobs/Absent Fathers

As explained in section 1, both Popenoe and Blankenhorn believe breadwinning is the defining function of fatherhood. As Blankenhorn states, "To be the primary breadwinner of the family is a bedrock responsibility of the good family man."[71] Popenoe tells us, "The most universal, and therefore arguably most fundamental, elements of the father role are the physical protection of the family unit and the provision of resources—breadwinning—necessary for the family's survival."[72] There is ample evidence for the claim that men understand providing as their core responsibility in the family. However, defining fatherhood in terms of breadwinning may actually pose an obstacle to strengthening ties between fathers and children. Many men face significant barriers to fulfilling the provider role, and this may discourage them from marrying, or if they are divorced or nevermarried, from remaining in close contact with their children. Men who feel they have failed to fulfill the provider role may experience feelings of inadequacy and shame when they are around their children. They may find it easier to drop out of their children's lives than to confront their feelings of failure.[73] In their defense of traditional gender roles, Popenoe and Blankenhorn fail to address the harsh economic realities of many men's lives in an economy that has fewer and fewer stable, well-paying jobs for workers without a college education. Researchers tell us that "fathering suffers disproportionately from negative social forces, such as racism, that inhibit opportunities in the environment."[74] However, Popenoe and Blankenhorn do not confront the close connection between father absence and job absence. There are a number of different ways in which poverty and unemployment affect the relationship between father and child. Many scholars argue that male unemployment contributes to low marriage rates in very poor communities. Research conducted on men who experience persistent poverty indicates that one of the primary factors that prevents a continuous relationship between unmarried, nonresidential fathers and their children is the inability of low-income fathers to provide for their children.[75] In addition, alcohol and drug use, physical and psychological trauma, depression, and anxiety, and domestic violence are associated with poverty and unemployment. All of these factors make it more difficult to sustain a marriage or a stable domestic union.[76]

While not all men respond to unemployment by feeling inadequate, the strong associations between masculinity, fatherhood, and providing for families can have devastating consequences for some men and their families. As Drucilla Cornell has pointed out, breadwinning is so tightly bound up with masculinity, that men who have been strong providers and who suddenly lose their jobs tend to blame themselves and are sometimes overcome by feelings of failure.[77] She argues that their failure to fulfill an idealized conception of masculinity can lead to separation or divorce. Both Cornell and Stacey suggest that men themselves are ultimately hurt by a definition of fatherhood based entirely on providing material goods. Stacey comments, "Male breadwinning is no longer an adequate (or widely attainable) definition of effective fathering, but we lack sufficient alternative models of socially desirable forms of masculinity and paternity that are both accessible and attractive to masses of male 'displaced breadwinners.'"[78] It is possible that if fatherhood were redefined to include child rearing, men experiencing financial difficulty might not believe that failing to obtain employment disqualified them from being good fathers.

The relationship between poverty and low marriage rates is not entirely clear. Rates of child bearing outside of marriage are certainly high in poor urban and rural communities. Indeed, in low-income black communities as many as 70 percent of births are to unmarried women. Wilson popularized the idea that black male joblessness is one of the primary causes of nonmarital child bearing in *The Truly Disadvantaged*.[79] Wilson argued that high rates of unemployment decreased the pool of marriageable men in poor black communities. However, in his more recent book, *When Work Disappears,* Wilson revised his thesis.[80] After reviewing recent studies on the relationship between unemployment and marriage, Wilson concludes that "even though the joblessness among black men is a significant factor in their delayed entry into marriage and in the decreasing rates of marriage after a child has been born, it can account for only a proportion of the decline in marriages in the inner city, including postpartum marriages."[81] Wilson now argues that the weakening of social sanctions against premarital sex, nonmarital child bearing, and single parenthood throughout the general society interact with joblessness in the inner city in a complex and subtle way. He states that while shifts in cultural norms have affected all socioeconomic groups, they have had distinct consequences for poor communities. For example, premarital sex is a universal phenomenon in the United States, but middle-class and upper middle-class young women (and men) have more reasons to avoid nonmarital pregnancy than their low-income peers do. Put simply, young women (and men) who expect to go to college and have a career wait until they have finished college, established their careers, and gotten married to get pregnant. Young women who do not expect such a future have little reason to wait. Neither they nor their sexual partners expect to go to college or to secure a well-paying job. Wilson explains that as "employment prospects recede, the foundation for stable relationships becomes weaker over time."[82] Joblessness may not be the direct cause of nonmarriage, but growing up in poor communities with no hope for a secure economic future provides little incentive for postponing pregnancy.

Men and women living in poor communities face multiple stresses that make establishing long-term plans and commitments difficult. The threat of violence, from both intimates and strangers, undermines the ability of individuals to establish trusting relationships. High rates of alcohol and drug addiction, race-based stigma, and the experience of physical trauma contribute to tensions in intimate relationships. High rates of incarceration for poor black and Latino men make establishing long-term, stable relationships more difficult. In addition, many people living in poor communities experience depression and anxiety, which also pose challenges to establishing trusting, long-term relationships. All of these life stresses interact to decrease the likelihood of stable relationships. Consequently, many men and women come to believe that marriage is an unattainable ideal.

The decline of marriage in low-income communities does not mean that fathers are entirely absent from the lives of their children. Various kinds of relationships are established between nevermarried mothers and fathers. Some unmarried couples live and raise their children together. Some parents who are living together at the time of their child's birth will eventually marry. Others maintain a romantic involvement, but do not live together. Finally, some parents split up as couples before or shortly after their child is born. Typically, low-wage, nevermarried fathers live with or see their children on a regular basis when they are young. Over time, however, contact between fathers and children drops off, and in many cases, fathers are eventually no longer a regular part of the lives of their children. Research conducted by Frank F. Furstenberg Jr., and Kathleen M. Harris on 400 teen parents from poor communities found that on average, youth spent half of their childhood years living with a biological or a surrogate father. As preschoolers, about half of youth lived with or saw fathers on a weekly basis, but by the end of their teens, only one third had regular contact with their fathers. Child support payments followed the same pattern of gradually decreasing as children grew up. The percentage of youth receiving child support payments from nonresidential fathers began at 80 percent when the children were one, declined to 30 percent by the time they were five, and decreased to 15 percent by their mid-adolescence.[83]

A significant number of low-income nonresidential fathers who have never been married to the mother of their children are simply not able to provide for their children. In-depth interviews conducted by Laura Lein, Kathryn Edin and Timothy Nelson with eighty-three low-wage male workers indicated that they did indeed see their ability to be good fathers in terms of their ability to provide for their children. Lein, Edin, and Nelson explain that "[m]en, according to the men we interviewed, need to do things for their children in order to feel good about being fathers."[84] However, while these men accepted the conventional gender-based definitions of fatherhood, and showed great interest in maintaining a connection with their children, many of them had only sporadic contact with their children. Lein, Edin, and Nelson argue that the inability of men to obtain steady employment cut them off from their children and their children's mothers. The men interviewed by Lein, Edin, and Nelson were not able to secure employment that provided them with a wage sufficient to avoid homelessness or hunger. Many of them were casual day laborers who were frequently unable to obtain year-round, full-time work. These men were often exploited by the men who hired them and faced many difficulties in maintaining steady employment such as failing health, the lack of reliable, year-round work, and the lack of transportation. Lein, Edin, and Nelson point out that many of the low-wage fathers they interviewed faced more severe and persistent material hardship than the low-wage mothers that they interviewed. For example, while many of the male interviewees had experienced periods of homelessness and did not have access to adequate health care, the same was not true for the female interviewees. This is in large part because men do not qualify for the welfare programs that have been available to impoverished mothers.

Defining fatherhood in terms of breadwinning is particularly inappropriate in the case of low-wage and impoverished men. Government policy, which has in past years devoted more resources to child support enforcement, has not paid sufficient attention to the needs of men who are not able to earn a living wage. As Edin, Lein, and Nelson point out, public policies aimed at preventing children and their mothers from going hungry and homeless have not addressed the needs of fathers. Instead of condemning poor men for not marrying the mothers of their children and for not supporting their children, politicians and policymakers should make a concerted effort to reform the low-wage labor market and to make it possible for men who lack education and training to support themselves and their families. Along with policies that would make decent jobs available to men, and provide them with income supports, transportation, and medical insurance, it is also necessary to reform the child support system so that underemployed men are not sanctioned for failing to pay their child support on time or burdened with unmanageable debt.[85]

The principle behind child support is sound. Nonresidential biological fathers should be held responsible for their part in bringing a child into the world. However, as we have seen, men with limited economic prospects are not always capable of meeting their child support responsibilities. As noted, this can make them feel shame and undermine their bond with their child. Several child support experts advocate reforming the system so that it facilitates, rather than hinders, the father-child relationship. The children of many low-income fathers receive welfare payments from the state. For these fathers, one of the most frustrating aspects of the child support system is that their child support payments go directly to the state in order to repay the state for the welfare payment received by the child. This is a bad policy for several reasons. First, it encourages mothers and fathers to agree to informal child support payments. Such agreements cannot be enforced and are illegal under welfare rules. Second, it prevents the father from feeling that he has made a contribution to the well-being of his child. Third, monthly welfare payments are extremely small. Based on their study of the budgets of women on welfare, Edin and Lein estimate that welfare payments and food stamps together cover only three-fifths of welfare-reliant mothers' expenses.[86] Women need both their welfare payment and child support in order to avoid material hardship.

Child support payments can either be viewed as an opportunity for the state to recover welfare and Medicaid costs, or as a mechanism for encouraging men to become responsible fathers. Vicki Turetsky of the Center for Law and

Social Policy points out that nearly "all state Transitional Aid to Needy Families (TANF) programs disregard some of the mother's earned income to encourage and support her effort to work. The same rationale justifies disregarding the father's earned income contributed to the family as child support."[87] Prior to the1996 welfare reform, all states were required to pass through the first fifty dollars of child support to welfare families. In other words, states could not keep all of a father's child support payment—fifty dollars went to the child's family. The Personal Responsibility and Work Opportunity Reconciliation Act (PRWORA) eliminated the fifty-dollar pass through as a federal requirement and thirty-two states now use child support to recoup state dollars. Eighteen states have retained the fifty-dollar pass-through, including the states of Nevada, Connecticut, and Wisconsin, which have increased it.[88] Paying child support directly to the father's children and disregarding it when calculating the mother's welfare benefits will allow men to feel that they are providing for their children. Fathers who feel they are fulfilling the role of breadwinner are more likely to remain involved in their children's lives. In addition, child support orders must be realistic and reflect the true income of men who have irregular work histories.

For a significant portion of the population, the strong connection between breadwinning and fatherhood functions to push men away from their children. Ashamed of themselves because of their inability to provide for their children, these men leave or stop visiting their families. Policymakers who are serious about keeping families together and strengthening fragile families must encourage responsible fatherhood through reforming the low-wage labor market. As I have argued throughout this book, helping families stay together means ensuring that men and women are able to earn a living wage. However, while it is essential to reform the low-wage labor market so that men can contribute to the well-being of their children, it is also important to broaden the definition of fatherhood so that men who are unemployed can still feel like good fathers. If providing for their family's financial support is out of reach for some men, it makes sense to give good fathering additional meanings. If men could be convinced that being a good father means providing physical care and emotional support, listening to and playing with their children, and providing them with love and encouragement, they might be less likely to disappear from their children's lives when they are not in a position to support them financially.

Are Fathers Necessary?

Popenoe and Blankenhorn both fear that in a society in which single mothers head 25 percent of all households with children, fathers will come to be viewed as superfluous to families. They support gender-specific parenting because they believe that fathers are necessary to families and that families without fathers are inherently deficient. If men and women contribute something very different to their children's development, then it stands to reason that all children need both a mother and a father. If men and women contribute something different to their children's development, then fathers can never be seen as inessential or be replaced by a grandmother or a lesbian co-parent.

As we have seen, many scholars of child development do not agree with Popenoe and Blankenhorn's conclusion that parenting is a gender-based activity and that men and women have different and complementary parenting styles. According to psychologists Louise Silverstein and Carl Auerbach, "Neither the sex of the adult(s) nor the biological relationship to the child has emerged as a significant variable in predicting positive development. We have found that the stability of the emotional connection and the predictability of the caretaking relationship are the significant variables that predict positive child adjustment."[89] On the topic of child development, the scholarly literature emphasizes the desirability of a warm and close nurturing relationship between parent or parents and child. Costs associated with father absence, such as declining household income or lack of emotional support for the mother, are not, strictly speaking, functions of masculinity. If a lesbian couple with children split up, these same problems would exist.

Nonetheless, abandoning the idea that fathers make a *distinctly masculine* contribution to their children in no way undermines the contributions that individual fathers make to their families. It simply means that what they contribute is not distinctly masculine or essentially different from what mothers contribute to their children. Parenting is not a gender-based task. Children are vulnerable and needy. They require care, guidance, moderate and consistent discipline, emotional support, love, and provision. Women and men are both capable of meeting these needs, not as men or women, but as mature adults. Given that this is the case, fathers are not absolutely necessary to families—but neither are mothers. As we have seen, studies of father-solo families indicate that fathers are as capable of being primary caretakers as mothers are. Thus, it is not the sex of the parent that matters, but the consistency and reliability of the care that he or she provides.

When Popenoe and Blankenhorn ask us if fathers are essential and irreplaceable, it is tempting to think of all the loving fathers we know of, and respond, Of course! However, we need to be careful because they are not really asking us if this or that particular father is necessary to his family. Instead, they are asking us if fathers *as men* are necessary to all families—including lesbian families and mother-solo families. In effect, they are asking us, Are families without fathers legitimate? Are fathers without families capable of raising healthy, happy children? If our answer to the latter questions is yes, we cannot accept the assertion that fathers *as men* are necessary to families.

CONCLUSION

This chapter has supported shared, or postgender, parenting because it will relieve women who participate in the labor force from working a second shift in the household, and open up their opportunities in the public sphere. If men take on greater responsibility for childcare and housework, women will be able to devote more time and energy to earning income, going to school, developing their careers, and engaging in community and public service. Becoming more involved in the care of their children could have tremendous benefits for men. Most mothers feel that caring for their children is deeply meaningful and satisfying. Men deserve the opportunity to experience the difficulties and rewards of taking responsibility for the care of their children.

However, postgender parenting is not for everyone. Even parents who are committed to gender equality are not always able to and do not always want to practice shared parenting. Some women want to stay home and take care of their children. Many times, but not always, these women have not found paid work satisfying or have not been able to find a well-paying job. Many men see breadwinning as essential to their sense of identity and do not want to withdraw from the labor force even temporarily. In addition, even couples who do not identify with traditional gender roles find that economic constraints make shared parenting an undesirable arrangement. The absence of affordable, high-quality day care is one of the reasons that women stay home with their children. In other families with stay-at-home moms, both parents believe that children should be raised within the home and are reluctant to send their children to day care. There are many different ways of organizing the care of children. What is essential is that parents—particularly women—should be aware of the costs and benefits of the parenting arrangement that they have chosen.

Public policy should aim at eliminating the economic and institutional constraints to shared parenting. This would mean making high-quality, affordable day care available, and increasing the flexibility of work schedules. It would also require guaranteeing paid parental leave to more men and women. Efforts to secure better pay for women would also facilitate shared parenting arrangements. As we have seen, when women command substantial economic resources, men are more likely to share child rearing responsibilities with them.

Persistent gender norms are perhaps the greatest barrier to the expansion of shared parenting. However, while masculine gender norms, in particular, are changing very slowly, there is some reason for optimism. Both Popenoe and Blankenhorn, but especially Blankenhorn, place great emphasis on how cultural norms and ideals shape parenting arrangements. Without accepting the distinction they make between natural mothers and cultural fathers, it is possible to endorse their argument that fatherhood (like motherhood) is a cultural invention. But if fatherhood was invented, then it can be reinvented. There is no reason that we cannot imagine a kind of masculinity that does not define itself in opposition to femininity. Nor is there any reason to think that providing direct care for children is somehow unmasculine. Redefining fatherhood would benefit men, women, and children.

NOTES

1. Christine Winquist Nord and Nicholas Zill, *Non-Custodial Parents' Participation in Their Children's Lives: Evidence from the Survey of Income and Program Participation, Volume II*, Department of Health and Human Services, Washington, D.C., 1996. http://fatherhood.hhs.gov/sipp/pt2.htm. (accessed 28 June 2000).

2. Frank F. Furstenberg Jr. and Kathleen M. Harris, "When and Why Fathers Matter: Impacts of Father Involvement on the Children of Adolescent Mothers," in *Young Unwed Fathers: Changing Roles and Emerging Policies*, ed. Robert I. Lerman and Theodora J. Ooms (Philadelphia: Temple University Press, 1993).

3. Elaine Sorensen and Ariel Halpern, "Child Support Is Working Better Than We Think," *New Federalism*, Series A, no. A-31 (Washington, D.C.: Urban Institute, 1999).

4. U.S. Department of Health and Human Services, *HHS Fact Sheet: Promoting Responsible Fatherhood, 2001*. http://www.hhs.gov/news/press/2001pres/01fsfatherhood.html (accessed 16 January 2002).

5. Nord and Zill, *Non-Custodial Parents' Participation*.

6. Michael E. Lamb, "The Changing Role of Fathers," in *The Father's Role, Applied Perspectives*, ed. Michael Lamb (New York: John Wiley, 1986), 16.

7. Frank F. Furstenberg Jr., S. Philip Morgan, and Paul D. Allison, "Paternal Participation and Children's Well-Being after Marital Dissolution," *American Sociological Review* 52, no. 5 (October 1987), 695–701.

8. Nord and Zill, *Non-Custodial Parents' Participation*.

9. Scott Coltrane, *Family Man: Fatherhood, Housework, and Gender Equity* (New York: Oxford University Press, 1996)

10. Sorensen and Halpern, "Child Support Is Working Better Than We Think."

11. David Blankenhorn, *Fatherless America* (New York: Basic Books, 1995); David Popenoe, *Life Without Father* (New York: Free Press, 1996).

12. Popenoe, *Life Without Father*, 1.

13. Blankenhorn, *Fatherless America*, 1.

14. Popenoe, *Life Without Father*, 197.

15. Daphne Spain and Suzanne M. Bianchi, *Balancing Act: Motherhood, Marriage and Employment Among American Women* (New York: Russell Sage Foundation, 1996), 110.

16. Arlie Hochschild with Anne Machung, *The Second Shift* (New York: Avon, 1989).

17. Coltrane, *Family Man*; and Lamb, "The Changing Role of Fathers."

18. Popenoe, *Life Without Father*, 65.

19. Popenoe, *Life Without Father*, 168.

20. Popenoe, *Life Without Father*, 168–69.

21. Popenoe, *Life Without Father*, 183.

22. Popenoe, *Life Without Father*, 176.

23. Popenoe, *Life Without Father*, 139.

24. Popenoe, *Life Without Father*, 146.

25. Popenoe, *Life Without Father*, 146–47.

26. Susan Moller Okin makes this point in *Women and Western Political Thought* (Princeton, N.J.: Princeton University Press, 1979).

27. Alice H. Eagly and Wendy Wood, "The Origins of Sex Differences in Human Behavior: Evolved Dispositions Versus Social Roles," *American Psychologist* 54, no. 6 (June 1999): 408–23.

28. Lamb, "The Changing Role of Fathers," 14.

29. Lamb, "The Changing Role of Fathers," 14.

30. Popenoe, *Life Without Father*, 183.

31. Popenoe, *Life Without Father*, 211.

32. Popenoe, *Life Without Father*, 213.

33. Popenoe, *Life Without Father*, 212.

34. Popenoe, *Life Without Father*, 213.

35. Lamb, "The Changing Role of Fathers"; and Coltrane, *Family Man*.

36. Blankenhorn, *Fatherless America*, 3.

37. Blankenhorn, *Fatherless America*, 3.

38. Blankenhorn, *Fatherless America*, 197.

39. Blankenhorn, *Fatherless America*, 121.

40. Robert Griswold, *Fatherhood in America: A History* (New York: Basic Books, 1993).

41. Michael Kimmel, *Manhood in America: A Cultural History* (New York: Free Press, 1996).

42. Blankenhorn, *Fatherless America*, 116.

43. Blankenhorn, *Fatherless America*, 217.

44. U.S. Bureau of the Census, *Fertility of American Women: June 1998, P20-526*, U.S. Department of Commerce, Economics and Statistics Administration (Washington, D.C., 1998); Spain and Bianchi, *Balancing Act*, 85.

45. Popenoe, *Life Without Father*, 183.

46. Popenoe, *Life Without Father*, 211.

47. Susan Moller Okin, *Justice, Gender, and the Family* (New York: Basic Books, 1989), 142.

48. Dana Canedy, "Troubling Label for Hispanics: 'Girls Most Likely to Drop Out,'" *New York Times*, 25 March 2001, A1.

49. Canedy, "Troubling Label for Hispanics."

50. Bureau of the Census, *Statistical Abstract of the United States*.

51. Coltrane, *Family Man*, 54.

52. Barbara J. Risman, and Danette Johnson-Sumerford, "Doing It Fairly: A Study of Postgender Marriages," *Journal of Marriage and Family* 60 (February 1998): 23–40.

53. Risman and Johnson-Sumerford, "Doing It Fairly," 27.

54. Coltrane, *Family Man*, 72.

55. Coltrane, *Family Man*, 78.

56. Risman and Johnson-Sumerford, "Doing It Fairly," 38.

57. Blankenhorn, *Fatherless America*, 3.

58. Blankenhorn, *Fatherless America*, 66.

59. Jean-Jacques Rousseau, *Emile or On Education*, intro. and trans. Allan Bloom (New York: Basic Books, 1979), 361.

60. Popenoe, *Life Without Father*, 186.

61. Frank F. Furstenberg Jr. and Andrew J. Cherlin, *Divided Families: What Happens to Children When Parents Part* (Cambridge, Mass.: Harvard University Press, 1991), 118.

62. Susan Chira, "War Over Role of American Families," *New York Times* 19 June 1994, A22.

63. Lamb, "The Changing Role of Fathers," 11.

64. Coltrane, *Family Man*, 60.

65. Coltrane, *Family Man*, 60.

66. Coltrane, *Family Man*, 81.

67. Graeme Russell, "Primary Caretaking and Role Sharing Fathers," in *The Father's Role, Applied Perspectives,* ed. Michael Lamb (New York: John Wiley, 1986), 29–57.

68. Russell, "Primary Caretaking and Role Sharing Fathers," 43–44.

69. Risman and Johnson-Sumerford, "Doing It Fairly," 51.

70. Nord and Zill, *Non-Custodial Parents' Participation*.

71. Blankenhorn, *Fatherless America*, 108.

72. Popenoe, *Life Without Father*, 171.

73. William J. Doherty, Edward F. Kouneski, and Martha F. Erickson, "Responsible Fathering: An Overview and Conceptual Framework," *Journal of Marriage and Family* 60 (May 1998): 277–92; Shirley Aisha Ray and Vonnie C. McLoyd, "Fathers in Hard Times: The Impact of Unemployment and Poverty on Paternal and Marital Relations," in *The Father's Role, Applied Perspectives*, ed. Michael Lamb (New York: John Wiley, 1986), 339–84.

74. Doherty, Kouneski, and Erickson, "Responsible Fathering," 287.

75. Kathryn Edin, Laura Lein, and Timothy Nelson, *Low-Income, Non-Residential Fathers: Off-Balance in a Competitive Economy, An Initial Analysis*, U.S. Department of Health and Human Services (Washington, D.C., 1998). http://fatherhood.hhs.gov/ELN/eln98.htm (accessed June 2001).

76. Ray and McLoyd, "Fathers in Hard Times," 348–51, 361–65.

77. Drucilla Cornell, "Fatherhood and Its Discontents: Men, Patriarchy and Freedom," in *Lost Fathers: The Politics of Fatherlessness in America*, ed. Cynthia R. Daniels (New York: St. Martin's Griffin, 1998), 183–202.

78. Judith Stacey, "Dada-ism in the 1990s: Getting Past Baby Talk about Fatherlessness," in *Lost Fathers: The Politics of Fatherlessness in America*, ed. Cynthia R. Daniels (New York: St. Martin's Griffin, 1998), 51–84.

79. William Julius Wilson, *The Transformation of Work* (Chicago: University of Chicago Press, 1987), 63–92.

80. William Julius Wilson, *When Work Disappears: The World of the New Urban Poor* (New York: Vintage Books, 1996), 87–110.

81. Wilson, *When Work Disappears*, 97.

82. Wilson, *When Work Disappears*, 110.

83. Frank F. Furstenberg Jr. and Kathleen M. Harris, "When and Why Fathers Matter: Impacts of Father Involvement on the Children of Adolescent Mothers," in *Young Unwed Fathers: Changing Roles and Emerging Policies*, eds. Robert I. Lerman and Theodora J. Ooms (Philadelphia: Temple University Press, 1993).

84. Edin, Lein, and Nelson, *Low-Income, Non-Residential Fathers.*

85. Vicki Turetsky, *Realistic Child Support Policies For Low Income Fathers* (Washington, D.C.: Center for Law and Social Policy, 2000). http://www.clasp.org/pubs/childenforce/kellogg.htm (accessed 8 June 2000).

86. Kathyrn Edin and Laura Lein, *Making Ends Meet: How Single Mothers Survive Welfare and Low-Wage Work* (New York: Russell Sage Foundation, 1997), 43.

87. Turetsky, *Realistic Child Support Policies.*

88. Sorensen and Halpern, "Child Support Is Working Better Than We Think."

89. Louise B. Silverstein and Carl F. Auerbach, "Deconstructing the Essential Father," *American Psychologist* 54, no. 6 (June 1999): 397–407.

Chapter Five

Do Welfare Recipients Have a Right of Privacy? A Public/Private Paradox

The 1996 Personal Responsibility and Work Opportunity Reconciliation Act (PRA hereafter) finds that government has an interest in decreasing out-of-wedlock pregnancy and instructs states to find ways to reduce nonmarital birth and promote marriage.[1] The PRA replaced Aid to Families with Dependent Children (AFDC) with Transitional Aid to Needy Families (TANF). In 2002, Congress will have the opportunity to reconsider and make changes to the TANF legislation.

Twenty-three states have incorporated child exclusion legislation into their welfare programs.[2] Under AFDC, welfare recipients received a small increase in their monthly cash grant if they bore an additional child while on welfare. The child exclusion policy eliminates this increase in benefits. The purpose of the child exclusion policy is to discourage births to women who are on welfare, most of whom are single and many of whom have never been married. Single mothers head about 81 percent of families receiving welfare; slightly over 55 percent of these women have never been married, and 26 percent are divorced or separated.[3] While the federal government does not require states to implement child exclusion regulations, this policy fulfills federal guidelines that call upon states to discourage out-of-wedlock birth and promote marriage.

Unlike chapters 3 and 4, this chapter does not respond to specific policies advocated by family communitarians. However, it furthers my analysis of their overarching claim, which is that law and policy should promote the two-parent family. The child exclusion provision raises important questions about the power of the state to influence how individuals order their intimate lives: Is it legitimate for the state to use its distributive power to discourage nonmarital childbirth and encourage marriage? Does the state have the authority to determine for its citizens the meaning and value of parenting and marriage?

I argue that the child exclusion provision violates a woman's right of privacy by interfering with her decisions regarding procreation and intimate association. The citizens of the United States hold differing beliefs regarding sexuality, marriage, and parenthood. The state should not use its distributive power to promote one conception of family over others.

Employing a right of privacy argument against family cap legislation opens up what appears to be a public/private paradox: The public is under no obligation to financially support "private" decisions. Advocates of privacy rights for welfare recipients are vulnerable to the argument that women have a right to procreate but that the public is under no obligation to subsidize a choice that was freely made. If women choose to exercise their right of procreative autonomy, they are responsible for supporting their children themselves.

My objective in this chapter is to show that the child exclusion policy illegitimately constrains the procreative and associational autonomy of women receiving welfare. Moreover, I argue that women who receive welfare are entitled to both procreative autonomy and public support. In section 1 of this chapter, "Welfare Reform and the Child Exclusion Policy," I describe the child exclusion policy and provide some background information on welfare-receiving women. In section 2, "Race, Class, Marital Status and Motherhood," I argue that the child exclusion policy is based on the principle that unmarried, low-income women, many of whom are women of color, do not deserve to have children. In section 3, "Welfare Recipients and the Right of Privacy," I argue that the family cap unjustly restricts procreative and associational autonomy. In section 4, "Reexamining the Public/Private Dilemma," I challenge the assumption that claiming privacy rights for welfare recipients opens up a public/private paradox. Simultaneously supporting public funding and privacy rights for single mothers only appears paradoxical when the social causes of poverty are ignored. When poverty is understood as a social problem, the alleged public/private paradox disappears.

I. WELFARE REFORM AND THE
CHILD EXCLUSION POLICY

President Clinton and the Republican-dominated Congress eliminated AFDC in 1996. AFDC was a means-tested cash assistance program funded by both federal and state governments, and administered by the states according to federal guidelines. Under AFDC, every dollar that a state appropriated for the program was matched by one to three federal dollars. AFDC was replaced by TANF, which abolishes this funding arrangement and substitutes for it an annual block grant. The block grant effectively limits the amount of money that states have to spend on poor women and their children. Under AFDC, families were entitled to aid as long as they met the eligibility requirements.[4] This is no longer case. If a state uses up its block grant, it will not receive additional funds from the federal government. In addition to this new funding arrangement, federal welfare reform mandates new time limits and work requirements. Under TANF, there is a cumulative lifetime sixty-month limit on cash benefits. Federal guidelines also require that welfare recipients begin employment after twenty-four months of receiving benefits. States are free to impose shorter time limits and stricter work requirements on welfare recipients, and many of them have.[5]

Cash welfare benefits vary widely from state to state. In 1993, a family of three received $120 dollars per month in Mississippi, and $680 dollars per month in Connecticut.[6] Welfare recipients also are eligible for food stamps, Medicare, and in some cases, housing subsidies.[7] In their comparative study of welfare-receiving and low-wage working women in four cities (Chicago, Charleston, Boston, and San Antonio), Edin and Lein found that, on average, cash welfare, food stamps, and Social Security Insurance (SSI) covered only about three-fifths of a family's expenses. Women receiving welfare made up the gap between their income from welfare and their living expenses by working in the informal economy and by accepting money from family or friends.[8] Over four-fifths of Edin and Lein's respondents lived below the federal poverty line, which was $11, 521 for a family of three in 1992.[9]

The PRA instructs states to devise welfare programs that will meet the following three goals: (1) provide families with time-limited assistance in order to end their dependency on government benefits and achieve self-sufficiency; (2) prevent and reduce out-of-wedlock pregnancies; and (3) encourage the formation and maintenance of two-parent families. To encourage states to promote marriage and discourage nonmarital birth, the federal government provided 100 million dollars to be divided each year among the five states that have lowered their illegitimacy ratio the most without increasing their abortion rate. The illegitimacy ratio is defined as the number of out-of-wedlock births that occurred in the state divided by the number of births. All births, not just births to women on welfare, are included in calculating the illegitimacy ratio.[10]

The child exclusion policy was a part of the GOP's "Contract with America" and was included in the House's original welfare reform bill, H.R. 4, which was passed overwhelmingly by Congress in 1995.[11] Opposition in the Senate caused the child exclusion policy to be eliminated from the final version of the PRA.[12] However, welfare reform has made it much easier for a state to institute the child exclusion policy. Under AFDC, states that wanted to adopt a family cap were required to obtain a waiver from the Health and Human Services Administration. Waivers are no longer required and twenty-three states have now enacted family cap regulations.[13] This means that the cash benefit women on welfare receive each month is no longer adjusted to reflect how the needs of their families change after they have an additional child. Under AFDC, the cash benefit a welfare recipient received would increase by anywhere from $30 to $100 depending on the state in which she resided.[14]

Conservatives writing in the 1980s popularized the idea that welfare benefits encourage nonmarital birth.[15] However, most scholars have found little or no association between state welfare benefits and births to unmarried mothers.[16] Moreover, during the time period when nonmarital births increased, the value of welfare benefits dropped dramatically. Wilson reports that AFDC payments lost 37 percent of their value between 1975 and 1995.[17] And lastly, given that the average family receiving welfare benefits is no larger than the average family that does not receive welfare benefits, it seems unlikely that welfare beneficiaries view the meager cash benefits provided by the government as an incentive to bear children. Seventy-three percent of families receiving welfare contain two or fewer children.[18]

Most low-income single mothers have a work history and should be considered a part of the working poor. Many tend to cycle from welfare to paid work and back again. Only about 15 percent of women stay on welfare for five years or more; 50 percent exit welfare after just one year and 75 percent are off of welfare after two years.[19] In their study comparing women receiving welfare with women working in the paid labor market, Edin and Lein found that most mothers who receive welfare have a work history and that most mothers who work for low wages have experienced periods of welfare receipt in their recent past. Edin and Lein report that the welfare recipients they studied had on average 5.6 years of work experience before they went on welfare,[20] while 60 percent of the working women that Edin and Lein interviewed had used welfare in the past.[21] The vast majority of women who leave welfare support themselves and their children through employment in the paid labor market. However, the work that poorly educated women find is often unstable, poorly paid, and rarely includes benefits. This means that women are often forced to return to welfare. According to Edin and Lein, the main distinction between women who are able to remain in the paid labor market and women who receive public aid is that the former either have older children than the latter, or they are able to secure low-cost childcare through a family member. Low-income working women who lose their low-cost childcare often have no alternative other than applying for welfare benefits.

Family cap supporters argue that once a woman begins to receive public aid, she should postpone having an additional child until she is sure she can afford it.[22] The problem with this position, as Jencks and Edin argue, is that the earning power of poorly educated women increases only incrementally over time. One study of poorly educated women that Jencks and Edin cite found that "women earned only 25 cents an hour more when they were 29 years old than when they were 21."[23] Wages for women without post-secondary education or training are so low that they cannot look forward to being able to afford to add to their families in the future. Given the lack of well-paid jobs for women and men without at least some college education or post-secondary training, telling welfare recipients to wait to have children until they can afford to is no different than telling them not to have children.

II. RACE, CLASS, MARITAL STATUS AND MOTHERHOOD

In 1970, single women headed 12 percent of all families with children and single men headed 1 percent. By 2000, the comparable percentages had risen to 26 percent and 5 percent.[24] While single parenthood occurs among women of all income groups and of all racial and ethnic groups, low-income families and families of color are more likely to consist of a single parent than middle- and upper-income or white families. Forty-seven percent of children living in low-income families, or families with incomes below 200 percent of the poverty line, live with two parents. In contrast, seventy-five percent of children in families with higher incomes live with two parents.[25] Black children are more likely to live in single-parent families than Hispanic or white children. In 1996, 57.4 percent of black children lived with one parent, 33.4 percent lived with two parents, and 9.3 percent lived in homes with no parent present. Among Hispanic children, 32.4 percent lived with one parent, 62.2 percent lived with two parents, and 5.4 percent lived in a home with no parent present. For white children, these proportions are 22.1, 74.7, and 3.2 percent.[26] In the middle and upper classes, divorce is the primary cause of single parenthood. In low-income communities, childbirth often precedes marriage and in an increasing number of cases, marriage does not occur. Consequently, a significant number of single-mother families are formed through nonmarital birth. According to figures from 1998, 67 percent of births to black women, 38 percent of births to Hispanic women, and 25 percent of births to white women were nonmarital.[27] However, it must be remembered that many unmarried women are cohabiting with a partner at the time of their child's birth, and many of them will marry or maintain their partnership with the child's father. Unmarried childbearing predominantly occurs among younger women. Forty-seven percent of births to women in their early twenties were out-of-wedlock, with the proportion declining to 11 percent for women thirty years and over.[28] Contrary to public opinion, the majority of births to unmarried women are not to teenagers. Over 70 percent of births to unmarried women are to adults. Teen childbearing rates, after reaching a peak in 1991, decreased to a record low by 1999.[29]

Race, class, and marital status have always played a role in how motherhood is perceived and evaluated. In *Killing the Black Body: Race, Reproduction, and the Meaning of Liberty*, Roberts argues that the devaluation of African American motherhood has a long history that includes slavery, racist eugenics doctrines, sterilization abuse, the criminal prosecution of pregnant women who use drugs, the imposition of birth control on women caught up in the criminal justice system, and efforts to control women's fertility through punitive welfare policies such as the family cap. Roberts links the prosecution of pregnant women who have used crack cocaine with the attempts of some judges to make long-acting birth control methods, such as Norplant, a condition of probation.[30] She claims that poor black women are perceived to be unfit mothers, and that their deficient mothering is held to be the cause of crime and drug abuse. According to Roberts, the child exclusion policy is part of a wave of government policies designed to punish poor black women for procreating. Roberts asserts that "modern-day reproductive punishments" are based on the idea that "social problems can be cured by keeping certain people from having babies and that certain groups therefore do not deserve to procreate."[31] Roberts concludes that social policies aimed at low-income mothers and their children have been strongly influenced by racial prejudice. For example, like other authors, Roberts argues that the public's hostility toward welfare is fueled by the perception that black women are its primary beneficiaries.[32]

Roberts is right to attribute the lack of respect accorded to some women's procreative decisions to a long history of distinguishing between good and bad mothers, valuable and expendable children.[33] These distinctions have been and are being made on the basis of race and ethnicity, as well as immigrant and economic status. However, there is an additional factor at play here: marital status. Women who have children and form families without being married to a man are widely understood to have broken an essential cultural code and to have challenged the ideal of the male-headed family. Martha Fineman explains:

> [While] many single mothers in both the divorced and never-married categories are also poor and this contributes to the societal designation of them as 'deviant,' their real offense—the 'true' indicia of their pathology—is their single-

ness. It is this demographic characteristic that embodies the challenge they present to the asserted necessity and inevitability of the heterosexual family in our society.[34]

Single motherhood is a vivid symbol of the decline of male rule. Even more so than divorced or separated mothers, who were once part of male-headed families, nevermarried women represent a rejection of the idea that the most basic form of social organization—the family—is based on a gender-based division of labor, women's economic dependence on men, and the (legal) union of a man and a woman.

Like lesbian mothers, nevermarried mothers have formed families without getting married to a man, and also like lesbian mothers, they generate a great deal of anxiety about the integrity and durability of the male-headed family. In her article "Family's Outlaws," Cheshire Calhoun argues that when the heterosexual nuclear family is perceived to be in crisis, the persecution of lesbians and gay men increases. Anxiety about the instability of the heterosexual family is displaced onto a group that can be "constructed as outsiders to the family."[35] According to Calhoun, this strategy of displacement accomplishes three goals: first, it externalizes the threat to the nuclear family; second, it disciplines rebellious heterosexuals by comparing their behavior to the practices of a group that is subject to social and criminal penalties; third, heterosexuals are better able to accept changes in gender roles and family arrangements if they can point to a group that has deviated even farther from conventional gender and family ideals. Heterosexual families, however transformed, can remain the norm as long as they can differentiate themselves from lesbian and gay families.[36]

Calhoun's assertion that lesbians and gay men are used as scapegoats whenever heterosexual families are perceived to be in crisis helps to explain derogatory images of nevermarried mothers. The anxiety generated by high rates of divorce, single parenthood, and blended families can be displaced onto women who are frequently portrayed to be undeserving of motherhood. Nevermarried mothers are stereotyped as too young, too poor, and as members of an irresponsible, primarily African American and Latino, underclass that relies on public assistance. Because welfare recipients are perceived to be neither white nor middle class, they can be viewed as outsiders and thus the threat to the white middle- and upper-class family can be externalized. Nevermarried mothers, while undeniably mothers, are often understood to be failed mothers by default. Their failure to marry makes them irresponsible mothers who have not taken the proper steps to ensure the well-being of their children. They function both to make divorced mothers more respectable and to remind women contemplating divorce of the penalties attached to mothering without a husband. Like lesbians and gay men, nevermarried mothers are stigmatized through their association with illegitimate sex. While the vast majority of young Americans engage in sex outside of marriage, labels of "promiscuous" or "sexually irresponsible" are reserved for the young black woman who becomes pregnant and has a child without getting married. Discomfort about one's own sexual behavior or that of one's child is eased when such behavior can be projected onto a group that is already viewed as different.

Nevermarried motherhood is a consequence of trends in sexual practice and family life that affect all race/ethnic and income groups. However, because their very existence poses a challenge to the male-headed family and because nevermarried mothers are often poor and disproportionately nonwhite, general anxiety about the stability of the traditional family and gender roles is projected onto them. Like other social policies of the past and present, the child exclusion policy is designed to calm these anxieties by defining one group of women to be unworthy of motherhood. It sends the clear message that some women do not deserve to be mothers because of their race, class, and marital status.

III. WELFARE RECIPIENTS AND THE RIGHT OF PRIVACY

The PRA explicitly promotes marriage. It states that "[m]arriage is the foundation of a successful society," and that "[m]arriage is an essential institution of a successful society which promotes the interests of children."[37] As we have already seen, the second stated purpose of the PRA is to prevent nonmarital birth and the third is to promote two-parent families. With these statements, the PRA promulgates a state-sanctioned view of the value of marriage and the two-parent family. It also announces that the federal government condemns births outside of marriage. The family cap punishes women who deviate from the federal government's understanding of when and under what conditions procreation is permissible.

Supporters of family cap legislation argue that refusing to fund women's procreative decisions is not the same as actively preventing women from having babies. This assertion does not respond to the claim that promoting one form of family over others is not a legitimate government purpose. The government should not attempt to influence a woman's decision to become pregnant or to carry a fetus to term. Many people believe that nonmarital birth is wrong and should not be supported with state funds. However, as I argued in chapter 2, the right of privacy is based on the moral idea that individuals should be able to disregard public opinion and convention when they make decisions that are deeply personal and that have a unique affect on independent identity formation. Supreme Court decisions have already stated that bearing or begetting a child is such a decision.[38]

In chapter 2, I argued that the right of privacy protects the individual's liberty in sexual and intimate relationships. When the state uses its power to influence the form that families take, it deprives its citizens of associational autonomy and denies them the right to form the families of their choice. It makes decisions for its citizens in the area of life that is most closely bound up with our feelings for others and that is most likely to have an enormous impact on our identity. Moreover, it denies us the freedom to decide on the meaning and value of sexuality, procreation, marriage, and parenting for ourselves.

Women should not have to marry in order to have children. Historically, the relationship between husband and wife has had a number of purposes. It has been viewed as a religious duty of the highest order, a method for controlling female sexuality and ensuring the creation of a legitimate male heir, a mechanism for building alliances between powerful families, and as an economic partnership. While it continues to perform important social and economic functions, it is currently understood as an emotional bond, voluntarily chosen on the basis of sexual desire and love. The decision to marry is a deeply personal one. It can affect the whole course of an individual's life and will certainly profoundly affect her daily life as well as her sense of self as long as she remains married. The very nature of the contemporary marital bond, particularly because it is an emotional relationship, suggests that it is not susceptible to coercion or external influence. It is wrong for the state to use its authority to allocate resources to influence the decision to marry.

State promotion of marriage ignores the fact that, in many cases, marriage continues to mandate women's dependence on and subservience to men. Historically, marriage law has given the husband unilateral power over his wife. While this is no longer the case in the United States, factors such as the continuing economic dependence of women on their husbands, religious beliefs and customs, and the gender-based division of labor ensure that most marriages are not equal partnerships. In many cases, marriage automatically confers power on the husband and obligates the wife to perform various services for him. While many single mothers may want to marry "the right man," it is possible that one reason behind some women's unmarried status is the growing discrepancy between how some men and women think about marriage and gender roles.[39] As we saw in chapter 4, some studies indicate that equal earning power is a prerequisite to equal decision-making power among married couples. Most women earn less than their male counterparts. Should women have to accept an unequal relationship with a man in order to have children?

If the decision to marry is a private one, involving tender personal feelings, so too is the decision to have a child and to be a parent. Until recently, sexual activity outside of marriage and nonmarital birth were heavily stigmatized, and in many states, illegal. Women who defied law and custom in most cases faced very severe penalties. In effect, women who wanted to be sexually active or to become mothers were forced to first become wives. The Supreme Court decisions on birth control and abortion undermined the government's authority to impose marriage on all women by decreasing the connection between unmarried sexual activity and pregnancy. But the ability to control fertility through the use of birth control and abortion is only one side of reproductive liberty. Black women, in particular, have long argued that the freedom to have a child is no less important than the freedom to control fertility. From their opposition to sterilization abuse in the 1960s to the present day, women of color have argued that reproductive freedom includes the ability to bear and raise a child. Indeed, both the freedom to control fertility and the freedom to bear and raise a child are included under the right to be self-determining in matters of sexuality and family formation.[40]

The government no more has the authority to use welfare rules to state a preference regarding nonmarital birth than it does to use welfare rules to state a preference regarding the importance of religious practice. Imagine the uproar that would be provoked if state governments announced that they would not increase the monthly cash benefit of welfare recipients who had an additional child while on welfare, unless the mother agreed to take her children to weekly religious services. The state could justify this policy by arguing that the children of welfare recipients are more likely to engage in crime or to become pregnant out-of-wedlock than the children of working families, and that additional measures must be taken to ensure proper moral conduct on their part. Such a policy would be rejected as an illegitimate constraint on religious freedom even though it does not force women to practice a religion but only penalizes them for refusing to do so. The freedom of religion is so deeply ingrained in our legal system and public culture that any effort on the part of government to influence religious belief is automatically assumed to be illegitimate. Government policies aimed at preventing nonmarital births are not immediately rejected because liberty in sexual and intimate relationships is not as securely established as the freedom of religion.

The citizens of the United States have different opinions on the benefits of marriage, the meaning and purpose of sexual intimacy, and the best way to raise children. When the state uses welfare reform to promote marriage, it discriminates against those citizens who believe that bearing and rearing children does not require marriage. The Supreme Court has ruled that parents have a constitutional right to raise their children in accordance with their own beliefs and values.[41] It also has held that children born out-of-wedlock should not be treated differently than children born to married women.[42] Nevermarried women who give birth to and raise children are expressing a belief about the legitimacy of parenthood and child rearing outside of marriage. The child exclusion policy penalizes women for not conforming to state supported beliefs regarding parenting and child rearing.

The right of privacy, properly understood, protects both reproductive freedom and the freedom of intimate association. Family cap legislation violates reproductive freedom by attempting to influence the decision to become pregnant and give birth. By clearly indicating its preference for marriage, the PRA threatens the procreative and associational autonomy of women who receive welfare. It stigmatizes women on welfare by declaring that their unmarried state makes them irresponsible reproducers and bad mothers. Moreover, it fails to respect their freedom to determine for themselves the meaning and value of marriage. Indeed, it actively insults them for daring to depart from state-approved ideas about the importance of marriage. The family cap reinforces the message that unmarried women do not deserve to be mothers by refusing to augment their resources when they have an additional child.

In the next section I turn to the public/private dilemma outlined in the introduction. It can be argued that the public is under no obligation to pay for the consequences of women's private procreative decisions. I argue that low-income single women are entitled to both public support and personal liberty.

IV. REEXAMINING THE PUBLIC/PRIVATE DILEMMA

All societies allocate duties among their major social institutions, including the family, the nonprofit sector, the market, and the state. While it is common to think of the functions performed by the family as unchanging or timeless, the distribution of duties between the family and state has changed over time according to the outcomes of political debates. Minow explains that our understanding of what family members owe each other is dependent on what we think the state owes its citizens. She claims that "despite a legal and cultural tradition distinguishing sharply between public and private realms, public and private duties end up tied together and mutually defining, as people actually struggle to address the needs of members of families."[43] Contests over where to draw public/private boundaries are fierce because they determine who will bear certain burdens or how these burdens will be shared. Moreover, altering public/private boundaries often involves the reallocation of resources and power. Martha Ackelsburg and Mary Lyndon Shanley assert that public/private boundaries are often renegotiated and that "[w]hen the issue of where to draw the line between public and private arises in legal and public policy debates, the deployment and configuration of political, economic, and social power is at stake."[44] The establishment of Social Security during the New Deal is a good example of how changing the relationship between government and citizens alters what family members owe each other. Before the creation of Social Security, retired persons who were not able to provide for their old age were expected to rely on their adult children. This federal program effectively shifted some of the responsibility for caring for the elderly from the private to the public.

Recent federal welfare reform reflects a particular understanding of the distribution of public and private duties and it therefore institutionalizes a particular allocation of power and resources. The key assumption behind welfare reform is that caring for dependents is a private responsibility that families should be able to accomplish on their own. Going back to the ancient Greek philosopher Aristotle, the household has been defined as a self-sufficient, productive unit that aims at supplying the daily material needs of its members. It is within families that dependents—the young, the old, the sick, and disabled—are cared for. This key assumption has almost never been entirely true. In modern societies, a variety of institutions and policies from public schools to tax deductible home mortgages support the caring work of families.[45] Nonetheless, the belief that families should be able to "take care of their own" is widely held. It is assumed that families, when properly configured, are self-sufficient in the sense that they do not require state aid. This assumption engenders the belief that single mothers' need for public support is illegitimate.

The Privatization of Poverty

The PRA asserts that poverty is caused by single parenthood and, like the family communitarians, proposes to reduce poverty by fostering marriage. Women's poverty is defined by the PRA as a consequence of refusing to conform to the nuclear family model. It is therefore described as a private problem that demands a private solution. Instead of designing public policies that would address why many single mothers are unable to support their families through work, welfare reform focuses on decisions that women make about their intimate lives. In the words of Joel Handler and Yeheskel Hasenfeld, welfare reform "is concerned with 'reformation' rather than redistribution."[46]

Mother-only families are frequently poor. In 1999, 60 percent of Latina, 55 percent of black, and 40 percent of white single-mother families lived in poverty.[47] However, it is misleading to assert that family structure is the *cause* of poverty.[48] Unemployment, involuntary part-time employment, and low wages in conjunction with racial and gender discrimination are the true causes of poverty. Many men and women who have only a high school degree or have not completed high school, particularly blacks and Latinos living in racially segregated, low-income neighborhoods, face great difficulty finding jobs that will lift them out of poverty. Even when the national unemployment rate dips below 4 percent, the unemployment rate in poor, racially segregated communities can remain as high as 15 percent.[49] Unemployment among blacks has historically been twice as high as unemployment among whites, and studies continue to document that employers routinely discriminate against African Americans.[50] In addition, those low-skilled workers who do find work are often not able to earn a living wage. According to Handler and Hasenfeld, 18 percent of full-time workers earned less than the poverty line in 1992.[51] In their study of 165 mothers who held low-wage jobs, Edin and Lein compared earnings with expenditures and found that jobs that pay less than seven dollars per hour typically cover only two-thirds of a mother's expenses.[52] Single mothers are poor primarily because the U.S. economy does not provide enough well-paying jobs with benefits for people who lack skills and education. In addition, women continue to face employment discrimination and to earn less than men do because of sex-based segregation in the labor market.[53] And, as I discuss in the next section, women are disadvantaged in the labor market because child rearing is assumed to be a woman's responsibility.

When failure to marry is said to be the cause of poverty, the fact that single mothers who enjoy real educational and economic opportunities are able to earn a living that supports their families is ignored. Single mothers who have a college degree, technical training, or a unionized job are capable of earning a family income. Women who work in male-dominated fields also are likely to earn a living wage. As we have seen, the PRA identifies marriage and the two-parent family as the only solution to women and children's poverty. However, the best way to respond to the poverty of single-parent families is to call for reforms that encourage unionization, raise the minimum wage, mandate equal pay for equal worth, expand the earned income tax credit, and increase educational and training opportunities for women in male-dominated occupations.[54] These economic reforms would lift the majority of single-parent families out of poverty without violating women's right of privacy.[55]

Blaming poverty on the failure to marry allows lawmakers to ignore their responsibility to provide all individuals, male and female, with the opportunity to work at a job that covers basic living expenses. In essence, policies that target how individuals conduct their intimate relationships are being used to replace economic policies aimed at full employment at an adequate wage for women and men. Focusing on individual behavior, in this case the failure to marry, shifts attention away from the dismal job prospects of low-skilled men and women living in poor neighborhoods. It places all of the responsibility for caring for dependents on low-income women without acknowledging the structural barriers to economic security that they face.

Liberals often respond to the assertion that marriage is the solution to poverty by asserting that there are simply not enough men with steady employment in very poor communities to supply every woman who wants to have children with a husband. While there is ample evidence of an imbalance in the sex ratio between men and women in poor African American communities, this is an incomplete response to the assertion that marriage is the best solution to poverty. It leaves open the possibility that if there were enough gainfully employed males to go around, it would be acceptable to pressure women into marrying. The conventional liberal response does not take a sufficiently strong stand in favor of the freedom of intimate association and women's procreative autonomy. Nor does it point out that marriage continues to condemn many women to economic dependence and domestic servitude. Advocates for low-income women and children should argue against economic policies that rely on a male wage earner to keep children out of poverty. Our economic and social arrangements should *not* presume that all women have or should have husbands.

Maintaining a full-employment economy and making sure that full-time work allows families, including single-parent families, to escape poverty is a public responsibility. If working men and women cannot earn enough money to support themselves and their children, policymakers must reform the low-wage labor market, and provide jobs and income supports to low-wage workers. Higher rates of marriage will not address the primary cause of poverty. Only the state and federal governments can intervene in the market and ensure that workers are paid a living wage. Shifting what is currently considered a private responsibility away from the family and toward the state would mean obligating policymakers to face up to the gap between what low-wage jobs pay, and what families, including those headed by single mothers, must earn to live decently.[56]

Real efforts to reduce poverty cannot occur unless public/private boundaries are redrawn. As long as it remains possible to blame poverty on the personal decisions that men and women make about their intimate lives, the economic and social reforms necessary to improving women's ability to earn a living wage will not be instituted. Given the proper economic conditions and social supports, single mothers are capable of supporting their children; the fact that so many single mothers cannot signals a failure—not on their part, but on the part of U.S. democracy.

The Privatization of Dependency Work

Contemporary feminist theorists have struggled both to make visible and dignify what they call dependency work or caretaking. These terms refer to the physical and emotional work necessary for caring for someone who is temporarily or permanently dependent. All societies must devote resources to dependency work, and further, establish social and economic arrangements that support caretaking. Historically, women have performed the bulk of dependency work in the privacy of the home. Low-income men and women, many of whom are from racially and ethnically disadvantaged groups, also have performed a disproportionate amount of dependency work in the homes of well-off people and in public and private institutions.[57]

Feminist theorists argue that arbitrarily assigning the vast majority of all caretaking, including the raising of children, on the basis of gender places an enormous burden on women.[58] As we have seen, mothers are now combining caretaking with providing. However, studies reviewed in chapter 4 show that most men have not substantially increased the amount of time they devote to caretaking. Women who work in the paid labor force, full- or part-time, and who do most of the housework and childcare at home, are doing far more than their fair share of work. Equally important, women's caretaking responsibilities limit the amount of time they can devote to education or paid work and reduce their lifetime earnings and savings. Single mothers often bear the costs of childcare and all of the other costs associated with raising children on their own. Women's caretaking responsibilities lead to gender-based inequities in the workplace and in politics and contribute to the low pay and economic insecurity of single women.

The unfair and inequitable allocation of dependency work has yet to be recognized as a pressing social issue that must be addressed.[59] Caring for loved ones is not thought of as work because it is not done for pay and takes place in the home. The assumption that it is women, and not men, who are best suited to meet the physical and emotional needs of dependents is one of the founding premises of our gender-based society. As Susan Moller Okin and Kittay have both argued, most discussions of justice ignore the question of caretaking.[60] According to Kittay, "the equitable distribution of dependency work, both among genders and among classes, has rarely been considered in the discussions of political and social justice which take as their starting point the public lives of men."[61] In addition, caretaking is widely perceived to be the responsibility of the private and ideally self-sufficient family. Fineman argues that conceiving of the family as self-sufficient makes the needs of the dependency worker invisible, and that the hidden nature of dependency work has especially harmful consequences for single mothers.[62]

According to Fineman and Kittay, dependency work has the inevitable effect of making the dependency worker dependent on others. It is difficult to give full-time care while simultaneously working full-time for pay. As Fineman puts it, "The very process of assuming caretaking responsibilities creates dependency in the caretaker—she needs some social structure to provide the means to care for others."[63] Currently, the husband-as-provider is the only widely accepted and *legitimate* support system available to the dependency worker. Women in two-parent families who perform dependency work full-time are sometimes permanently and often temporarily dependent on their husbands; they either take time off from paid work, do not work outside the home, or work outside of the home part-time. However, a wife's economic dependence on her husband is not seen as dependence by the larger society. It is seen, instead, as part of the "natural" order of the family. A woman with children who is economically dependent on her husband is praised for sacrificing her career interests and economic independence for the sake of her family. In contrast, low-income single women with children who turn to the government for support are chastised for their dependence on public assistance. Fineman explains that when measured against the nuclear family norm, low-income, single-mother families are viewed as inadequate because they lack self-sufficiency. But this assessment, Fineman insists, is hypocritical at best. Married women's dependence on their husbands is expected and approved of. Why, then, are single mothers criticized for lacking self-sufficiency? Why isn't it understood that they, too, need a support system if they are going to care for their children?

When single women with children are not able to provide care and provision simultaneously, they are often perceived to be at fault. Indeed, as we have seen, they are pressured to find a husband or to forgo having additional children. However, marriage is not an adequate solution to the gender-based distribution of caretaking responsibilities. As I have explained, it requires too high a cost to personal liberty. The proper solution is to reorganize our basic institutions so that the costs of caretaking are redistributed. As Kittay puts it, "For a society to be characterized by care, we need something other than the affirmation of the importance of family integrity. We need structures that will assure that dependency work, whether done in families or other social institutions, can be carried out under non-exploitative conditions."[64] Dependency work is necessary to the reproduction of human society and should not be viewed as an entirely private responsibility. As Kittay points out, all individuals are dependent at one or more points in their lives. We therefore all have a responsibility to contribute in one way or another to caring for dependents. Additionally, our society will lack future citizens and workers if children are not cared for and socialized. The establishment of public schools for children and Medicare and Social Security for the elderly shows that the public is willing to socialize some forms of dependency work. It is time to relieve women of some of the costs of raising children. Establishing high quality, affordable childcare, paid parental leave, and reducing the employment hours of parents of infants would effectively redistribute some of the costs associated with raising children from the private to the public sphere. Working and middle-class two-parent families would benefit from these reforms as well as single mothers. In those cases in which single women are unable to find work, or in which they have a health problem or a disability or their child has a health problem or a disability, mothers should receive a guaranteed income to support their caretaking.[65]

Supporters of the child exclusion policy argue that if the decision to have a child is private, then the repercussions of this decision should not fall on all citizens. If women want the freedom to make up their own minds regarding whether they should have a child, those who choose to have a child must accept full responsibility for rearing it. Taxpayers, they argue, should not have to pay for the misguided or irresponsible procreative decisions of individual women. At first glance, this position appears to make sense. But placing procreative decisions in a broader social and economic context undermines this commonsense conclusion. First, as we have already seen, the realities of the low-wage labor market make it impossible for low-skilled single women to raise a family without external assistance. It is the duty of policymakers to ensure that full-time, year-round work pays a living wage. Reforming the low-wage labor market and making income supports, health care, and housing and childcare subsidies available to those who earn low wages is necessary to fulfilling the quintessential American ideal of equal opportunity. Second, dependency work, including caring for and raising children, is essential to a well-ordered society. Today's children are tomorrow's taxpayers, workers, and citizens. Women, married and unmarried, currently do far more than their fair share of dependency work. One way to redistribute some of the burdens associated with dependency work is to provide women with a public alternative to the provider-husband. When child rearing is seen as socially necessary work, it becomes clear that the public bears some of the responsibility for the cost of raising the next generation of citizens.

CONCLUSION

I have argued in this chapter that the state should not use its distributive power to influence procreative or associational choices. The citizens of the United States hold differing views on sexuality, marriage, and parenting. Neither state nor federal government should have the authority to decide for its citizens that one model of family is preferable to all others. Intimate relationships, including the relationship between mother and child, are our greatest source of comfort and love. It is through our relationships with others that we form personal identities, gain a sense of personal worth, and develop the sustaining emotional ties that reinforce our sense of self. The state should not have the authority to influence decisions as deeply personal as the choice to have a child. The family cap policy violates the right of privacy and should be abolished.

Another, more subtle, way that our society violates the right of privacy, or a woman's freedom to decide whether she will marry, is by organizing its economic and social arrangements as if the provider-husband were the only possible support structure for dependency workers. Public policies implicitly support and privilege marriage by *not* providing dependency workers with an alternative to it. Government policy is perfectly capable of replacing the provider-husband with affordable childcare, paid parental leave, flexible work schedules, and reduced hours in the paid workplace for those who care for infants. Low-income single mothers and their children face severe material hardship because of our national commitment to marriage. If the right of privacy were understood properly and fully recognized, external preferences, like the belief that child rearing must take place within marriage, would not be allowed to interfere with the making of public policy. Moreover, if we fully appreciated the importance of dependency work, we would be compelled to acknowledge that supporting low-income single women is a public responsibility.

In this chapter, I introduced the feminist claim that the costs of caretaking need to be redistributed. In the final chapter of this book, I examine debates between feminists regarding how best to accomplish this goal. Some feminist authors argue for a postgender or egalitarian family model that requires men and women to share breadwinning and caretaking responsibilities. Other feminists believe that rearing children always will be women's role, and that the best way to compensate mothers for taking on this responsibility is to provide them with a guaranteed income. These opposing feminist family models are analyzed in chapter 6.

NOTES

1. P.L. 104-193, [H.R. 3734] Title I, Section 101, August 22, 1996.
2. NOW Legal Defense and Education Fund, "Update on Recent Child Exclusion Developments," *Welfare and Poverty*, 2000. http://www.nowldef.org/html./issues/wel/chexdv.htm (accessed 16 January 2002).
3. Joel J. Handler and Yeheskel Hasenfeld, *We the Poor People: Work, Poverty, and Welfare* (New Haven: Yale University Press, 1997), 45.

4. Prior to the Welfare Rights Movement in the 1960s and 1970s, states invented many ways to restrict welfare payments to "deserving" families. These restrictions were aimed at black women, particularly those who had their children without getting married. See Rickie Solinger, *Wake Up Little Suzie: Single Pregnancy and Race Before Roe v. Wade* (New York: Routledge, 1992).

5. On the recent history of welfare reform and current eligibility requirements see Charles Noble, *Welfare As We Knew It: A Political History of the American Welfare State* (New York: Oxford, 1997); Gwendolyn Mink, *Welfare's End*, (Ithaca, N.Y.: Cornell University Press, 1998); and Handler and Hasenfeld, *We the Poor People.*

6. Kathyrn Edin and Laura Lein, *Making Ends Meet: How Single Mothers Survive Welfare and Low-Wage Work* (New York: Russell Sage Foundation, 1997), 35.

7. According to Wilson, in 1992 only 23 percent of welfare beneficiaries received some form of housing subsidy or lived in public housing. See William Julius Wilson, *When Work Disappears: The World of the New Urban Poor* (New York: Vintage Books, 1996), 166.

8. Edin and Lein, *Making Ends Meet*, 43.

9. Edin and Lein, *Making Ends Meet*, 47.

10. In 1999 and again in 2000, the Department of Health and Human Services distributed $100 million to those states with the lowest nonmarital birth rates. In 2000, four states (Alabama, Arizona, Illinois, and Michigan) and the District of Columbia each received $20 million. See Tamar Lewin, "Cut Down on Out-of-Wedlock Births, Win Cash," *New York Times* 24 September 2000; and Patricia Donovan, "The 'Illegitimacy Bonus' and State Efforts to Reduce Out-of-Wedlock Birth," *Family Planning Perspectives* 31, no.2 (March/April 1999): 94–7.

11. Noble, *Welfare As We Knew It*, 128.

12. Elizabeth Shogren, "Senate, House on Own Paths in Welfare Debate," *Los Angeles Times*, 16 September 1995, A4.

13. New Jersey was the first state to institute the child exclusion policy under a waiver obtained from the Department of Health and Human Services in 1992. On September 5, 1997, NOW Legal Defense and Education Fund, the ACLU of New Jersey, and the law firm of Gibbons, Del Deo, Dolan, Griffinger, and Vecchione filed a suit in New Jersey State Court challenging the constitutionality of the child exclusion provision. The case alleges that the child exclusion provision violates both the right of privacy and the equal protection clauses of New Jersey's Constitution (*Sojourner A. v. New Jersey Department of Human Services*, 1997). The case was dismissed in August 2000. The plaintiffs may appeal. For more information, see NOW Legal Defense and Education Fund, "Background on Child Exclusion Proposals," *Welfare and Poverty*, 2000. http://www.nowldef.org/html/issues/wel/childep.shtml (accessed 16 January 2002).

14. NOW Legal Defense and Education Fund, "Background on Child Exclusion Proposals."

15. Charles Murray, *Losing Ground: American Social Policy, 1950–1980* (New York: Basic Books, 1984).

16. William Julius Wilson, *The Transformation of Work* (Chicago: University of Chicago Press, 1987), 77–81.

17. Wilson, *When Work Disappears*, 165.

18. Handler and Hasenfeld, *We the Poor People*, 45.

19. Handler and Hasenfeld, *We the Poor People*, 46.

20. Edin and Lein, *Making Ends Meet*, 63.

21. Edin and Lein, *Making Ends Meet*, 221.

22. Wayne R. Byrant, "The Art of Welfare Reform," *New Jersey Reporter* 25, no. 4 (November/December 1995): 46–47; NOW Legal Defense and Education Fund, "Update on Recent Child Exclusion Developments."

23. Christopher Jencks and Kathryn Edin, "Do Poor Women Have the Right to Bear Children?" *The American Prospect* 20 (Winter 1995): 43–52.

24. Bureau of the Census, *America's Families and Living Arrangements: Population Characteristics, 2000, P20-537*, U.S. Department of Commerce, Economics and Statistics Administration (Washington, D.C., June 2001).

25. Sharon Vandivere, Kristin Anderson Moore, and Martha Zaslow, "Children's Family Environment: Findings from the National Survey of America's Families," *Snapshots of America's Families II, 1999* (Washington, D.C.: Urban Institute, 2000). http://newfederalism.urban.org/nsaf/family-environ.html (accessed 28 January 2002).

26. Bureau of the Census, *Marital Status and Living Arrangements: March 1996, P20-496*, U.S. Department of Commerce, Economics and Statistics Administration (Washington, D.C., 1998).

27. Bureau of the Census, *Fertility of American Women: June 1998, P20-526*, U.S. Department of Commerce, Economics and Statistics Administration. (Washington, D.C., 1998).

28. Bureau of the Census, *Fertility of American Women: June 1998, P20-526*.

29. Richard Wertheimer, Justin Jager, and Kristin Anderson Moore, "State Policy Initiatives for Reducing Teen and Adult Nonmarital Childbearing: Family Planning to Family Caps," *New Federalism: Issues and Options for States*, Series A, no. A-43 (Washington, D.C.: Urban Institute, 2000). http://newfederalism.urban.org (accessed 3 January 2000).

30. On the criminal prosecution of pregnant women for drug use see also Lynn M. Paltrow, "Punishment and Prejudice: Judging Drug-Using Pregnant Women," in *Mother Troubles: Rethinking Contemporary Maternal Dilemmas*, ed. Julia E. Hanigsberg and Sara Ruddick (Boston: Beacon, 1999). The Supreme Court ruled on March 21, 2001, that involuntary testing of pregnant women for drug use is unconstitutional. See Linda Greenhouse, "Justices, 6-3, Bar Some Drug Tests," *New York Times*, 22 March 2001, A1.

31. Dorothy Roberts, *Killing the Black Body: Race, Reproduction, and the Meaning of Liberty*. (New York: Pantheon Books, 1997), 200.

32. On racial prejudice and welfare policy, see Wilson, *When Work Disappears*; Solinger, *Wake Up Little Suzie*; Jill Quadagno, *The Color of Welfare* (New York: Oxford Press, 1994); and Mink, *Welfare's End*.

33. Rickie Solinger chronicles the vastly different treatment black and white pregnant teenagers received from the 1940s through the 1960s. Solinger documents the efforts of politicians to punish young, black women for procreating. She also shows that the recent family cap policy has its antecedents in state laws passed in the 1950s and

1960s that denied welfare benefits to women who had a child out-of-wedlock while they were on welfare. These laws passed in states that had large populations of low-income black residents. See Solinger, *Wake Up Little Suzie*, especially chapter 6. On prejudice directed at black women who receive welfare, see also Wahneema Lubiano, "Black Ladies, Welfare Queens, and State Minstrels: Ideological War by Narrative Means," in *Race-ing Justice, En-gendering Power: Essays on Anita Hill, Clarence Thomas, and the Construction of Social Reality*, ed. Toni Morrison (New York: Pantheon, 1992).

34. Martha Fineman, *The Neutered Mother, The Sexual Family and Other Twentieth Century Tragedies* (New York: Routledge, 1995), 101–102.

35. Cheshire Calhoun, "Family Outlaws: Rethinking the Connections between Feminism, Lesbianism, and the Family," in *Feminism and Families*, ed. Hilde Lindeman Nelson (New York: Routledge, 1997), 131–50.

36. Calhoun, "Family Outlaws," 138.

37. 1996 Personal Responsibility and Work Opportunity Act [H.R. 3734], P.L. 104-193, Title I, Section 1, August 22, 1996.

38. *Eisenstadt v. Baird*, 405 U.S. 438 (1972).

39. Frank F. Furstenberg Jr., "Divorce and the American Family," *Annual Review of Sociology* 16, 1990: 379–403.

40. Roberts, *Killing the Black Body,* 294–312.

41. *Meyer v. Nebraska*, 262 U.S. 390 (1923); and *Pierce v. Society of Sisters*, 268 U.S. 510 (1925).

42. *Gomez v. Perez*, 409 U.S. 535 (1973); and *Mills v. Habluetzel*, 456 U.S. 91 (1982).

43. Martha Minow, "All in the Family and In all Families: Membership, Owing, and Loving," in *Sex, Preference, and Family: Essays on Law and Nature*, ed. David M. Estlund and Martha C. Nussbaum (New York: Oxford University Press, 1997), 249–76.

44. Martha Ackelsburg and Mary Shanley, "Privacy, Publicity and Power: A Feminist Rethinking of the Public-Private Distinction" in *Revisioning the Political: Feminist Reconstructions of Traditional Concepts in Western Political Thought*, ed. Nancy J. Hirshmann and Christine Di Stefano (Boulder, Colo.: Westview Press. 1996), 213–34.

45. On the many ways that traditional families have depended on public support see Stephanie Coontz, *The Way We Never Were: American Families and the Nostalgia Trap* (New York: Basic Books, 1992), 68–92.

46. Handler and Hasenfeld, *We the Poor People*, 10.

47. Child Trends, "Poverty, Welfare and Children," *Research Brief* (Washington, D.C.: Child Trends, 1999). http://www.childtrends.org (accessed 3 January 2000).

48. Andrew J. Cherlin, *Marriage, Divorce, Remarriage* (Cambridge, Mass.: Harvard University Press, 1992), 114.

49. In 1999, when the national unemployment rate was around 4 percent, the unemployment rate for Ocean-Hill Brownsville, an African American community in East Brooklyn, was 15.9 percent. This information was obtained by the author from the New York State Department of Labor on September 7, 2000. The figures are on file with the author.

50. Thomas J. Sugrue, "Poor Families in an Era of Urban Transformation: The 'Underclass' Family in Myth and Reality," in *American families: A Multicultural Reader*, ed. Stephanie Coontz with Maya Parson and Gabrielle Raley (New York: Routledge, 1999).

51. Handler and Hasenfeld, *We the Poor People*, 41.

52. Edin and Lein, *Making Ends Meet*, 90.

53. Daphne Spain and Suzanne M. Bianchi, *Balancing Act: Motherhood, Marriage and Employment Among American Women* (New York: Russell Sage Foundation, 1996), 107–40.

54. Heidi Hartmann and Roberta Spalter-Roth, *The Labor Market, The Working Poor, and Welfare Reform: Policy Suggestions for the Clinton Administration* (Washington, D.C.: Institute for Women's Policy Research, 1992).

55. Roberta M. Spalter-Roth, Heidi I. Hartmann, and Linda M. Andrews, "Mothers, Children, and Low-Wage Work: The Ability to Earn a Family Wage," in *Sociology and the Public Agenda*, ed. William Julius Wilson (London: Sage, 1993), 316–38.

56. I provide a more detailed account of what economic and social policies are needed to improve the economic security of single mothers and their children in chapter 6.

57. Eva Feder Kittay, "Taking Dependency Seriously: The Family and Medical Leave Act," *Hypatia: A Journal of Feminist Philosophy* 10, no. 1 (1995): 8–30; Fineman, *The Neutered Mother*.

58. Arlie Hochschild with Anne Machung, *The Second Shift* (New York: Avon, 1989); and Susan Moller Okin, *Justice, Gender, and the Family* (New York: Basic Books, 1989).

59. Fortunately, two new books on this topic, aimed at a general audience, have been recently published: Mona Harrington, *Care and Equality: Inventing a New Family Politics* (New York: Knopf, 1999), and Ann Crittenden, *The Price of Motherhood* (New York: Metropolitan Books, 2001).

60. Okin, *Justice, Gender and the Family*; Kittay, "Taking Dependency Seriously."

61. Kittay, "Taking Dependency Seriously," 9.

62. Fineman, *The Neutered Mother*.

63. Fineman, *The Neutered Mother*, 163.

64. Kittay, "Taking Dependency Seriously," 24.

65. Feminist scholars such as Fineman and Mink argue that all mothers should receive public funding that would allow them to stay home and care for their children. I respond to this argument and provide a more detailed program for supporting low-income single mothers in chapter 6.

Chapter Six

Feminist Family Policies: A Comparison of the Egalitarian and Caregiver Models

Since the early days of the Women's Liberation Movement, feminists have argued for an egalitarian model of family in which wife and husband share the duties of breadwinning and caretaking equally. Susan Moller Okin, a well-known advocate of the egalitarian model and the author of *Justice, Gender and the Family*, argues that the elimination of the gender-based division of labor in the family is essential to the realization of gender justice for two reasons.[1] First, if women and men were both equally devoted to paid work, women would no longer be economically dependent on men. Men would no longer be the only or the main providers of household income. Consequently, they would no longer be able to claim the title of head of the household. Second, the reallocation of caretaking from women to men would eliminate one of the chief barriers to equal employment opportunity for women. The unpaid work that women have traditionally performed in the home—caring for children, the elderly, the sick, and disabled—has limited their ability to work full-time for pay or to pursue education or training. If men took up their fair share of caretaking *and* if childcare were affordable, high quality, and readily available, women would have more time to work for pay or invest in their careers. In addition, if a marriage ended in divorce, women would be better prepared to support themselves and their children. The egalitarian model has been embraced by many feminists because it reallocates some of the burdens of childcare and housework from women to men, eliminates those aspects of traditional marriage that have given men power over women, and decreases barriers to women's full participation in the economy, civil society, and politics.

While the egalitarian model is attractive to many women (and men) committed to gender equality, it is not without its feminist critics. Legal theorist Martha Fineman has developed a critical, and yet clearly feminist, analysis of the egalitarian model in her book *The Neutered Mother, The Sexual Family and Other Twentieth Century Tragedies*.[2] According to Fineman, the egalitarian model has three interrelated flaws. First and foremost, the egalitarian model fails to address the needs of single mothers, especially poor mothers without education or job skills. Requiring men to do their fair share of caretaking will not help women who parent on their own. Second, the egalitarian model gives priority to working for pay and thus underestimates the importance of both caretaking and caretakers. Because it is based on the assumption that women can raise children and provide for a family at the same time, the egalitarian model suggests that caretaking is not demanding, time-consuming work. Third, the egalitarian model perpetuates the popular idea that caring for family members is a private responsibility and should not be subsidized by the state.

Fineman seeks to replace what she sees as the failed egalitarian model with her own caregiver model. The caregiver model accepts the current gender-based division of labor and seeks to raise the status of caretaking and caretakers. Fineman proposes to do this by abolishing marriage as a legal institution and redefining the family so that its core unit is the mother and child. According to Fineman, it is the mother and child, not the sexual couple, that law and policy should privilege and protect. Currently, Fineman argues, the sexual couple (husband and wife) is seen as the core family unit. Families without fathers are perceived to be incomplete and inadequate. This allows politicians and policymakers to blame nonmarital birth for child poverty. Instead of providing needed public support for single mothers and their children, policymakers fashion laws designed to encourage marriage and discourage nonmarital birth. Fineman argues that as long as the provider-husband is perceived to be the only legitimate form of support for caretakers, single motherhood will be stigmatized and the needs of single mothers will be ignored. Eliminating the husband-as-provider role and turning all mothers into single mothers will compel the general public to acknowledge that caretakers cannot reasonably be asked to both provide for and care for their children.

In this chapter, I compare Okin's and Fineman's family models. My analysis will highlight three questions that feminists concerned with family policy must address. First, should feminist family policy strive to eliminate gender differences, or should it aim at elevating the status of what is currently gender-specific work? Will a feminist family policy that seeks to eliminate gender differences inevitably lead to the devaluation of caretaking and caretakers? Second, how can the needs of single mothers best be addressed? Should all mothers receive a guaranteed income that will allow them to care for their children in their own homes, or should mothers be expected to work as long as they are provided with childcare, income supports, and subsidies? And third, what role should marriage and men have in feminist family policy? Is the elimination of marriage as a legal institution the only way to decrease the stigma experienced by single mothers? Should feminists encourage men to be caretakers, or should we acknowledge that most men would never be involved in the direct care of children? In sections 1 and 2, I present brief summaries of, respectively, Okin's and Fineman's family policies. In section 3, I analyze how these two authors respond to the questions listed above, and provide my own views on how these questions can best be addressed.

I. OKIN'S EGALITARIAN MODEL

In *Justice, Gender, and the Family*, Okin argues that the distribution of unpaid labor within the two-parent family is unequal, unfair, and arbitrary. Okin argues that "the heavy weight of tradition" and "the effects of socialization" maintain a division of labor in the home based on gender. She defines gender as "the deeply entrenched institutionalization of sexual difference."[3] According to Okin, the gender-structured family is the greatest obstacle to equal opportunity for women in the public world of politics, civil society, and work. As a consequence of the gender-based division of labor in the home, women have less access to paid labor, education and leisure, decision-making power, and physical safety, than men. Because they are primarily responsible for the daily care of infants and small children, women devote more time than their husbands to unpaid labor, and less time than their husbands to paid work, training, or education. This, in turn, means that women are less able to invest in their jobs and careers than men are. Consequently, even though women have decreased their economic dependence on men in recent years by working in the paid labor force, wives are more likely than husbands to work part-time or to leave the labor market for lengthy periods of time. Women's childcare responsibilities, in combination with employment discrimination based on gender and gender-segregated labor markets, help to explain why wives usually make less money than their husbands.

Okin claims that men's greater earning capacity, in combination with traditional notions of male leadership in the home, creates power differentials between husbands and wives. In addition, because their caretaking duties make wives financially dependent on their husbands, women often have more to lose if a marriage dissolves than men do. As a result, women who fear the economic insecurity that often affects women and their children after a divorce are likely to submit to the wishes of their husbands. In some cases, women's economic dependence on men may heavily influence their decision to stay with a husband or boyfriend who is abusing them physically or emotionally.

In sum, the gender-based division of labor does not simply give men and women different tasks to perform. It gives men more decision-making power within the home and more opportunities for earning and self-development outside of the home. It contributes to the poverty that divorced mothers and their children experience because women who lead gender-based lives are not prepared to support a household on their own earnings when their marriage ends. In addition to exposing children to economic insecurity if the marriage of their parents dissolves, gender-structured marriages teach boys and girls to take up gender-specific roles when they begin their own families. The socialization they receive in the gender-structured family prepares girls to be caretakers and boys to be providers. Consequently, young women fail to prepare themselves for well-paying careers.

Okin's solution to the inequalities generated by the gender-structured family is to eliminate the gender-based division of labor in the home. If men and women share child rearing and housework equally, the organization of labor in the home will be just and women will enjoy greater opportunities in the public world of paid work and politics. If men and women share the tasks of breadwinning and child rearing equally, women will not be dependent on men and husbands will no longer hold power over their wives. If a marriage ends, Okin claims that men who have been as involved in the daily care of their children as their wives will be less likely to drop out of their children's lives, as often happens following a divorce today. Divorced and separated women who have shared breadwinning responsibilities with their husbands will be better prepared to earn a good living.

Okin's ultimate goal is a gender-free society. She defines such a society as one in which "no assumptions would be made about 'male' and female' roles, and men and women would participate in more or less equal numbers in every sphere of life, from infant care to different kinds of paid work to high-level politics."[4] Okin recognizes that distributing child rearing and housework equally between men and women will require large changes in all major social institutions, including workplaces and schools. Employers and schools will no longer be able to maintain policies that are based on the assumption that all employees have a stay-at-home wife. Policies including a shorter work week, flex-time, job sharing, extended and paid parental leave, and more on-site childcare centers are necessary if all men and women with children are to combine working in the paid labor force with parenting. Schools must adjust to the fact that there is no one to pick the children up at two or three in the afternoon or to stay home with children during the summer and winter vacations. In short, major social institutions must be organized as if all citizens have parenting responsibilities. Perhaps the single most important condition that must be met in order to achieve Okin's genderless society is the creation of federally regulated and subsidized childcare centers. However, Okin's plan clearly does not call for the reallocation of all caring work to the public sphere. Instead, Okin envisions a society in which husband and wife alternate taking time off from work when their children are very young, or in which each parent works a shortened work week thus ensuring that one parent is always at home with his or her children. As children grow older, many parents will choose to use childcare centers so that they can spend more time doing paid work.

II. FINEMAN'S CAREGIVER MODEL

The foundation of Fineman's argument in *The Neutered Mother, The Sexual Family and Other Twentieth Century Tragedies* is that despite feminist hopes and dreams, the family remains our most gender-based institution and women remain our society's caretakers. Feminist-inspired policies that ignore this fact can often harm mothers, particularly single mothers. While Fineman's criticisms are not directed specifically at Okin, her target is the egalitarian model of family that Okin advocates. Writing about feminist efforts to reform family law, Fineman argues that "equality as an overarching goal continues to have severe limitations, both practical and theoretical—particularly in the context of the family. Feminist legal reformers naively assumed that sharing could and would happen."[5] Fineman claims that changes in custody law sought by liberal feminist lawyers have placed mothers at a disadvantage in the divorce process. Up until recently, mothers had an advantage in custody disputes because the "tender years" doctrine, on which judges based their custody decisions, held that young children needed to be with their mothers. Liberal feminist lawyers, intent on abolishing gender bias in the law, have led and won a fight for gender-neutral family law. Unfortunately, Fineman explains, creating laws based on the idea that either mother or father could be the primary parent does not change the fact that it is women who care for and nurture children. Eliminating the original preference for mothers in divorce cases has lead to joint custody and has given men additional leverage in the division of common property. Fineman objects to joint custody because she believes that in most cases it gives fathers rights without giving them responsibilities, while giving mothers both rights and responsibilities. Fineman also argues that with the elimination of maternal preference, husbands are able to use the threat of a custody battle to get their wives to agree to unfair property settlements.

According to Fineman, as long as parenting remains a deeply gender-based practice, creating gender-neutral laws will harm women who have devoted themselves to caretaking. Feminist lawyers, Fineman contends, are committed to gender-neutral language because of its symbolic importance. They lobby for gender-neutral language out of the belief that it will prepare the way for our gradual transformation into a society that ascribes little importance to sex. But according to Fineman, the use of gender-neutral language undermines respect for caretaking by erasing the unequal investment that men and women currently make in caring for children. When our language assumes that there are no significant differences between men and women as parents, we make the emotional, intellectual, and physical energy necessary to caring for children disappear. This, in turn, allows for a change in how custody decisions are made. While at one time the mother's role as primary parent determined the outcome of custody decisions, the application of gender-neutral language to family law has paved the way for other considerations, such as which parent can best financially support the child, to take precedence.

Fineman's most serious criticism of the egalitarian model is that it perpetuates essential elements of "the natural family." Fineman employs the term "natural family" to capture two assumptions that she claims govern how a wide variety of academic, religious, scientific, and policy-making discourses conceptualize the family. These two assumptions are that the sexual couple, or husband and wife, form the "basic core of family life," and that the family is solely responsible for caring for its dependent members.[6] According to Fineman, instead of challenging these assumptions, the egalitarian model reinforces them. She states that to "a large extent, the new visions of the family merely reformulate basic assumptions about the nature of sexual intimacy . . . retaining the centrality of sexual affiliation to the organization and understanding of intimacy."[7] While acknowledging that feminists concentrate on the heterosexual two-parent family because of their legitimate concern with gender inequality, Fineman claims that by placing the husband and wife at the center of its theorizing about family, feminists unwittingly contribute to the marginalization of single mothers. Fineman argues that as long as the sexual affiliation of husband and wife is taken to be definitive of the family, single-mother families will be perceived as deviant. The stigma attached to the divorced or unmarried mother, but especially the latter, make punitive welfare policies popular with politicians and the public.

The egalitarian model also perpetuates the assumption that the private family is solely responsible for the care of dependent family members. Fineman explains that the "ideal of the natural family—the unit to which responsibility for inevitable dependency is referred—establishes a relationship between 'public' state and 'private' family. Dependency is allocated away from the state to the private grouping."[8] As we saw in chapter 5, Fineman argues that caring for a dependent causes inevitable and derivative dependency on the part of the caretaker. Those who care for others require a social support system that will allow them to devote their time and energy to caretaking. The only social structure that currently exists to support the caretaker is the traditional marriage in which the wife/mother cares for children and other dependent family members, and the husband/father provides for the material needs of wife and children. Thus, the traditional family solves the problem of dependency by requiring men to specialize in breadwinning and women to specialize in caretaking.

Fineman argues that the natural family in either its traditional or egalitarian forms can no longer provide an adequate solution to the inevitable and derivative dependency of the caretaker. The traditional family cannot be considered an adequate solution because it requires women to be dependent on men and violates the principle of gender equality. However, according to Fineman, attempts to reform the traditional family are doomed to failure. This is primarily because men and employers will resist the shift to a shared parenting-shared breadwinning model of family. As a result, less time and energy will be devoted to caring for children in the home. Indeed, the egalitarian model does not face up to the fact that parents are forced to compete with nonparents in the marketplace. This places additional pressure on parents to spend less time at home and more time at work. According to Fineman, the egalitarian model simply does not accord sufficient value to unpaid caretaking. It may bring women into the paid workforce, but it does little to make up for the time they once spent in the home. Fineman fears that the two-parent family will become an institution with "potentially No available caretakers."[9] She concludes that "the private-natural family is no longer viable as the sole, or even primary, institutional response to dependency."[10] As Fineman sees it, the egalitarian model converts all caretakers into workers, but does not convert all workers into caretakers.

Fineman's greatest concern is that the egalitarian model does no better than the traditional model when it comes to supporting single low-income mothers. As dependency workers, single mothers require a viable support system. They need external support if they are to continue to care for dependents. However, if the providing-husband is the only legitimate form of social support recognized by the greater society, women without husbands will be left in a state of perpetual crisis. The power of the natural family as a norm, combined with the refusal to recognize caretaking as time-consuming and energy-draining work, de-legitimizes the needs of the single mother trying to care for her children. While the egalitarian model attempts to reallocate caring work between men and women, it does not do enough, according to Fineman, to re-allocate caring work between the family and the state. Consequently, it offers little help to women who do not have husbands.

Fineman rightly points out that although single mothers are often in dire need of material support, they also suffer from the lack of respect shown to them by both the greater society and the social service bureaucracy on which they are often dependent. Single mothers are often assumed to be bad mothers simply because of their unmarried or divorced status. Politicians, policy-makers, and social service administrators use the stigma attached to single motherhood to justify the regulation of poor women's mothering. One of the most important goals of Fineman's family model is to decrease the stigma attached to single motherhood and to increase the control that single mothers have over the social conditions of mothering.

In sum, Fineman criticizes the egalitarian model because it does not address the needs of single mothers, it does not accord sufficient respect to care-taking, and it does not do enough to challenge traditional boundaries between private and public. The expectation that women will transfer 50 percent of their child rearing responsibilities to men will not help single mothers who do not have a partner with which to share caretaking. The expectation that married and unmarried women will become breadwinners fails to recognize the important contribution that caretaking makes to a well-ordered society. Failing to redefine child rearing as a public responsibility leaves single women without social support.

Fineman's original and provocative solution to the economic vulnerability of single mothers and the devaluation of caretaking is to redefine the family's core unit. Fineman proposes that marriage should be abolished and that the mother-child relationship should take its place as the core family unit. According to Fineman, sexual affiliation "would be governed by the same rules that regulate other interactions in society—specifically those of contract and property, as well as tort and criminal law."[11] Couples could use privately negotiated contracts similar to antenuptual agreements to regulate their relationships. Ending marriage as a legal relationship would eliminate its privileged status as the only legitimate and state sanctioned form of sexual affiliation. All sexual relationships would be rendered equal with each other, and most important to Fineman, all intimate relationships would be rendered equal to the sexual relationship. What Fineman hopes to accomplish by deregulating marriage is to transform our definition of family in such a way that single motherhood is no longer perceived to be deviant.

By ending marriage as a legal concept, Fineman proposes to displace the only support system that currently meets the needs of the dependency worker—the provider-husband. If all women were to become, in effect, single mothers, the public would recognize its obligation to pay for the caretaking work that women have historically performed within the private family. According to Fineman, we would then "become a society that recognized and accepted the inevitability of dependency. We would face, value, and therefore subsidize, caretaking and caretakers."[12] What Fineman calls "the caregiving family" would be "entitled to special, preferred treatment by the state."[13] However, it would not be subject, as it is now, to public regulation. Public support for "the caregiving family" would not come with strings attached. Fineman suggests that if marriage as a legal concept were eliminated, and if the value of caretaking were elevated, mothers would be accorded greater respect and enjoy greater independence. Historically, Fineman argues, motherhood always has been situated within the patriarchal family, under the supervision of men. In addition to raising the social value of caretaking, Fineman's proposals also aim at giving mothers greater independence from individual patriarchs and a patriarchal social service bureaucracy.

III. A COMPARATIVE ANALYSIS
OF FEMINIST FAMILY POLICIES

The accounts that I have provided of the egalitarian and the caregiver models demonstrate that while Okin and Fineman believe that current social arrangements exploit and disadvantage women, they disagree on which reforms will improve women's situation. Okin's chief goal is gender equality, and she argues that the only way it can be achieved is through the elimination of the gender-based division of labor in the home. Fineman's chief goal is increasing the respect accorded to caretakers. She believes that a policy of gender neutrality such as Okin advocates is bound to decrease the value of caretaking. Therefore these two authors disagree on whether the exploitation of women can best be rectified by affirming or undermining gender differences. Because they do not agree on what the greatest barrier to bettering women's situation is, Okin and Fineman focus on different forms of family. Okin is primarily concerned with ending the power imbalance between men and women and consequently, her analysis targets the two-parent family. Fineman, in contrast, is more concerned with the poverty and powerlessness of single mothers, and she criticizes the egalitarian model for ignoring their needs. As we have seen, in order to provide single mothers with an alternative means of support, Fineman argues for socializing the costs associated with child rearing, thereby radically redefining public and private responsibilities. Okin also seeks to socialize some of the costs associated with child rearing, but she does not call for quite as thoroughgoing a change as does Fineman. Okin and

Fineman also disagree on the role that men and marriage should play in family life. While Okin affirms egalitarian marriages and exhorts men to take on more responsibility for the direct care of their children, Fineman seeks to abolish marriage and defines the mother and child as the core family unit.

I have organized my comparative analysis of the egalitarian and caregiver models into three interrelated sections: (1) Gender Differences and the Social Value of Caretaking, (2) Meeting the Needs of Single Mothers, and (3) Men and Marriage.

Gender Differences and the Social Value of Caretaking

As we have seen, Okin and Fineman differ on the question of whether feminists should work for a world without rigid gender distinctions, or for one in which the gender-specialized work performed by men and women receives equal value. Okin envisions a gender-free society in which "most men would be—and would be expected to be—as capable of nurturance as most women."[14] In contrast, Fineman's policy is built on the assumption that women will continue to be our society's caretakers.

The question of whether feminist family policy should reinforce or undermine gender differences is directly tied to the question of how best to establish the social worth of caretaking. Nancy Fraser has argued that caretaking is most valued when it is conceptualized as a gender-neutral activity, that men and women, parents and nonparents have an obligation to perform.[15] According to Fraser, exempting men from caretaking conveys the idea that it is not really important or valuable work. However, Fineman argues that family policies that focus on fostering gender equality between men and women place too much emphasis on paid work. The egalitarian model requires women to give up full-time caretaking and to work part- or full-time in the paid labor market. These policies may increase women's economic independence, but they also function to raise the status of paid work and to lower the value of unpaid caretaking.

In examining the relationship between gender differences and the social value of caretaking, it is helpful to refer to Fraser's typology of three feminist family models in her essay, "After the Family Wage: A Postindustrial Thought Experiment": (1) universal caregiver, (2) universal breadwinner, and (3) caregiver parity. According to Fraser, the universal breadwinner model aims at fostering gender equality by integrating women into the paid labor market and by shifting as much caretaking as possible out of the home and into the marketplace. Fraser warns that providing affordable and universal access to childcare allows women to work outside of the home, but does not necessarily increase men's involvement in caretaking. Neither does the caregiver parity model, which provides women with a child allowance or guaranteed income that covers their family's basic needs so that they can stay at home and care for their children. Like Fineman's model, caregiver parity reinforces the gender-based division of caretaking, while allocating part of the financial burden associated with raising children to the public sphere. Fraser claims that only universal caregiver, a version of Okin's egalitarian model, can foster gender equality and raise the status of caretaking.

Fraser shares Fineman's fear that feminist family policies that focus solely on turning women into workers will lead to the devaluation of caretaking. Fraser explains that universal breadwinner "valorizes men's traditional sphere—employment—and simply tries to help women fit in. Traditionally female caretaking, in contrast, is treated instrumentally; it is what must be sloughed off in order to become a breadwinner. It is not itself accorded social value."[16] Fraser explains that the universal breadwinner model leads both to "workerism," or the elevation of paid work over caretaking, and "androcentrism," or the elevation of the work traditionally performed by men over the work traditionally performed by women.

Unlike Okin, Fineman is not anxious to send women out into the paid workforce. Instead, Fineman claims that what women need most is greater freedom to determine how and under what conditions they will mother and greater public support so that their economic needs are met while they care for their children. Given men's and employers' successful resistance to the reallocation of caretaking, Okin's model is more likely to turn women into full-time workers than it is to turn men into part-time caregivers. Thus, according to Fineman, there is no difference *in practice* between universal breadwinner and Okin's egalitarian model. If women as well as men are expected to do paid work, caretaking will not be seen as full-time, demanding work. The workerism and androcentrism inherent to the egalitarian model will ultimately require both two-parent and single-parent families to cut back on time spent caring for children and other dependents.

If Fineman's analysis is accepted, the feminist goals of elevating the status of caretaking and of integrating women into the paid labor market appear to conflict. If caretaking is as valuable and important as feminists like Fineman say it is, feminists like Okin should not push for all women to devote themselves to jobs and careers. However, it is not the case that Okin values caretaking less than paid work. Instead, feminists like Okin and Fraser embrace a different strategy for elevating caretaking's value. Like Fraser, Okin argues that caring for dependents must be seen as a universal responsibility. Valuing caretaking, Fraser explains, means requiring that everyone take part in it. Fraser and Okin both argue that all careers and forms of employment must be structured as if *all* employees were parents. This means that everyone would be on the "mommy track" and that parents as well as nonparents would spend less time at work and more time caring for dependent members of their community. Fraser even suggests that nonparents would be expected to devote some of their free time to caring for others by volunteering at community childcare centers or elder care centers. In this sense, Fraser's policies go further than Okin's do in redistributing caretaking. Fraser argues that all people, men and women, parents and nonparents, should be direct providers of care. Her model requires that capacities long associated with women—the ability to nurture and comfort and the ability to comprehend and respond to another's needs, for example—be distributed as widely as possible.

It is true that unless adequate attention is paid to the structure of paid work, Okin's egalitarian model could begin to look like Fraser's account of the universal breadwinner model. The egalitarian model cannot succeed unless a radical transformation of the workplace, based on a widely held and deeply felt appreciation of family life and caretaking, is accomplished. A society in which all parents work forty hours or more per week throughout their children's infancy is not an attractive one. However, this is not what the egalitarian model envisions. Instead, as Fraser explains, the egalitarian model calls for women's current life pattern, a pattern that combines work and caretaking, to become the norm. The universalization of caretaking would ensure respect for caretakers and social recognition of caretaking.

One of the chief drawbacks of building a family policy on gender differences, as Fineman's model does, is that it is likely to leave political decision-making overwhelmingly in the hands of men. This could undermine one of Fineman's most important goals, which is to increase mothers' control over the social conditions of caretaking. According to Fineman's model, caretaking remains women's work, but the poverty that so often accompanies single parenthood will no longer exist. Mothers will be provided with generous subsidies so that they can care for their children at home. Given the value ascribed to caretaking in Fineman's ideal society, we might expect to see professional caretakers—including daycare workers, nurses, and primary school teachers—better compensated than they are now. However, most of the people holding these positions will be women. Consequently, while poverty among single women and their children will have been eliminated, the gender-based division of labor will have been left intact. As Fraser argues in her discussion of the caregiver parity model, increasing the value of caretaking will not empower women politically. Even if women are better compensated for their private and public caretaking, political and economic positions attached to high levels of status and power are unlikely to be held by women. These positions are currently organized so as to exclude persons who plan on devoting a significant amount of time to caretaking. As a result, the people who exercise power and who make decisions that affect caretakers and the social conditions of caretaking will continue to be men without extensive childcare experience. Furthermore, the gender-based division of labor always has been associated with a gender-based division of capacities and behaviors. If it continues to be assumed that women are inherently nurturing and caring, it is equally likely that men will continue to be seen as inherently decisive and authoritative. Fineman's policy would leave intact a division of labor and a division of capacities that has prevented women from holding positions of authority. In contrast, since all work in Okin's gender-free society would be organized to accommodate parents, people with significant caretaking responsibilities would be able to hold positions of power. Consequently, in many cases the people making decisions that would directly affect the social conditions of caretaking would be caretakers themselves. In addition, while laws and regulations cannot restructure behaviors and capacities as easily as they can restructure the workplace, if men are involved in caretaking and women are involved in making political decisions, the association between women and nurturing, and men and decisiveness, will gradually erode. Over time, we will come to realize that there is nothing inherently feminine about feeding a baby, nor is there anything essentially masculine about exercising public authority.

Fineman's model is appealing in part because she demands that all mothers receive the respect they deserve and that their hard work as caretakers be recognized. She forces her readers to confront the fact that many, if not most, women continue to live highly gender-based lives and that women remain society's caretakers. However, it is equally true that many, if not most women have benefited in a variety of ways from a decreased emphasis on traditional gender norms. Women still do most of the dependency work in our society, but the new economic opportunities opened up to women in the last thirty years have improved the lives of many women. While it is important to give women credit for all of the caretaking they have done and continue to do, it is dangerous to envision a future where women, and women alone, are assumed to have the capacities necessary to caring for dependent others. The egalitarian model is preferable to the caregiver model because it conceives of caretaking as gender-neutral work and requires men and the workplace to change.

Meeting the Needs of Single Mothers

One of Fineman's chief objections to the egalitarian model is that it does not fully address the needs of single mothers. While Okin's call for subsidized childcare, universal health care, government-backed child support, generous parental leave, and flexible work schedules will clearly be of great help to single mothers, Fineman is right to argue that the egalitarian model does not provide a comprehensive solution to the economic vulnerability of women who do not have access to a male wage. In contrast to Okin, Fineman does provide a plan that could, if it was enacted, eliminate single women's economic insecurity. However, Fineman's policy undermines an important feminist principle and should not be supported for that reason. Okin's family model can be made to meet the needs of single mothers if it is integrated into a strong antipoverty policy.

As we have seen, Fineman argues that the best way to address the needs of single mothers is to provide them with public support so that they are not compelled to be both providers and caretakers. Reallocating some of the costs of raising children to the general public is also a way of recognizing single mothers' work as caretakers. While Fineman fails to specify the exact form that this public support would take, it appears that she has something like a guaranteed income in mind. Such a policy has been proposed in *An Immodest Proposal: Rewarding Women's Work to End Poverty*, a document written and distributed by a group of feminist scholars and activists, the Women's Committee of 100/Project 2002 (WC100), who seek to reform the current welfare system.[17] The WC100 share Fineman's commitment to recognizing the value of caretaking. An examination of their proposal will allow me to show why I do not think that providing all mothers or all single mothers with a guaranteed income is the best way to respond to their needs.

The WC100 describe themselves as a group of scholars and activists "who are concerned with the relationship between women, economic survival and the work of caregiving."[18] They do not adopt Fineman's call for the deinstitutionalization of marriage, but they echo her assertion that caregivers make an essential contribution to society and that they should be rewarded for their work. The WC100 proposes a universal caregiver's allowance that would go to all primary caregivers, with payments varying according to total household income. Their proposal aims to both eliminate women's poverty by providing all primary caregivers with a guaranteed income and to recognize the contribution that caregivers make to society. The universal caregiver's allowance would function like Social Security benefits for surviving parents and minor children. It would provide a regular, automatic, and guaranteed income for caregivers and their children, and would not allow for government intrusion into the personal lives of beneficiaries.

The proposal offered by the WC100 is attractive because it combines recognition for caregiving with an antipoverty program for single mothers. Moreover, as its supporters emphasize, the universal caregiver's allowance gives women the choice of working outside the home and using the allowance to pay for high-quality childcare, or staying home to raise their children and using the allowance to pay their bills. Thus, it does not rule out women's participation in the paid workforce, but it does give low-income women the opportunity to stay at home with their children either part-time or full-time. Because it empowers women to make their own choices, recognizes the value of caregiving, and addresses the needs of single mothers, the universal caregiver's allowance appears to be the ideal solution to the unjust distribution of dependency work and the economic need of many single mothers. However, despite its many attractive features, I will argue that it is difficult to defend a guaranteed income for mothers while at the same time supporting the feminist principle that working for pay is compatible with good parenting. I will illustrate this difficulty by examining Gwendolyn Mink's defense of a guaranteed income for single mothers in *Welfare's End*.[19]

According to Mink, the unjust and gender-based distribution of caretaking often leads to one of two undesirable outcomes: dependence on men for married women or poverty for single women. Mink asserts that both dependence and poverty are barriers to full and equal citizenship. She argues that the only way to enable women to be equal citizens is to provide public funding for primary caretakers.[20] Welfare, she asserts, should be reconceived "as the income owed to persons who work inside the home caring for, nurturing, and protecting children."[21] Mink criticizes the 1996 federal welfare reform for undermining both women's rights (especially women's reproductive rights and their right to family privacy) and gender equality. She recommends that TANF be replaced with a guaranteed income for single mothers.

Mink argues that it is wrong to compel welfare beneficiaries to work outside of the home. Married women, Mink argues, have the option of staying at home; it is therefore unfair to expect single women to place their children in day care and to seek work in the paid labor market. As part of her defense of the right of welfare beneficiaries and other single mothers to raise their children at home, Mink attempts to derail the popular argument that since most married mothers work outside of the home, women receiving welfare benefits must work too. Mink claims that most married mothers only work part-time and that few, if any, "sacrifice care-giving to wage-earning, as their labor force patterns seem to accommodate family needs; and one-third of married women with children under six do not participate in the labor force at all."[22] While Mink admits that some married mothers do work year-round and full-time outside of the home, her argumentative strategy relies on diminishing married mothers' participation in the labor force. Mink accuses the American public of taking a hypocritical stance toward welfare beneficiaries. She states that Americans expect married mothers to stay at home with their children, while at the same time supporting welfare policies requiring single mothers to work outside of the home. Mink argues that if the public believes that children benefit when their mothers do not work outside of the home, then they must find a way to provide single mothers with the material means to forego paid work. Anything less indicates a profound disrespect for poor children and their mothers.

Mink is undoubtedly right that many Americans support work requirements for welfare beneficiaries because they want to punish unmarried women for having sex and having babies. She is also right to argue, as do I in chapter 5, that attitudes toward welfare beneficiaries are strongly influenced by racial prejudice. However, she is wrong to downplay married mothers' commitment to the paid labor force. Recent figures show that 77 percent of married women with children between the ages of six and seventeen work part- or full-time in the labor market, while 81.2 percent of single women with children between the ages of six and seventeen do. This is a difference of four percentage points.[23] However, it is the case that separated, divorced, or widowed women are more likely to work full-time (50.2 percent) than married women (39.3 percent). This is a difference of eleven percentage points. Nevermarried mothers are least likely to work full-time (24.2 percent). Educational achievement appears to have a strong impact on whether and to what extent mothers participate in the labor force. Mothers with only a high school education are less likely to work full-time than those with one or more years of college.[24]

These figures demonstrate that the labor force participation of married mothers and single mothers is similar. They do not support Mink's assertion that it is normative for married mothers to care for their children in their homes. Instead, they support the very different idea that a majority of married mothers and single mothers are combining caregiving with wage work. While many Americans are still uncomfortable with mothers working outside the home, the vast majority accepts mothers' labor force participation as inevitable. Some regret that mothers work outside the home but concede that most households require two wage-earners. Others believe that becoming a mother should not force women to give up their careers or their economic independence. Despite remaining ambivalence, fewer and fewer Americans are strongly opposed to the participation of mothers in the labor market. Gaining public support for a family policy that would provide low-income mothers with a guaranteed income would be very difficult given the widespread expectation that mothers, married or single, will work outside of the home.

Mink's argument in *Welfare's End* illustrates how support for a caregiver's allowance or a guaranteed income can end up undermining the idea that women can be both providers and caretakers. Diminishing married mothers' participation in the paid market is a bad move because it encourages the idea that providing and caretaking are incompatible. By claiming that married mothers *are not* combining caretaking and providing, and that single women *should not have to* combine caretaking and providing, Mink encourages the idea that mothers *should not* combine caretaking and providing. This position flies in the face of years and years of feminist agitation. Feminists have long pointed to statistics that show mothers' increased labor force participation as proof that good mothering is compatible with working outside the home. Moreover, Mink comes perilously close to asserting that women who work outside the home are not able to provide their children with the best care. In defending welfare beneficiaries' right to stay home with their children, Mink argues that working outside the home undermines the ability of mothers to care for and nurture their children. She asserts that work requirements create "significant barriers to care-giving by single mothers for their own children." Mink explains that the key barrier is time, and that single mothers' loss of time with their children "directly injures children's welfare."[25] It is a short distance from Mink's assertion that work requirements harm children to the conservative argument that mothers should not work outside the home. Mink's real interest lies in meeting the needs of low-income single mothers and their children, but the argument she adopts states that paid work is incompatible with good mothering.

When social support for mothers takes the form of a guaranteed income, as it does for the WC100, Mink, and Fineman, it runs counter to the emphasis that most feminists have placed on paid work as the foundation of women's economic independence and gender equality. Since the late sixties, feminists have endeavored to persuade the public that mothers have a right to engage in paid work and that those who receive good childcare and other forms of support are quite capable of combining work and caretaking. In their effort to defend low-income women's caretaking, Fineman and Mink call into question the desirability of combining work and caretaking and undermine the importance of women's participation in the paid labor market.

It will be difficult for feminists to simultaneously push for an agenda that calls for subsidized, high-quality childcare, reduced work hours for parents with infants, and paid parental leave, while at the same time advocating a guaranteed income for all mothers who wish to stay at home and raise their children themselves. These two policies are based on two different images of motherhood. The latter is based on the desirability of mothers withdrawing from the paid labor market. It suggests that full-time mothering is best for children. The former is based on the idea that motherhood is compatible with paid work. It says that mothers with the proper supports can be workers, too. Thus, feminists who want to support both childcare and the universal caregiver's allowance are caught in a paradox. Should they argue for the desirability of stay at home mothering, or should they assert that motherhood is compatible with wage work? We have already seen that Mink, who believes that mothers should be able to work outside the home if they so choose, was forced to argue that wage work is incompatible with providing the best care for children in order to defend a guaranteed income for single mothers. Thus, advocating for the universal caregiver's allowance can lead even feminists to base their argument on a conservative image of motherhood.

There is a second drawback to using some version of the universal caregiver's allowance to respond to the economic needs of single mothers. Women, particularly single women, who opt to stay at home for long periods of time, increase their vulnerability to poverty. Few women now spend their entire adult lives raising children. Women who have children in their late teens and early twenties will have completed their child raising by their early forties. Having spent a significant period of time outside of the labor force, these women will not have the kind of skills, work experience, or work record that will allow them to earn a livable wage. What will happen to these women once they are no longer eligible for the universal caregiver's allowance? Fineman's response to this question is to adopt a proposal advanced by Richard T. Gill and T. Brandon Gill.[26] According to Gill and Gill, parents who leave the labor market for long periods of time to care for their children at home should be rewarded with public funds that they could use toward education or professional training. The idea behind the Parental Bill of Rights is that it would encourage parents to provide care in the home and would protect parents from costs associated with leaving the labor market. While the Parental Bill of Rights is an innovative way to reward caretaking, it is not clear that it would actually achieve its goal. Earning power is not simply a function of training and education. It is also a consequence of on-the-job experience and uninterrupted participation in the labor force. Additional years of education do not provide potential employees with management or supervisory experience, nor does it establish a stable work record. The value of Social Security benefits and pensions are also determined by years of labor force participation. Providing parents returning to the work force with education and training will give them an advantage in the labor market that they otherwise would not have had, but it cannot compensate for their lack of a work history. Parents who choose to leave the work force for long periods of time will still be disadvantaged when they return to paid work. In addition, as Barbara Bergmann points out, family policies that allow women who want to stay home to do so affect women who would like to work in the paid labor market. She claims that "all women workers have better job opportunities when the custom is for most new mothers to return to work very soon after the birth of a child."[27] Bergmann explains that women's economic opportunities will shrink if employers expect them to leave the labor market to care for their children. Historically, employers have discriminated against women because they believed it was likely that they would quit their jobs to bear and rear children. While this practice has abated in recent years, a policy that encouraged women to leave the workforce for long periods of time could revive it.

The final problem with the universal caregiver's allowance is that it is built on an inadequate conception of single mothers' poverty. Fineman claims that the poverty experienced by many single mothers stems from the lack of social value accorded to caretaking and the widespread assumption that rearing children is a private function. Single women who are caring for dependents, Fineman argues, are not in a position to provide for themselves and their families. They experience material hardship because they are compelled to be full-time caretakers and full-time providers. Single mothers are poor because the only legitimate support system available to mothers in the United States is the provider-husband. Therefore, as we have seen, Fineman's solution to single mothers' poverty is to replace the provider-husband with public funds.

The problem with Fineman's analysis is that the lack of a provider-husband is not the only, or even the primary, cause of single mothers' poverty. It does not fully account for the poverty of single mothers who grow up in poor neighborhoods and who have little schooling or skills. Their poverty, like the poverty of their peers without children, is due to the lack of jobs for low-skilled workers (especially women workers) that pay a decent wage and include benefits. While the disproportionate amount of caretaking performed by women clearly disadvantages them in the paid labor market, caretaking itself is not the primary cause of single mothers' poverty. Skilled and well-educated single mothers are capable of providing for their families if they are able to secure reliable childcare. The single most important cause of poverty is the paucity of good jobs for women who lack skills and education.[28] Consequently, any family policy aimed at meeting the needs of single women and their children must focus on reforming the low-wage labor market and increasing the education and skill level of women who grow up in poverty. The women Fineman and Mink want to protect are those who are least likely to possess what economists like to call human capital. Removing low-skilled women from the work force is not the solution to their poverty; improving their ability to earn a good wage is.

Many scholars argue that the best way to address the needs of single mothers is to increase their earning power. Roberta M. Spalter-Roth, Heidi I. Hartmann, and Linda M. Andrews of the Institute for Women's Policy Research argue that lack of human capital is one of the primary causes of single mothers' low wages. They claim that the key to improving low-skilled women's earning potential is to increase their training and educational opportunities.[29]

It is especially important to train women for higher wage fields that traditionally have been closed to women. Many of the jobs that men without a college degree currently hold provide good wages, but women are seldom encouraged to pursue these occupations. Spalter-Roth, Hartmann, and Andrews also argue that race and immigrant status have a large impact on earnings. White women consistently average higher wages than black and Latino women, and are more likely to be found in the more stable and better paying kinds of jobs such as clerical and administrative employment. Thus, increasing all women's wages means eliminating race-based wage inequities through pay equity policies, and the stronger enforcement of existing equal employment opportunity laws. The Institute for Women's Policy Research reports that encouraging collective bargaining can have an important influence on the ability of women to earn a wage that will support their families: unionized women earn an average of $2.50 more per hour than non-unionized women.[30] Raising the minimum wage also would strengthen the earning power of low-wage women workers. In addition, part-time and temporary work needs to be regulated to include benefits and the same hourly wages as full-time jobs.[31]

Given the lack of well-paying jobs for persons with low educational attainment, it is inevitable that even if training for nontraditional jobs and unionization is increased, many women will not be able to earn a wage that will keep them out of poverty. Even when they work full-time and year-round, women employed at low-wage jobs such as cashiers, nursing aids, factory workers, domestic servants, and food service workers are unlikely to earn enough to avoid material hardship. They will be trapped in jobs with no benefits and little opportunity for advancement. Several scholars have proposed plans to supplement the incomes of low-wage workers.[32] They have called for an expansion of the earned income tax credit, expanded unemployment insurance, and in the event of high unemployment, the creation of public jobs. According to the Institute for Women's Policy Research, under current eligibility requirements, many low-income women do not qualify for unemployment insurance. This is because single mothers often work at jobs that are part-time, or because their childcare duties make it difficult to hold the same job continuously. The Institute for Women's Policy Research argues that unemployment insurance must be reformed so that it can accommodate the employment patterns of low-skilled workers who are caring for young children.[33] Workers, both male and female, in the low-wage labor market will also require food stamps and housing subsidies. The lack of affordable housing is a serious problem in both urban and rural areas.[34] While these programs would not be targeted specifically at single mothers, supplementing wages and providing subsidies to low-income working people would have tremendous benefits for single mothers. These programs add a strong antipoverty program to Okin's proposals for subsidized child-care, universal health care, flexible work schedules, parental leave, and government-backed child support.

I would add three recommendations to the policies described above. First, following Kittay, I propose an expansion of the Family and Medical Leave Act.[35] Currently, family members are allowed to take six weeks of unpaid leave for the birth or adoption of a child or to care for an ill family member. Unpaid leave is of little use to single mothers who have no spouse on whom to rely. The Family and Medical Leave Act should be expanded so that it provides parents and caretakers with at least twelve weeks of paid leave. Two-parent families should be able to take twelve weeks of paid leave if (and only if) each parent agrees to take a six-week leave. Single mothers should be entitled to twelve weeks of paid parental leave. In large firms, the cost of this leave program should be paid for by employers; it is likely that the government will have to fund paid parental leave in smaller private firms. In addition, each partner in a two-parent family should be able to decrease his or her paid working hours by five hours per week during the first two years of his or her child's life. A single mother should be able to decrease her work week by ten hours. Single mothers (or two-parent families) earning below 200 percent of the poverty line would receive a child allowance or a tax credit that would cover their lost wages.

Second, more attention must be paid to the fact that a significant number of low-income single mothers (and non-custodial fathers) have problems, such as chronic illnesses, psychiatric disorders, alcohol and drug addiction, and post-traumatic stress disorder, which will prevent them from working in the paid labor market, at least temporarily.[36] These mothers (and fathers) will need more than income supports and subsidies, and may not be in a position to care for their children while holding down a job. Women who suffer from an addiction or from a mental or physical disability or illness, or are caring for a child with a mental or physical disability or illness, should receive a guaranteed income that will allow them to live above the poverty line and to care for their children at home.

Third, one of the greatest threats to low-income mothers' ability to care for their children stems from the deterioration of the communities in which they live. Low-income mothers are not able to secure adequate housing or good schools for their children. They are not able to provide their children with clean, attractive, and safe places to play. One of the best ways to support the caretaking work of low-income mothers would be to invest in their communities by removing or renovating abandoned housing, building new housing and attractive parks and playgrounds, restoring schools and hiring more teachers, and investing in community-based businesses. Investing in the infrastructure of poor communities also means providing needed social services such as health care (especially prenatal care) and mental health and substance abuse treatment clinics. One of the most effective ways to increase single mothers' control over the social conditions of mothering is to improve the communities in which they care for their children.

Fully addressing the needs of single mothers clearly means going beyond Okin's call for childcare, parental leave, government-backed child support, and flexible work schedules. Taken on their own, these policies will meet the needs of married couples and single professional mothers. Okin's proposals will provide important help to single mothers, but will not increase the low earning potential of women who have grown up in impoverished communities. Fully addressing the needs of single mothers requires situating childcare and family friendly work policies within a broader antipoverty policy. The problems that low-income mothers face are influenced, but not solely determined, by their gender or their status as caretakers. Low-income single mothers don't just need husbands or an alternative to husbands. Like their childless peers, they need economic reforms that will make work pay and they need opportunities to improve their earning potential. While it is true that antipoverty policies must always keep gender differences in mind, it is equally true that family policies must always be coupled with strong antipoverty policies.

In contrast to Fineman's caregiver model, the revised version of Okin's egalitarian model that I have recommended—let's give it the inelegant title of the antipoverty/egalitarian model—would compel low-income, single mothers to be both providers and caretakers. It would not give low-income, single mothers the opportunity to choose between caring for their children within their homes and placing them in childcare and seeking paid work. Staying home with your children full-time for more than twelve weeks would be a luxury that only a minority of well-off, two-parent families could afford. Feminists such as Fineman and Mink would undoubtedly argue that the revised policy, like the original egalitarian model, fails to fully recognize the social value of caretaking. And, they might add that the antipoverty/egalitarian family model capitulates to a male-centered value system that places too much emphasis on independence and self-sufficiency, and denies the inevitability of dependence. Using Fraser's language, the antipoverty/egalitarian family policy could be accused of both workerism and androcentrism. These are serious objections, but the policy I am recommending can be defended against them.

The antipoverty/egalitarian family policy recognizes the value of caretaking in several ways. First, it provides single mothers with paid parental leave and reduced work hours in the first two years of a child's life. Second, it aims at giving low-income mothers greater control over the social conditions of caretaking by investing in their communities. Third, the antipoverty/egalitarian family policy supports caretaking by providing free or subsidized high-quality childcare. Now, it can be argued that placing children in childcare centers does not support caretaking, but in fact further devalues it. I reject this assertion on the grounds that treating parenting as a full-time occupation is not the only way to demonstrate respect for caretaking and caretakers. It is also possible to demonstrate support for caretaking by providing working mothers (and fathers) with the resources (i.e., childcare) that will allow them to effectively combine parenting and work.

Feminists such as Fineman, Kittay, and Iris Marion Young have argued that our society places inordinate value on independence defined as economic self-sufficiency and denies the pervasiveness of relations of dependence.[37] This ordering of values is the product of a male-dominated society in which men have been historically associated with independence, while caring for dependents has been assigned to women. It follows from this analysis that instead of urging women to become economically independent, feminists should work to change how dependence and independence are perceived. Sending women with children out into the workforce signals capitulation to a value system that refuses to recognize the important contribution that caretakers make to society.

Fineman and other feminists are right to argue that dependency is a necessary part of human life, that caring for dependents is an essential public function, and that caring for dependents inevitably gives rise to legitimate needs. However, while the stigma attached to dependence is clearly wrong, economic independence remains a worthy goal for women because it provides them with one of the most important bases of self-determination. Maintaining steady participation in the workforce remains the most likely route to economic security for women as well as for men. While there is merit to the argument that low-paying jobs are no more likely to lead to true self-sufficiency than receiving benefits from the state, this does not mean that caregiving allowances are preferable to work. Instead, this argument shows why greater training and educational opportunities, income supports, unionization, health care, childcare, and an array of earning policies that would make it more likely that women would earn higher wages must be implemented.

The antipoverty/egalitarian model is preferable to Fineman's caregiver model because it is based on the principle that caretaking and providing are compatible. This principle has been, and will continue to be, the foundation of women's progress toward economic equity with men. While Fineman is right to accuse the egalitarian model of not doing enough to address the needs of single mothers, this accusation cannot be made against the antipoverty/egalitarian model. The policy I am recommending demonstrates that the caregiver model is not the only way to provide low-income single mothers with the means to care for their families. Moreover, when compared to the caregiver model, the antipoverty/egalitarian model is based on a more accurate analysis of the main cause of single mothers' poverty.

Marriage and Fathers

Fineman's family policy is built on the assumption that most women will not be able to achieve an egalitarian marital partnership with a man. According to Fineman, feminists should not continue to work for an unattainable ideal while so many single mothers live in poverty. Instead, feminists should face up to the fact that women are our society's caretakers and direct their activities toward securing greater recognition of and greater public support for mothers. Accomplishing this goal requires the elimination of marriage because as long as marriage exists, politicians and policymakers will continue to hold it up as the best solution to single mothers' poverty. Fineman claims that the only way to create an alternative support system for unmarried mothers is to turn all mothers (legally speaking) into single mothers. She claims that the general public will not recognize the legitimacy of single mothers' needs as long as marriage and the natural family remain the ideal.

While Fineman is certainly correct about the need to support single mothers, it does not make sense to eliminate one form of support (marriage) in order to generate another. It makes more sense to keep the old support system while adding to it by recognizing other family forms and, as I argue for in the section above, expanding economic opportunities, income supports, and subsidies for low-income mothers. If our goal is to find ways to care for our society's caretakers, marriage—which has proven effective in accomplishing this goal—should be maintained.

Opponents of marriage often argue that the law and employer policy privileges married couples by making health insurance and other benefits contingent on marital status. They argue that eliminating marriage is the only way to treat nontraditional family forms and intimate relationships equally.[38] However, as I argued in chapter 3, the goal of treating family forms equally can be met by instituting a system of universal health care and by expanding our definition of family. Abolishing marital privilege does not require eliminating a legal and social institution that has great sentimental and religious value for many men and women.

Feminists oppose marriage because of the role it has historically played in maintaining male domination and female subordination. Given religious tradition, custom, the gender-based division of labor, and the unequal earning power of men and women, there is little reason to think that contemporary marriage is an egalitarian institution. At the same time, it also should be acknowledged that progress has been made toward greater gender equality within marriage, and that women's continued presence in the workforce will increase the number of men and women living together as equal partners. As a legal, as opposed to a conventional, arrangement, marriage no longer brings with it fixed gender roles or relations of dominance and subservience. While some women (and men) may believe that it is necessary to reject an institution that has contributed so much to women's subordination, others believe that marriage can be transformed so that it is consistent with the principle of equality.[39] In addition, whether marriage is a legal institution or a social convention, women and men will continue to live together and raise children. Eliminating marriage will not abolish gender inequality, but only deregulate it. While current divorce laws do not provide women who have devoted themselves to caretaking with adequate income protection, deregulating marriage would not improve—and could have a negative effect—on women's economic security.

Marriage is not for everyone. Unmarried adults currently constitute a larger portion of all adults than in 1970. In 1996, 63 percent of white adults were married, in comparison to 73 percent in 1970. Fifty-eight percent of Hispanic adults were married in 1996, while 72 percent were married in 1970. For African American adults, the comparable figures are 42 percent in 1996 and 64 percent in 1970.[40] Not all adults are single by choice, but these figures do indicate that a greater proportion of adults are choosing to postpone or forgo marriage. At the same time, many adults do get married, and the majority of the adults that divorce eventually remarry.[41] Men and women marry for many different reasons. Some get married because it is customary, and others believe it is a religious duty. Some people believe that marriage provides the only appropriate legal and social arrangement for rearing children. And some individuals (including individuals who are not able to legally marry because of their sexual preference) believe that marrying is the best way to communicate their commitment to each other to family, friends, and the community at large. In an era in which the proportion of men and women marrying has declined, many individuals are choosing cohabitation over marriage; though over 40 percent of marriages end in divorce, marriage continues to have a strong, easily recognizable social meaning. Marriage still signifies commitment. For some men and women, although not for all, receiving social recognition for their commitment is important. As I argued at greater length in chapter 3, the legal institution of marriage facilitates and protects valuable relationships of interdependence. Abolishing marriage as a legal institution will make it more difficult for individuals to act in unison and to protect their joint interests. Marriage is beneficial to the couple and to the wider society because it obligates adults to care for and support one another in times of illness and economic insecurity. It protects individuals from facing the exigencies of modern life all on their own. Those who want to should be able to marry.

Fineman's proposal to redefine the family in terms of the caretaker-dependent relationship of mother and child fails to recognize that marriage, too, is a relationship between caretaker and dependent. Marriage is based on the assumption that individual adults lack self-sufficiency and require emotional and material support and companionship. While marriage is certainly not the only way that adults can find the support and companionship they need, as long as it works for a large number of people we should keep it. In the ideal egalitarian marriage, spouses are dependent on each other and alternate caring for one another. While most adults are not needy in the same ways that children are, and require less care than children do, they are seldom truly self-sufficient and independent.

Fineman claims that expanding marriage to include same-sex couples will not radically alter the exclusionary nature of marriage. Same-sex marriage, she argues, will only reinforce the idea that the sexual relationship is the paradigm of intimacy. It will not challenge, but will instead promote the belief that the sexual relationship is the foundation of the family. Fineman is right to call for a redefinition of what counts as family. However, it is not clear that the goal of generating greater acceptance of and support for diverse forms of family is best met by eliminating marriage. After all, Fineman's plan simply replaces one form of intimacy with another; it does not increase the number of legitimate family forms. Fineman is wrong to dismiss the legalization of lesbian and gay marriage. Lesbian marriages, like single-mother families, undermine the assumption that families without male heads are incomplete and inadequate. Gay marriages, like single-mother families, challenge the assumption that marriage is based on the fundamental interdependence of men and women. Friends who coparent or adopt children together also displace the hegemony of the married couple. Multiplying the number and kinds of families that receive legal sanction is the best way to displace the power of the heterosexual marital norm.

In addition, deregulating marriage has the effect of denying the role that sexuality plays in family formation. The sexual desire for a particular other brings individuals together. It can inspire and form the basis of their commitment to live together and take care of one another. Contemporary, egalitarian marriage can be understood as a way of recognizing and affirming sexual intimacy. Abolishing it would suggest that we do not value sexuality or recognize its importance in the lives of many individuals.

Fineman's policy on the relationship between fathers and children grows out of her primary goal, which is to affirm the value of caretaking. Fineman argues that the legal status of father is not something that should be automatically conferred on biological fathers. She explains, "Biology *plus* should be the prerequisite for all paternal-rights claims. The nurturing or caretaking connection should be a requirement for all fathers, married as well as unwed."[42] Men must earn the right to fatherhood by taking responsibility for the physical and emotional care of their children. The source of women's motherhood status also would be the performance of caretaking responsibilities. However, while Fineman does not address this point, she would probably want to consider carrying a fetus to term as a form of caretaking, as well it should be. Therefore, women who give birth to a child would be entitled to the legal status of mother. Fineman's definition of parental rights raises the question of whether the traditional male role of provider or breadwinner is an important dimension of caretaking. Should men who do not participate in the daily and routine physical and emotional care of infants and young children be accorded the status of "fathers" on the basis of the economic support they offer to both mother and child? Should the efforts they made to provide for their wife and children be considered evidence of caretaking during custody disputes? These are difficult questions. On the one hand, providing the resources essential to life is clearly one way to take care of others. On the other hand, it also makes sense to define parenthood as more than supplying children and their caretakers with material goods. Is a man who provides for his child but cannot or will not comfort or feed her on a regular basis truly a parent in the fullest and most complete sense? Do irregular acts of physical and emotional caretaking qualify a man as a good parent, or does care have to be performed daily? We might want to define parenthood in its fullest and more complete sense as including the parent's ability to understand and respond to the child's needs for physical and emotional care and comfort. Parenting, it could be said, should be defined as having established a caretaking relationship—it should be linked to the performance of regular caretaking duties. However, it also seems wrong to fail to recognize men who work hard to put food on the table for their children. While we might want to stipulate that in custody disputes preference should be given to the parent who performed the majority of the physical and emotional caretaking, and who therefore established a caretaking relationship with the child, breadwinning also should be recognized as making an important contribution to a child's well-being. Thus, men who have provided for their biological children should be entitled to the legal status of fathers.

The majority of women continue to raise children with a spouse or a live-in partner who is often the father of their children. The best way to relieve these women of some of the daily tasks associated with raising children, and to make more time available to them for paid work, leisure, or training and education, would be to persuade their partners that they, too, can care for young children. But to accomplish this, we must think of and encourage men to be caretakers. And we must expect them to care for their children, physically, emotionally, and economically, after divorce or separation, and in cases when parents do not continue their relationship after the child's birth.

Fineman's challenge to basing fatherhood on biology would probably decrease men's already low level of involvement in caring for children. Stripping men of their parenting rights simultaneously relieves them of their parenting responsibilities. While it is true that men who want to can claim their fatherhood rights by actively participating in the care of the infant they helped to conceive, Fineman's redefinition of the family exonerates men who do not want to take up the responsibilities of fatherhood and discourages those who are ambivalent about becoming caretakers. The legally enshrined presumption that women are children's primary caretakers will do little to encourage the small steps that many men already have taken toward becoming more involved in raising their children. It also eliminates one of the most powerful incentives men have for using birth control themselves or cooperating with their female partners' use of birth control. Currently, men who fail to use birth control do not face the same life changing consequences for engaging in sex that women do. It would be a mistake to completely excuse them from all responsibility for taking care of their offspring.

Fineman makes a strong argument against paternity policies that aim at maintaining the connection between biological fathers and their children in cases of nonmarital birth. She rightly asserts that paternity policies, which aim at identifying fathers in order to compel them to pay child support, often end up harming single mothers. Women who are welfare beneficiaries and do not cooperate in paternity proceedings often find that their benefits have been cut or eliminated altogether. These women often have good reason to avoid identifying the fathers of their children. First, most state governments treat child support payments as an opportunity to recoup state funds spent on welfare beneficiaries. Consequently, when a noncustodial parent of a child who receives welfare benefits pays child support, his money goes to the state and not to the child. Custodial and noncustodial parents often work out informal child support arrangements so that the mother can keep both her welfare benefits and the money she receives from the child's father. A welfare beneficiary who identifies the father of her child to child support enforcement officials will usually see her monthly income decrease.[43] She also risks angering or alienating the father. Second, in some cases, a mother may feel that the biological father of her child could be dangerous to her or her child. She may want to cut off all connection with him for fear that he may be abusive. However, noncustodial parents who pay their child support obligations are almost always given visitation rights. A mother who identifies the biological father of her child may find that she is forced to stand aside while her child goes on an unsupervised visit with a man she fears. In some cases, a mother may even be forced to give up custody of her child to a man who has abused her.[44]

Due to the reasons described above, I agree with Fineman that feminists should oppose mandatory paternity policies. But, abolishing mandatory paternity policies does not mean that we should eliminate voluntary paternity establishment. Federal and state governments should help mothers to collect child support from biological fathers. Indeed, as discussed in chapter 4, we must design public policies that aim at maintaining connections between biological fathers and their children in cases of nonmarital birth and in cases of divorce and separation. Since this goal is more important than recouping state dollars, child support payments should go directly to mothers and their children. In addition, the child support enforcement system needs to be reformed so that low-income men can afford to live up to their child support obligations. This, in turn, necessitates providing noncustodial fathers with training and employment opportunities. Many men can and will play a positive role in the lives of their children if they themselves receive the proper social supports.

Fineman's proposed definition of parenthood is appealing because it heightens the respect given to caretaking by making it the source of legal rights. It states that being biologically related to a child does not in and of itself constitute parenthood. The true basis of parenthood is providing care. It is tempting to agree with Fineman's assertion that since women always have been and continue to be the caretakers of children, the status and rights of parenthood more clearly belong to women than to men. But it would be a mistake to exempt biological fathers from the responsibilities of parenthood. Such a move would reaffirm the idea that women are natural caretakers and men are not. If feminists seek to reallocate some of the responsibilities and burdens of caretaking from women to men, then they must support policies based on the assumption that men can make valuable contributions to the care of their children. We must act as if most men will some day be caretakers. Increasing men's participation in the care of their children cannot be accomplished without extending parental rights to men in cases of divorce and nonmarital birth. This can be done safely as long as paternity proceedings are entirely voluntary and the privacy rights of mothers are carefully guarded.

CONCLUSION

Fineman's caregiver model makes an essential contribution to feminist thinking on family policy by moving single mothers from the margins to the center of

feminist theorizing on the family. In addition, Fineman highlights the importance of caretaking in a dramatic and important way. She insists that caretaking
should be seen as a vital public service and that the costs of raising children
should be socialized. But Fineman's goal is not limited to securing public support for mothers. She also seeks to raise the level of respect accorded to caretakers. Public support, Fineman argues, should not come with strings attached.
Truly respecting mothers and the work that they do require us to guarantee their
freedom to mother independently, unsupervised by individual patriarchs or a
patriarchal bureaucracy.

However, despite its strengths, Fineman's caregiver model points feminist
thinking on family policy in the wrong direction. Fineman's model reinforces
gender differences, perpetuates the association of men with the public sphere
and women with the private sphere, suggests that caretaking and providing
are incompatible, threatens to undermine the progress that women have made
toward economic and political equality, and discourages male involvement in
child rearing. While there may be good reason to doubt that men will ever
take on a full 50 percent of all child-rearing duties, feminists must continue
to assert that the gender-based division of labor in the family is arbitrary and
illegitimate. If they do not, the power of gender norms to determine the life
choices that women and men make will be strengthened.

Okin's egalitarian model is based on the principle that men can and should
be caretakers. It seeks to realize gender equality through the reallocation of
caretaking from women to men. However, as Fineman brings to our attention,
the egalitarian model does not do enough to assist single women and is vulnerable to the accusation that it contributes to androcentrism and workerism.
As I argued above, the needs of single women can best be addressed by combining the policies Okin calls for with antipoverty policies. The fact that
women remain our society's caretakers has undoubtedly increased the obstacles to economic security and self-sufficiency faced by many single women.
However, in most cases, having children without getting married is not what
makes women and their children poor. Poverty is largely the effect of a labor
market that does not provide enough well-paying jobs for low-skilled people.
Consequently, family policy cannot be separated from economic policy. Our
economic policies must pay special attention to the needs of parents for childcare and health care, and our family policies must include an analysis of the
low-wage labor market and how to reform it. Finally, encouraging the economic independence of single mothers also means providing services to and
investing in the infrastructure of poor communities. For too long public programs aimed at families have targeted mothers in isolation from their intimate
relationships with other adults and their community. But mothers cannot ensure the well-being of their children in neighborhoods that are deteriorating.
A commitment to families requires a commitment to the entire community,

including the unmarried adult men who live in the community and who often contribute to the emotional and financial support of their children and their girlfriends' children.

The success of the egalitarian model necessitates a thoroughgoing transformation of the workplace and work schedules. A future in which infants and toddlers spend a full eight to ten hours in childcare centers and away from their parents is not an attractive one. If the egalitarian model is to avoid workerism and to affirm the value of caretaking, employers must make a much greater commitment to providing lengthy parental leaves and more flexible work schedules for both their male and female employees. Moreover, as Fraser suggests, caretaking in its many different forms must come to be seen as a fundamental civic duty. Nonparents should be encouraged to volunteer at childcare and elder care centers, or homes for the mentally ill and disabled. If we do not find some way to universalize caretaking, parenting men will share the burdens of parenting women, while nonparents, both men and women, will be free to devote themselves exclusively to their careers and leisure pursuits. Replacing the mommy track with the parent track will do little to affirm the social value of caretaking.

Ultimately, instituting family policies that will bring about greater gender equality and liberation from traditional gender roles means rethinking public/private boundaries and rejecting the widespread conviction that families should be self-supporting. As Fineman convincingly argues, families can only maintain their self-sufficiency if women perform caretaking for free while depending on their husbands for economic support. All other forms of family, including traditional two-working-parent families, egalitarian two-working-parent families, and single working parent families, are torn between the demands of the workplace and the demands of caring for their children. The only solution to this dilemma is to raise the status of caretaking and to socialize *some* of the costs of raising children. As I have argued, I do not think this means providing all mothers with a guaranteed income. But it does mean subsidizing high-quality, affordable childcare and altering the way that we work. We will not be able to achieve these two goals unless we politicize caretaking by popularizing the view that it is a public responsibility.[45]

NOTES

1. Susan Moller Okin, *Justice, Gender, and the Family* (New York: Basic Books, 1989).

2. Martha Fineman, *The Neutered Mother, The Sexual Family and Other Twentieth Century Tragedies* (New York: Routledge, 1995).

3. Okin, *Justice, Gender and the Family*, 6.

4. Susan Moller Okin, "Sexual Orientation, Gender, and Families: Dichotomizing Differences," *Hypatia: A Journal of Feminist Philosophy* 11, no. 1 (Winter 1996): 1–48.

5. Fineman, *The Neutered Mother*, 159.

6. Fineman, *The Neutered Mother*, 160.

7. Fineman, *The Neutered Mother*, 147.

8. Fineman, *The Neutered Mother*, 161.

9. Fineman, *The Neutered Mother*, 165.

10. Fineman, *The Neutered Mother*, 165.

11. Fineman, *The Neutered Mother*, 229.

12. Fineman, *The Neutered Mother*, 232.

13. Fineman, *The Neutered Mother*, 231.

14. Okin, "Sexual Orientation," 23.

15. Nancy Fraser, ed., "After the Family Wage: A Postindustrial Thought Experiment," in *Justice Interruptus: Critical Reflections on the "PostSocialist" Condition* (New York: Routledge, 1997), 41–68.

16. Fraser, "After the Family Wage," 54.

17. A copy of *An Immodest Proposal: Rewarding Women's Work to End Poverty* by the Women's Committee of 100/Proposal 2002 is on file with the author. It has been widely circulated among feminist academics and activists.

18. Women's Committee of 100/Proposal 2002, *An Immodest Proposal: Rewarding Women's Work to End Poverty.* The document is on file with the author.

19. Gwendolyn Mink, *Welfare's End* (Ithaca, N.Y.: Cornell University Press, 1998). Mink served as a cochair of the Women's Committee of 100.

20. Mink, *Welfare's End*, 8.

21. Mink, *Welfare's End*, 19.

22. Mink, *Welfare's End*, 119.

23. U.S. Bureau of the Census, *Statistical Abstract of the United States*: 119th edition (Washington, D.C., 1999).

24. Bureau of the Census, *Statistical Abstract of the United States*.

25. Mink, *Welfare's End*, 113.

26. Fineman, *The Neutered Mother*, 216.

27. Barbara R. Bergmann, "Subsidizing Child Care by Mothers at Home," *Feminist Economics* 6, no. 1, (2000): 77–88.

28. Joel J. Handler and Yeheskel Hasenfeld, *We the Poor People: Work, Poverty, and Welfare* (New Haven, Conn.: Yale University Press, 1997); Roberta M. Spalter-Roth, Heidi I. Hartmann, and Linda M. Andrews, "Mothers, Children, and Low-Wage Work: The Ability to Earn a Family Wage," in *Sociology and the Public Agenda*, ed. William Julius Wilson (London: Sage, 1993), 316–38; William Julius Wilson, *When Work Disappears: The World of the New Urban Poor* (New York: Vintage Books, 1996).

29. Spalter-Roth, Hartmann, and Andrews, "Mothers, Children, and Low-Wage Work."

30. Institute for Women's Policy Research, "What Do Unions Do For Women?" *Research-in-Brief* (Washington, D.C.,1994).

31. Institute for Women's Policy Research, "What Do Unions Do for Women."

32. Handler and Hasenfeld, *We the Poor People*; Spalter-Roth, Hartmann, and Andrews, "Mothers, Children, and Low-Wage Work"; Wilson, *When Work Disappears.*

33. Institute for Women's Policy Research, "Women and Unemployment Insurance." *Fact Sheet* (Washington, D.C., 1999).

34. Harvard Joint Center for Housing Studies, *The State of the Nation's Housing: 2000* (Cambridge, Mass.: Harvard University, 2000).

35. Eva Fedder Kittay, "Taking Dependency Seriously: The Family and Medical Leave Act," *Hypatia: A Journal of Feminist Philosophy* 10, no. 1 (1995): 8–30

36. Sandra Danziger et al., *Barriers to the Employment of Welfare Recipients* (Ann Arbor, Mich.: University of Michigan, Poverty Research and Training Center, 2000).

37. Fineman, *The Neutered Mother*; Kittay, "Taking Dependency Seriously"; Iris Marion Young, "Mothers, Citizenship, and Independence: A Critique of Pure Family Values," *Ethics* 105 (April 1995): 535–56.

38. Iris Marion Young, "Reflections on Families in the Age of Murphy Brown: On Gender, Justice, and Sexuality," in *Revisioning the Political: Feminist Reconstructions of Traditional Concepts in Western Political Thought*, ed. Nancy J. Hirshmann and Christine Di Stefano (Boulder, Colo.: Westview Press, 1996), 251–70.

39. Nan Hunter, "Marriage, Law and Gender: A Feminist Inquiry" in *Sex Wars: Sexual Dissent and Political Culture*, ed. Lisa Duggin and Nan Hunter (New York: Routledge, 1995), 107–22.

40. Bureau of the Census, *Marital Status and Living Arrangements: March 1996, P20-496*, U.S. Department of Commerce, Economics and Statistics Administration (Washington, D.C., 1998).

41. Frank F. Furstenberg Jr., "Divorce and the American Family," *Annual Review of Sociology* 16, no. 1 (1990): 379–403.

42. Fineman, *The Neutered Mother*, 206.

43. Vicki Turetsky, *Realistic Child Support Policies For Low Income Fathers* (Washinton, D.C.: Center for Law and Social Policy, 2000). http://www.clasp.org/pubs/childenforce/kellogg.htm (accessed 8 June 2000).

44. Annia Ciezadlo, "Failure to Protect," *City Limits: New York's Urban Affairs News Magazine* 25, no. 8 (September/October 2000): 21–25. Mink provides a strong argument against mandatory paternity in *Welfare's End*.

45. Stephanie Coontz, *The Way We Never Were: American Families and the Nostalgia Trap* (New York: Basic Books, 1992).

Conclusion

This book argues for the compatibility of the following two principles: (1) well-functioning families and intimate associations are essential to the physical and emotional health of their members and to the larger society; and (2) the ability to choose the form and nature of our families and intimate associations is a fundamental right. As we have seen, family communitarians argue that these two principles are irreconcilable. They believe that strengthening families means promoting the two-parent family and limiting personal liberty.

In contrast, I have argued that personal liberty is a precondition to meaningful, intimate relationships. Today's marriages and partnerships, unlike marriages in the past, are based primarily on feelings of affection and love. The voluntary nature of adult partnership has made it both fragile and strong. It is fragile because feelings are notoriously changeable. However, freely chosen relationships have an integrity and dignity that relationships upheld by even the subtlest forms of coercion do not. The development of a new intimacy ideal is a tremendous historic achievement because it allows individuals to be self-determining in matters of the heart. If we value emotionally rich relationships, we must protect personal liberty.

Greater personal liberty has contributed to increased family instability and diversity. Higher rates of divorce and single parenthood are associated with emotional suffering and economic hardship for children. However, there are a variety of ways of responding to new family forms. I've argued that a comprehensive antipoverty program is the best way to help fragile families stay together and to decrease the economic hardship experienced by single mothers and their children. Addressing racial, economic, and gender inequality will not eliminate family instability. Adult relationships are subject to disruption even when families are economically secure. Nonetheless, providing families with the resources and opportunities they need will go a long way toward strengthening them. And, it will not involve the serious costs to personal liberty that are required by the policies advocated by family communitarians.

PUBLIC/PRIVATE BOUNDARIES

My proposal for greater public support for single parents and other low-income families brings us to a second set of allegedly irreconcilable principles. Conventional ways of thinking about public/private boundaries entail the assumption that once a decision has been declared "private," any obligation on the part of the state to provide support for the decisionmaker ceases to exist. After all, a majority of the citizenry may disagree with the decisions that some individuals make. It is also frequently assumed that individuals who rely on public aid do not deserve the same rights and freedoms as those that do not. As a student from Columbia University once said to me in regards to welfare recipients' right of procreative autonomy: "It is my money, so I can tell them what they can and cannot do."

The alleged contradiction between ensuring personal liberty and providing public funding can be responded to in several ways. First, whether the public approves or disapproves of unmarried women becoming mothers, it has a responsibility to provide all men and women with *real* equality of opportunity. The main reason that mothers with children are struggling to make ends meet is that there are not enough well-paying jobs available for women or men with low educational achievement and/or few skills. Employees who currently work in the low-wage labor market deserve two kinds of publicly funded reforms: (1) greater opportunities for education and training, and (2) income supports and subsidies that will allow them to live with dignity on the low wages offered by the current labor market. These reforms are not based on the principle that when low-income women decide to give birth the public is obligated to pay for the care of their children. Indeed, these reforms are not even targeted at single mothers. Providing single mothers with the resources to increase their own earning power and to live comfortably does not require the public to subsidize private decisions. Instead, it requires policymakers and the public to make good on our national commitment to equality of opportunity.

Second, caring for dependents is essential to the well-being of our society. Historically, caretaking has been performed by women for free in the private home. However, the social structure (provider-husband) that once allowed some women to refrain from paid work so that they could devote themselves to caretaking in the private home no longer provides reliable support. Moreover, the vast majority of women, married or unmarried, now work outside of the home for pay. In addition, the gender-based division of labor that women's unpaid caretaking is based on is unfair to women because it makes them dependent on men and limits their opportunities in the public sphere. Consequently, we must find a way to socialize some of the costs associated with caring for dependents. At a minimum, this means high-quality, affordable childcare, generous parental leaves, reduced work schedules for parents with infants, divorce laws that protect women and children from experiencing a sharp decrease in income after a divorce, and government-enforced child support. Again, these policies are not based on the principle that the public is obligated to fund the private decisions of individuals. They are not targeted at low-income mothers. Instead, they are based on the principle that caretaking must be equitably allocated and that the costs of caretaking cannot be distributed on the basis of gender. If women are to enjoy real equality of opportunity, some of the costs associated with caretaking must be redistributed to men and to taxpayers.

Third, fundamental rights should not become less secure when individual bearers of rights are economically needy or politically powerless. Women who receive welfare benefits have the same right to procreative autonomy as women who support themselves through wage work. Their fundamental rights should not be taken away simply because they have become temporarily dependent on state aid. Women who receive welfare benefits are not asking the citizenry to fund their private decisions. Instead, they are asking for economic assistance during a period of their lives in which they are not able to support themselves and their children. Bearing a child is one among many factors, such as unemployment, illness, old age, or accident, that may force a citizen to rely on state aid.

Fourth, in some cases the state may be obligated to take positive action to enable citizens and residents to exercise their rights. When rights are recognized as fundamental but distributed unequally, they are immediately transformed into privileges. This seriously compromises democracy. If all women are to enjoy procreative freedom, there must be public support for prenatal and pediatric health care, including treatment for substance abuse, sex education, birth control, and abortion. If all citizens are to enjoy the same rights, resources such as education and health care must be distributed equally.

STRENGTHENING CONNECTIONS AND COMMUNITIES

Strengthening low-income families is not simply a matter of supplementing their incomes. The Annie E. Casey Foundation, a major supporter of programs for children and their families, has recently reported that social isolation and disconnection from "core opportunities, resources and institutions" is one of the most serious problems faced by many low-income families. For a number of reasons, including lack of trust in government agencies and workers, lack of transportation, and lack of funding for services and programs, low-income parents are not engaged with the institutions that could help them and their children. These institutions include schools, community-based organizations, clinics, social service agencies, religious associations, and after school youth programs. The Annie E. Casey Foundation argues for a new strategy for strengthening families that they believe goes beyond providing "subsidies, charity or welfare."[1] This new strategy, which accords well with some of the policies I have called for, focuses on connecting families to local institutions. According to the Annie E. Casey Foundation, "Children succeed when their families are strong, and families get stronger when they live in neighborhoods that connect them to the economic opportunities, social network supports, and services they need."[2] Strengthening families means creating strong, politically empowered social networks within low-income communities.

In most low-income neighborhoods there are at least some nonprofit community-based organizations (CBOs) serving local families. Strengthening families means providing political support and adequate funding for these locally controlled organizations. Economic development projects that bring together private and public funding and place it in the hands of CBOs controlled by community residents are one of the most effective ways to build communities. Not only do such projects funnel resources into needy communities, they also serve to mobilize local residents and generate community-based leaders. They build the kinds of social relationships that empower citizens to take charge of their communities.

Families are *small* mutual aid associations. As Aristotle realized, they are incapable of self-sufficiency and need to be embedded in larger associations. Fostering healthy families means rejecting the ideology that families can "take care of their own." Instead, it requires forging supportive relationships between families and schools, social service agencies, and CBOs. Our poorest families simply cannot meet all of the needs of their dependent members themselves. While families must give their children care and moral guidance, larger associations can supplement the work of parents. This point is well-illustrated by an advertisement in New York City designed to encourage parents to sign their children up for government-funded medical insurance. It says simply, "You provide the love, we'll provide the health care."

It can of course be objected that what I have proposed is both expensive and politically unpopular. My response to the first objection is that many of the policies I have called for are already in place in other industrialized countries, especially in France, Sweden, and Norway.[3] While they will undoubtedly be very expensive, it is political will and not cost that is the greatest obstacle to their implementation. The second objection is impossible to refute. However, my objective in this book has been to explain why we should base our family policies on the principles of liberty, equality, and diversity, and not to come up with a plan that could easily win political support. In addition, while it is true that large-scale funding for low-income families and communities is unlikely to become available any time soon, issues such as welfare reform, childcare, and balancing work and family will continue to be potent political concerns for years to come. It is essential to provide a feminist and progressive response to these concerns. If it is not vocal and strong, the policies supported by family communitarians and conservative advocates of traditional family values will continue to gain influence.

The sweeping changes that have altered family life in the last thirty years are in large part due to the incomplete transformation of gender roles and the gender-based division of labor. As our gender-based beliefs and practices changed, the package deal came undone and with it the social arrangements that once regulated sexuality, procreation, and child rearing. We should not be sorry that a gender structure that required the subordination of women and the persecution of lesbians and gay men has been partially torn down. Indeed, we should move forward and complete its disassembly. At the same time, we also must acknowledge that it was this gender structure that nurtured and provided for children in the past. And we must recognize that not even feminists agree on how to create a new set of social arrangements for raising children. However, even though the egalitarian model of family may appear out of reach, we should not accept the argument that the gender revolution can never be completed. Nor should we accept the argument that whatever else they are or will become, women will always be our society's primary caretakers. Our family policies should be built on a vision of the future in which caretaking, providing, and decision making are not distributed according to gender.

NOTES

1. Annie E. Casey Foundation, *Kids Count Data Book, 2000* (Baltimore, Md.: Annie E. Casey Foundation, 2000), 9.

2. Annie E. Casey Foundation, *Kids Count Data Book*, 18.

3. Barbara Bergmann, *Saving Our Children From Poverty* (New York.: Russell Sage Foundation, 1996).

Bibliography

Ackelsburg, Martha, and Mary Shanley. "Privacy, Publicity and Power: A Feminist Rethinking of the Public-Private Distinction." In *Revisioning the Political: Feminist Reconstructions of Traditional Concepts in Western Political Thought*, edited by Nancy J. Hirshmann and Christine Di Stefano. Boulder, Colo.: Westview Press, 1996.

Alan Guttmacher Institute. *Sex and America's Teenagers*. New York: The Alan Guttmacher Institute, 1994.

Allen, Anita. "Privacy at Home: The Twofold Problem." In *Revisioning the Political: Feminist Reconstructions of Traditional Concepts in Western Political Thought*, edited by Nancy J. Hirshmann and Christine Di Stefano. Boulder, Colo: Westview Press, 1996.

Allen, M., and N. Burrell. "Comparing the Impact of Homosexual and Heterosexual Parents on Children: Meta-Analysis of Existing Research." *Journal of Homosexuality* 32 (1996): 19–35.

Amato, Paul R., and Bruce Keith. "Parental Divorce and the Well-Being of Children: A Meta-Analysis." *Psychological Bulletin* 110, no. 1 (1991): 26–46.

American Civil Liberties Union. *ACLU Fact Sheet: Overview of Lesbian and Gay Parenting, Adoption and Foster Care*. New York: American Civil Liberties Union, 1999. http://www.aclu.org/issues/gay/parent.html (accessed 1 December 2000).

———. *New Jersey Supreme Court Grants Visitation Rights to Former Partner of Lesbian Mom, Establishes "Psychological Parenthood."* New York: American Civil Liberties Union, 2000. http://www.aclu.org/news/2000/n040600a.html (accessed 1 December 2000).

American Psychological Association. *Lesbian and Gay Parenting: A Resource for Psychologists*. Washington, D.C.: American Psychological Association, 1995. http://apa.org/pi/parent.html (accessed 1 December 2000).

Amott, Teresa. *Caught in the Crisis: Women and the U.S. Economy Today*. New York: Monthly Review Press, 1993.

Annie E. Casey Foundation. *Kids Count Data Book, 2000*. Baltimore, Md.: Annie E. Casey Foundation, 2000.

Aries, Phillipe, and Andre Bejin, eds. *Western Sexuality: Practice and Precept in Past and Present Times*. Translated by A. Forster. New York: Basil Blackwell, 1985.

Aristotle. *The Politics*. Edited by Stephen Everson and translated by Jonathan Barnes. Cambridge: Cambridge University Press, 1988.

Bergmann, Barbara R. *The Economic Emergence of Women*. New York: Basic Books, 1986.

———. *Saving Our Children from Poverty*. New York: Russell Sage Foundation, 1996.

———. "Subsidizing Child Care by Mothers at Home." *Feminists Economics* 6, no. 1 (2000): 77–88.

Benn, Stanley, I. "Privacy, Freedom, and Respect for Persons." In *The Philosophical Dimensions of Privacy*, edited by Ferdinand D. Shoeman. Cambridge: Cambridge University Press, 1984.

Berlin, Isaiah. "John Stuart Mill and the Ends of Life." In *J. S. Mill: On Liberty in Focus*, edited by John Gray and G.W. Smith. New York: Routledge, 1991.

Bianchi, Suzanne, and Daphne Spain. "U.S. Women Make Workplace Progress." *Population Today* 25, no. 1 (January 1997): 1–2.

Blankenhorn, David. *Fatherless America*. New York: Basic Books, 1995.

Blankenhorn, David, Steven Bayme, and Jean Bethke Elshtain, eds. *Rebuilding the Nest: A New Commitment to the American Family*. Milwaukee: Family Service America, 1990.

Blasius, Mark, and Shane Phelan, eds. *We Are Everywhere: A Historical Sourcebook of Gay and Lesbian Politics*. New York: Routledge, 1997.

Brooks-Gunn, Jeanne, and George J. Duncan, eds. *Consequences of Growing up Poor*. New York: Russell Sage Foundation, 1997.

Brooks-Gunn, Jeanne, Greg J. Duncan, and Nancy Maritato. "Poor Families, Poor Outcomes: The Well-Being of Children and Youth." In *Consequences of Growing Up Poor*, edited by Jeanne Brooks-Gunn and Greg J. Duncan. New York: Russell Sage Foundation, 1997.

Bumpass, Larry L. "What's Happening to the Family? Interactions between Demographic and Institutional Change." *Demography* 27, no. 4 (November 1990): 483–98.

Byrant, Wayne R. "The Art of Welfare Reform." *New Jersey Reporter* 25, no. 4 (November/December 1995): 46–47.

Byrne Gregory. "Father May Not Know Best, But What Does He Know?" *Population Today* 25, no. 10 (October 1997): 1–3.

Calhoun, Cheshire. "Family Outlaws: Rethinking the Connections between Feminism, Lesbianism, and the Family." In *Feminism and Families*, edited by Hilde Lindeman Nelson. New York: Routledge, 1997.

Canedy, Dana. "Troubling Label for Hispanics: 'Girls Most Likely to Drop Out.'" *New York Times* (25 March 2001): Al.

Center of Law and Social Policy. *Caps on Kids: Family Cap in the New Welfare Era*. Washington, D.C.: Center on Law and Social Policy, 1999. http://www.clasp.org/pubs/caps_on_kids.htm (accessed 16 February 2000)

Cherlin, Andrew J. *The Changing American Family and Public Policy*. Washington, D.C.: Urban Institute Press, 1998.

Cherlin, Andrew J., "Going to Extremes: Family Structure, Children's Well-Being, and Social Science." *Demography* 36, no. 4 (November 1999): 421–28.

———. *Marriage, Divorce, Remarriage*. Cambridge, Mass: Harvard University Press, 1992.

Cherlin, Andrew J., P. Lindsay Chase-Lansdale, and Christine MacRae. "Effects of Parental Divorce on Mental Health Throughout the Life Course." *American Sociological Review* 63, no. 2 (April 1998): 239–49.

Child Trends, "Poverty, Welfare and Children." *Research Brief*. Washington, D.C.: Child Trends, 1999. http://www.childtrends.org (accessed 5 December 1999).

Chira, Susan. "War Over Role of American Families." *New York Times* (19 June 1994): A22.

Ciezadlo, Annia. "Failure to Protect." *City Limits: New York's Urban Affairs News Magazine* 25, no. 8 (September/October 2000): 21–25.

Clark, Charles S. "Marriage and Divorce." *CQ Researcher* 6, no. 18 (May 1996): 409–32.

Cohen, Jean. "Redescribing Privacy: Identity, Difference, and the Abortion Controversy." *Columbia Journal of Gender and Law* 3 (1994): 43–116.

Collins, Patricia Hill. "Shifting the Center: Race, Class and Feminist Theorizing about Motherhood." In *American Families: A Multicultural Reader*, edited by Stephanie Coontz with Maya Parson and Gabrielle Raley. New York: Routledge, 1999.

Collier, Jane, Michelle Rosaldo, and Sylvia Yanagisako. "Is There a Family? New Anthropological Views." In *Rethinking the Family: Some Feminist Questions*, edited by Barrie Thorne with Marilyn Yalom. Boston: Northeastern University Press, 1992.

Coltrane, Scott. *Family Man: Fatherhood, Housework, and Gender Equity*. New York: Oxford University Press, 1996.

Coontz, Stephanie. *The Way We Never Were: American Families and the Nostalgia Trap*. New York: Basic Books, 1992.

———. *The Way We Are Now*. New York: Basic Books, 1997.

Coontz, Stephanie, with Maya Parson and Gabrielle Raley, eds. *American Families: A Multicultural Reader*. New York: Routledge, 1999

Cornell, Drucilla. "Fatherhood and Its Discontents: Men, Patriarchy and Freedom." In *Lost Fathers: The Politics of Fatherlessness in America*, edited by Cynthia R. Daniels. New York: St. Martin's, 1998.

Council on Families in America, "Marriage in America: A Report to the Nation." In *Promises to Keep: Decline and Renewal in America*, edited by David Popenoe, Jean Bethke Elshtain, and David Blankenhorn, 293–318. Lanham, Md.: Rowman & Littlefield Publishers, 1996.

Crittenden, Ann. *The Price of Motherhood*. New York: Metropolitan Books, 2001.

Daniels, Cynthia R., ed. *Lost Fathers: The Politics of Fatherlessness in America*. New York: St. Martin's, 1998.

Danziger, Sandra et al. *Barriers to the Employment of Welfare Recipients*. Ann Arbor, Michigan: University of Michigan, Poverty Research and Training Center, 2000.

Dao, James. "Ruling Lets Unwed Couples Adopt." *New York Times* (3 November 1995): B16.

Darling, Carol A, David J. Kallen, and Joyce E. VanDusen. "Sex in Transition, 1900–1980." In *Family in Transition: Rethinking Marriage, Sexuality, Child Rearing, and Family Organization*, edited by Arlene S. Skolnick and Jerome H. Skolnick, 151–57. Glenview, Ill: Scott, Foresman and Co., 1992.

Darroch, Jacqueline E., David J. Landry, and Susheela Singh. "Changing Emphases in Sexuality Education in U.S. Public Secondary Schools, 1988–1999." *Family Planning Perspectives* 32, no. 5 (September/October 2000): 212–19.

de Tocqueville, Alexis. *Democracy in America.* New York: Knopf, 1994.

Degler, Carl D. *At Odds: Women and the Family in America from the Revolution to the Present.* New York: Oxford University Press, 1980.

D'Emilio, John. *Sexual Politics, Sexual Communities: The Making of a Homosexual Minority in the United States, 1940–70.* Chicago: University of Chicago Press, 1983.

Dill, Bonnie Thorton. "Fictive Kin, Paper Sons, and Compadrazgo: Women of Color and the Struggle for Family Survival." In *American Families: A Multicultural Reader*, edited by Stephanie Coontz, with Maya Parson and Gabrielle Raley. New York: Routledge, 1999.

Dill, Bonnie Thorton, Maxine Baca Zinn, and Sandra Patton. "Feminism, Race, and the Politics of Family Values." *Philosophy and Public Policy* 13, no. 3 (Summer 1993): 13–19.

Di Stefano, Christine. "Autonomy in the Light of Difference." In *Revisioning the Political: Feminist Reconstructions of Traditional Concepts in Western Political Thought,* edited by Nancy J. Hirshmann and Christine Di Stefano. Boulder, Colo.: Westview Press, 1996.

Doherty, William J., Edward F. Kouneski, and Martha F. Erickson. "Responsible Fathering: An Overview and Conceptual Framework." *Journal of Marriage and Family* 60 (May 1998): 277–92.

Donovan, Patricia. "The 'Illegitimacy Bonus' and State Efforts to Reduce Out-of-Wedlock Birth." *Family Planning Perspectives* 31, no. 2 (March/April 1999): 94–97.

Driscoll, Annie K. et al., "Nonmarital Childbearing among Adult Women." *Journal of Marriage and the Family* 61, no. 1 (February 1999): 178–87.

Duggin, Lisa, and Nan Hunter. *Sex Wars: Sexual Dissent and Political Culture.* New York: Routledge, 1995.

Duncan, Greg J., and Jeanne Brooks-Gunn. "Income Effects Across the Life Span: Integration and Interpretation." In *Consequences of Growing Up Poor*, edited by Jeanne Brooks-Gunn and Greg J. Duncan. New York: Russell Sage Foundation, 1997.

Dupree, Allen, and Wendell Primus. *Declining Share of Children Lived with Single Mothers in the Late 1990s.* Washington, D.C.: Center on Budget and Policy Priorities, 2001. http://www.cbpp.org (accessed 15 June 2001).

Dworkin, Ronald. *Life's Dominion.* New York: Knopf, 1993.

———. *A Matter of Principle.* Cambridge, Mass: Harvard University Press, 1985.

———. *Taking Rights Seriously*. Cambridge, Mass.: Harvard University Press, 1977.

Eagly, Alice H., and Wendy Wood. "The Origins of Sex Differences in Human Behavior: Evolved Dispositions Versus Social Roles." *American Psychologist* 54, no. 6 (June 1999): 408–23.

Echols, Alice. *Daring to be Bad: Radical Feminism in America, 1967–1975*. Minneapolis, Minn.: University of Minnesota, 1989.

Edin, Kathyrn, and Laura Lein. *Making Ends Meet: How Single Mothers Survive Welfare and Low-Wage Work*. New York: Russell Sage Foundation, 1997.

Edin, Kathryn, Laura Lein, and Timothy Nelson. *Low-Income, Non-Residential Fathers: Off-Balance in a Competitive Economy, An Initial Analysis*. Washington, D.C.: U.S. Department of Health and Human Services, 1998. http://fatherhood.hhs.gov/ELN/eln98.htm. (accessed 20 June 2001).

Eichbaum, June Aline. "Towards an Autonomy-Based Theory of Constitutional Privacy: Beyond the Ideology of Family Privacy." *Harvard Civil Rights-Civil Liberties Law Review* 14 (1979): 360–84.

Eisenstein, Zillah. "Equalizing Privacy and Specifying Equality." In *Revisioning the Political: Feminist Reconstructions of Traditional Concepts in Western Political Thought*, edited by Nancy J. Hirshmann and Christine Di Stefano, 181–92. Boulder, Colo.: Westview Press, 1996.

Ellwood, David. *Poor Support*. New York: Basic Books, 1998.

Elshtain, Jean Bethke. "Accepting Limits." *Commonweal* 18 (November 22, 1991): 685–86.

———. "A Call to Civil Society." *Social Science and Modern Society* 36, no. 5 (July/August 1999): 11–19.

———. "The Family and Civic Life." In *Power Trips and Other Journeys: Essays in Feminism and Civic Discourse*, edited by Jean Bethke Elshtain, 45–60. Madison, Wis.: University of Wisconsin Press, 1990.

———. "Feminism, Family and Community." *Dissent* 30, no. 1 (winter 1983).

Emerson, Ralph Waldo. *Self-Reliance and Other Essays*. Mineola, N.Y.: Dover Publications, 1993.

Etzioni, Amitai, ed. *Rights and the Common Good*. New York: St. Martin's, 1995.

Federal Interagency Forum on Child and Family Statistics. *America's Children 2000: Key National Indicators of Well-Being, 2000*. Washington D.C., 2000.

Feinberg, Joel. "Autonomy, Sovereignty, and Privacy: Moral Ideals in the Constitution?" *The Notre Dame Law Review* 58, no. 3 (1983): 44–92.

Fineman, Martha. *The Neutered Mother, The Sexual Family and Other Twentieth Century Tragedies*. New York: Routledge, 1995.

Fitchen, Janet M. *Endangered Spaces, Enduring Places: Change, Identity, and Survival in Rural America*. Boulder, Colo.: Westview Press, 1991.

Flandrin, Jean-Louis. *Families in Former Times: Kinship, Household, and Sexuality*. Cambridge: Cambridge University Press, 1979.

Fraser, Nancy, ed. "After the Family Wage: A Postindustrial Thought Experiment." In *Justice Interruptus: Critical Reflections on the "PostSocialist" Condition*, 41–68. New York: Routledge, 1997.

————. *Justice Interruptus: Critical Reflections on the "PostSocialist" Condition.* New York: Routledge, 1997.

Fraser, Nancy, and Linda Gordon. "A Genealogy of 'Dependency': Tracing a Key word of the U.S. Welfare State." In *Justice Interruptus: Critical Reflections on the "PostSocialist" Condition*, 121–50. New York: Routledge, 1997.

Freedman, Estelle B., and John D'Emilio. *Intimate Matters: A History of Sexuality in America.* New York: Harper and Row, 1988.

Friedman, Marilyn. "Feminism and Modern Friendship: Dislocating the Community." In *Feminism and Political Theory*, edited by Cass R. Sunstein. Chicago: Chicago University Press, 1990.

Furstenberg, Frank F. Jr. "Divorce and the American Family." *Annual Review of Sociology* 16, no. 1 (1990): 379–403.

————. "Is the Modern Family a Threat to Children's Health?" *Social Science and Modern Society* 36, no. 5 (July/August 1999): 31–37.

Furstenberg, Frank F. Jr., and Andrew J. Cherlin. *Divided Families: What Happens to Children When Parents Part.* Cambridge, Mass.: Harvard University Press, 1991.

Furstenberg, Frank F. Jr., and Gretchen A. Condran. "Family Change and Adolescent Well-Being: A Re-examination of U.S. Trends." In *The Changing American Family and Public Policy*, edited by Andrew J. Cherlin. Washington, D.C.: The Urban Institute Press, 1988.

Furstenberg, Frank F. Jr., and Kathleen M. Harris. "When and Why Fathers Matter: Impacts of Father Involvement on the Children of Adolescent Mothers." In *Young Unwed Fathers: Changing Roles and Emerging Policies*, edited by Robert I. Lerman and Theodora J. Ooms. Philadelphia: Temple University Press, 1993.

Furstenberg, Frank F. Jr., S. Philip Morgan, and Paul D. Allison. "Paternal Participation and Children's Well-Being after Marital Dissolution." *American Sociological Review* 52, no. 5 (October 1987): 695–701.

Galston, William A. "Divorce American Style." *The Public Interest* 124 (Summer 1996): 12–26.

————. "Needed: A Not-So-Fast Divorce Law." *New York Times* (27 December 1995).

————. "A Liberal Case for the Two-Parent Family." In *Rights and the Common Good*, edited by Amitai Etzioni. New York: St. Martin's, 1995.

————. *Liberal Purposes: Goods, Virtues and Diversity in the Liberal State.* Cambridge: Cambridge University Press, 1991.

Garrow, David J. *Liberty and Sexuality.* New York: Macmillan, 1994.

Gilligan, Carol. *In a Different Voice: Psychological Theory and Women's Development.* Cambridge, Mass.: Harvard University Press, 1982.

Glendon, Mary Ann. *Rights Talk.* New York: Free Press, 1991.

Glendon, Mary Ann, and David Blankenhorn. *Seedbeds of Virtue.* Lanham, Md.: Madison House Books, 1995.

Goldberg, Carey. "Vermont Gives Final Approval to Same-Sex Unions." *New York Times* (26 April 2000): A14.

Gray, John, and G. W. Smith, eds. *J. S. Mill: On Liberty in Focus.* New York: Routledge, 1991.

Greenhouse, Linda. "Justices, 6-3, Bar Some Drug Tests." *New York Times* (22 March 2001): A1.

Griswold, Robert. *Fatherhood in America: A History*. New York: Basic Books, 1993.

Guy-Sheftall, Beverly, ed. *Words of Fire: An Anthology of African-American Feminist Thought*. New York: New Press, 1995.

Hacker, Andrew. *Two Nations*. New York: Ballantine Books, 1995.

Haningsberg, Julie E., and Sara Ruddick. *Mother Troubles: Rethinking Contemporary Maternal Dilemmas*. Boston: Beacon Press, 1999.

Handler, Joel J., and Yeheskel Hasenfeld. *We the Poor People: Work, Poverty, and Welfare*. New Haven, Conn.: Yale University Press, 1997.

Harrington, Mona. *Care and Equality: Inventing a New Family Politics*. New York: Knopf, 1999.

Hartmann, Heidi. "The Unhappy Marriage of Marxism and Feminism." In *Women and Revolution,* edited by Lydia Sargeant. Boston, Mass.: South End Press, 1981.

Hartmann, Heidi, and Roberta Spalter-Roth. *The Labor Market, The Working Poor, and Welfare Reform: Policy Suggestions for the Clinton Administration*. Washington, D.C.: Institute for Women's Policy Research, 1992.

Harvard Joint Center for Housing Studies. *The State of the Nation's Housing: 2000*. Cambridge, Mass.: Harvard University, 2000.

Hirshmann, Nancy J. *Rethinking Obligation: A Feminist Method for Political Theory*. Ithaca, N.Y.: Cornell University Press, 1992.

Hirshmann, Nancy J., and Christine Di Stefano, eds. *Revisioning the Political: Feminist Reconstructions of Traditional Concepts in Western Political Thought*. Boulder, Colo.: Westview Press. 1996.

Hochman, Anndee. *Everyday Acts and Small Subversions: Woman Reinventing Family, Community and Home*. Portland, Oreg.: Eighth Mountain Press, 1994.

Hochschild, Arlie, with Anne Machung. *The Second Shift*. New York: Avon, 1989.

Hochschild, Jennifer L. *Facing Up to the American Dream*. New Jersey: Princeton University Press, 1995.

Hoffman, Saul D., E. Michael Foster, and Frank F. Furstenberg Jr. "Reevaluating the Costs of Teenage Childbearing." *Demography* 30, no. 4 (February 1993): 1–13.

Hunter, Nan. "Identity, Speech and Equality." In *Sex Wars: Sexual Dissent and Political Culture*, edited by Lisa Duggin and Nan Hunter. New York: Routledge, 1995.

Institute for Women's Policy Research. "What Do Unions Do for Women?" *Research-in-Brief*. Washington, D.C.: Institute for Women's Policy Research, 1994.

———. "Women and Unemployment Insurance." *Fact Sheet*. Washington, D.C.: Institute for Women's Policy Research, 1999.

Jencks, Christopher. *Rethinking Social Policy: Race, Poverty, and the Underclass*. New York: HarperPerennial, 1993.

Jencks, Christopher, and Kathryn Edin. "Do Poor Women Have the Right to Bear Children?" *The American Prospect* 20 (Winter 1995): 43–52.

Kaplan, Morris. "Intimacy and Equality: The Question of Lesbian and Gay Marriage." *The Philosophical Forum* 25 (1994): 333–66.

———. *Sexual Justice: Democratic Citizenship and the Politics of Desire*. New York: Routledge, 1997.

Karst, Kenneth L. "The Freedom of Intimate Association." *Yale Law Journal* 89 (1980): 624–92.

Kateb, George. *The Inner Ocean: Individualism and Democratic Culture.* New York: Cornell University Press, 1992.

Kiecolt, Jill K., and Mark A. Fosset. "The Effects of Mate Availability on Marriage among Black Americans." In *Family Life in Black America*, edited by Robert Joseph Taylor, James S. Jackson, and Linda Chatters. Thousand Oaks, Calif.: Sage, 1997.

Kimmel, Michael. *Manhood in America: A Cultural History.* New York: Free Press, 1996.

Kiss, Elizabeth. "Alchemy or Fool's Gold?: Assessing Feminist Doubts about Rights." In *Reconstructing Political Theory from a Feminist Perspective*, edited by Mary Lyndon Shanley and Uma Narayan. University Park, Pa.: Pennsylvania State University Press, 1995.

Kittay, Eva Feder. "Taking Dependency Seriously: The Family and Medical Leave Act." *Hypatia: A Journal of Feminist Philosophy* 10, no. 1 (1995): 8–30.

Kozol, Jonathan. *Amazing Grace.* New York: Crown Publishers, 1995.

Kymlicka, Will. *Contemporary Political Philosophy: An Introduction.* Oxford: Clarendon Press, 1990.

Laird, J. "Lesbian and Gay Families." In *Normal Family Processes*, edited by Froma Walsh. New York: Guilford Press, 1993.

Lamb, Michael E., ed. *The Father's Role, Applied Perspectives.* New York: John Wiley, 1986.

Lambda Legal Defense and Education Fund. *Adoption by Lesbians and Gay Men: An Overview of the Law in the 50 States*, 1997. http://www.lambdalegal.org/sextions/library/adoption.pdf (accessed 28 January 2002).

Lerman, Robert I, and Theodora J. Ooms, eds. *Young Unwed Fathers: Changing Roles and Emerging Policies.* Philadelphia: Temple University Press, 1993.

Levin-Epstein, Jodie. *Open Questions: New Jersey's Family Cap Evaluation.* Washington, D.C.: Center on Law and Social Policy, February 1999. http://www.clasp.org/pubs/teens/OpenQuestions.htm (accessed 23 March 2000).

Lewis, Tamar. "Cut Down on Out-of-Wedlock Births, Win Cash." *New York Times* (24 September 2000).

Locke, John. *A Letter Concerning Toleration.* Edited by James H. Tully. Indianapolis, Ind.: Hackett Publishing Company, 1983.

——. *Two Treatises of Government: A Critical Edition with an Introduction and Apparatus Criticus by Peter Laslett.* London: Cambridge University Press, 1967.

Los Angeles Times. "Laws Discouraging Divorce Spreading Slowly if at All." (11 February 2001): A41.

Lubiano, Wahneema. "Black Ladies, Welfare Queens, and State Minstrels: Ideological War by Narrative Means." In *Race-ing Justice, En-gendering Power: Essays on Anita Hill, Clarence Thomas, and the Construction of Social Reality*, edited by Toni Morrison. New York: Pantheon, 1992.

Ludtke, Melissa. *On Our Own: Unmarried Motherhood in America.* New York: Random House, 1997.

Luker, Kristen. *Dubious Conceptions: The Politics of Teenage Pregnancy.* Cambridge, Mass.: Harvard University Press, 1996.

MacKinnon, Catherine. *Feminism Unmodified*. Cambridge, Mass.: Harvard University Press, 1987.

Marx, Karl. *Selected Writings*, edited by Lawrence H. Simon. Indianapolis, Ind.: Hackett, 1994.

Mason, Mary Ann, Arlene Skolnick, and Stephen D. Sugarman, eds. *All Our Families: New Policies for a New Century*. New York: Oxford University Press, 1998.

McLanahan, Sara. "The Consequences of Single Motherhood." In *Sex, Preference, and Family: Essays on Law and Nature*, edited by David M. Estlund and Martha C. Nussbaum. New York: Oxford University Press, 1997.

McLanahan, Sara, and Gary Sandefur. *Growing Up with a Single Parent: What Helps, What Hurts*. Cambridge, Mass.: Harvard University Press, 1994.

Mead, Lawrence. *The New Politics of Poverty*. New York: Basic Books, 1992.

Milbank, Dana. "Blame Game: No-Fault Divorce Law is Assailed in Michigan and Debate Heats Up." *Wall Street Journal* (5 January 1996): A1.

Mill, John Stuart. *On Liberty*. Edited by David Spitz. New York: Norton, 1975.

———. "On the Subjection of Women." In *Essays on Sex Equality*, edited by Alice S. Rossi. Chicago: University of Chicago Press, 1970.

Mink, Gwendolyn. *Welfare's End*. Ithaca, N.Y.: Cornell University Press, 1998.

Minow, Martha. "All in the Family and In all Families: Membership, Owing, and Loving." In *Sex, Preference, and Family: Essays on Law and Nature*, edited by David M. Estlund and Martha C. Nussbaum. New York: Oxford University Press, 1997.

Minow, Martha, and Mary Lyndon Shanley. "Relational Rights and Responsibilities: Revisioning the Family in Liberal Political Theory and Law," *Hypatia: A Journal of Feminist Philosophy* 11 no. 1 (winter 1996): 4–29.

Morrison, Toni, ed. *Race-ing Justice, En-gendering Power: Essays on Anita Hill, Clarence Thomas, and the Construction of Social Reality*. New York: Pantheon, 1992.

Murray, Charles. *Losing Ground: American Social Policy, 1950–1980*. New York: Basic Books, 1984.

Murray, Pauli. "The Liberation of Black Women." In *Words of Fire: An Anthology of African-American Feminist Thought*, edited by Beverly Guy-Sheftall, 186–97. New York: New Press, 1995.

Nelson, Hilde Lindeman, ed. *Feminism and Families*. New York: Routledge, 1997.

New York Times, 19 June 1994–25 March 2001.

Newman, Katherine. *No Shame in My Game: The Working Poor in the Inner City*. New York: Vintage Books, 2000.

Newton, Esther. *Cherry Grove, Fire Island: Sixty Years in America's First Gay and Lesbian Town*. Boston: Beacon Press, 1993.

Noble, Charles. *Welfare as We Knew It: A Political History of the American Welfare State*. New York: Oxford University Press, 1997.

Nicholson, Linda, ed. *The Second Wave*. New York: Routledge, 1997.

Nord, Christine Winquist, and Nicholas Zill. *Non-Custodial Parents' Participation in Their Children's Lives: Evidence from the Survey of Income and Program Participation, Volume II*. Washington, D.C.: Department of Health and Human Services, 1996. http://fatherhood.hhs.gov/sipp/pt2.htm. (accessed 28 June 2000).

NOW Legal Defense and Education Fund. "Background on Child Exclusion Proposals." *Welfare and Poverty*, 2000. http://www.nowldef.org/html/issues/wel/childep.shtml (accessed 16 January 2002).

———. "Update on Recent Child Exclusion Developments." *Welfare and Poverty*, 2000. http://www.nowldef.org/html/issues/wel/chexdv.htm (accessed 16 January 2002).

Okin, Susan Moller. *Justice, Gender, and the Family*. New York: Basic Books, 1989.

———. "Sexual Orientation, Gender, and Families: Dichotomizing Differences." *Hypatia: A Journal of Feminist Philosophy* 11, no. 1 (Winter 1996): 1–48.

———. *Women in Western Political Thought*. Princeton, N.J.: Princeton University Press, 1980.

Olsen, Frances E. "The Family and the Market: A Study of Ideology and Legal Reform." *Harvard Law Review* 96, no. 7 (1983): 1497–576.

———. "Unraveling Compromise." *Harvard Law Review* 103, no. 1 (1989): 105–35.

Paine, Thomas. "Common Sense." In *Collected Writings*. New York: Literary Classics of the United States, 1995.

Paltrow, Lynn M. "Punishment and Prejudice: Judging Drug-Using Pregnant Women." In *Mother Troubles: Rethinking Contemporary Maternal Dilemmas*, edited by Julia E. Hanigsberg and Sara Ruddick. Boston: Beacon, 1999.

Pateman, Carol. "Feminist Critiques of the Public/Private Dichotomy." In *Feminism and Equality*, edited by Anne Phillips. Oxford: Blackwell, 1987.

Phillips, Anne, ed. *Feminism and Equality*. Oxford: Blackwell, 1987.

Polikoff, Nancy. "This Child Does Have Two Mothers: Redefining Parenthood to Meet the Needs of Children in Lesbian-Mother and Other Nontraditional Families." *Georgetown Law Review* 78, no. 3 (1990): 459–575.

Popenoe, David. "Can the Nuclear Family Be Revived?" *Social Science and Modern Society* 36, no.5 (July/August 1999): 28–30.

———. *Life Without Father*. New York: Free Press, 1996.

Popenoe, David, Jean Bethke Elshtain, and David Blankenhorn, eds. *Promises to Keep: Decline and Renewal in America*. Lanham, Md.: Rowman & Littlefield, 1996.

Quadagno, Jill. *The Color of Welfare*. New York: Oxford Press, 1994.

Rachels, James. "Why Privacy Is Important." In *Philosophical Dimensions of Privacy*, edited by Ferdinand Schoeman. Cambridge: Cambridge University Press, 1984.

Rawls, John. *Political Liberalism*. Cambridge, Mass.: Harvard University Press, 1994.

———. *A Theory of Justice*. Cambridge, Mass.: Harvard University Press, 1971.

Ray, Shirley Aisha, and Vonnie C. McLoyd. "Fathers in Hard Times: The Impact of Unemployment and Poverty on Paternal and Marital Relations." In *The Father's Role, Applied Perspectives*, edited by Michael Lamb. New York: John Wiley and Sons, 1986.

Reiman, Jeffry H. "Privacy, Intimacy and Personhood." *Philosophy and Public Affairs* 6, no. 1 (1976): 26–44.

Rimer, Sara. "Tradition of Care for the Elderly Thrives in Black Families." *New York Times* (10 March 1998), A9.

Risman, Barbara J., and Danette Johnson-Sumerford. "Doing It Fairly: A Study of Postgender Marriages." *Journal of Marriage and Family* 60 (February 1998): 23–40.

Roberts, Dorothy. *Killing the Black Body: Race, Reproduction, and the Meaning of Liberty.* New York: Pantheon Books, 1997.

Rosenblum, Nancy. *Another Liberalism: Romanticism and the Reconstruction of Liberal Thought.* Cambridge, Mass.: Harvard University Press, 1987.

Rossi, Alice S., ed. *Essays on Sex Equality.* Chicago: University of Chicago Press, 1970.

Rousseau, Jean-Jacques. *Emile or On Education.* Translated by Allan Bloom. New York: Basic Books, 1979.

Rubin, Gayle. "The Traffic in Women." In *The Second Wave*, edited by Linda Nicholson, 27–61. New York: Routledge, 1997.

Russell, Graeme. "Primary Caretaking and Role Sharing Fathers." In *The Father's Role, Applied Perspectives,* edited by Michael Lamb. New York: John Wiley and Sons, 1986.

Sack, Kevin. "Louisiana Approves Measure to Tighten Marriage Bonds." *New York Times* (24 June 1997).

Sandel, Michael. *Democracy's Discontents: America in Search of a Public Philosophy.* Cambridge, Mass.: Harvard University Press, 1996.

——. *Liberalism and Its Critics.* New York: New York University Press, 1996.

Sargent, Lydia, ed. *Women and Revolution.* Boston: South End Press, 1981.

Schemo, Diana Jean. "Sex Education with Just One Lessons: No Sex." *New York Times* (28 December 2000).

Schneir, Miriam, ed., *Feminism in Our Time.* New York: Vintage Books, 1994.

Seidman, Steven. *Romantic Longings: Love in America, 1830–1980.* New York: Routledge, 1991.

Shanley, Mary Lyndon. "Lesbian Families: Dilemmas in Grounding Legal Recognition of Parenthood." In *Mother Troubles: Rethinking Contemporary Maternal Dilemmas*, eds. Julie E. Hanigsberg and Sara Ruddick. Boston: Beacon Press, 1999.

Shanley, Mary Lyndon, and Uma Narayan, eds. *Reconstructing Political Theory from a Feminist Perspective.* University Park, Pa.: Pennsylvania State University Press, 1995.

Shoeman, Ferdinand D., ed. *The Philosophical Dimensions of Privacy.* Cambridge: Cambridge University Press, 1984.

Shogren, Elizabeth. "Senate, House on Own Paths in Welfare Debate." *Los Angeles Times* (16 September 1995): A4.

Shorter, Edward. *The Making of the Modern Family.* New York: Basic Books, 1977.

Silverstein, Louise B., and Carl F. Auerbach. "Deconstructing the Essential Father." *American Psychologist* 54, no. 6 (June 1999): 397–407.

Skolnick, Arlene S. and Jerome H. Skolnick, eds. *Family in Transition: Rethinking Marriage, Sexuality, Child Rearing, and Family Organization.* Glenview, Ill: Scott, Foresman and Co., 1995.

Smothers, Ronald. "Accord Lets Gay Couples Adopt Jointly." *New York Times* (18 December 1997): 134.

Solinger, Rickie. *Wake Up Little Suzie: Single Pregnancy and Race Before Roe v. Wade.* New York: Routledge, 1992.

Sorensen, Elaine and Ariel Halpern. "Child Support Is Working Better Than We Think." *New Federalism Series*, no. A-31. Washington, D.C.: Urban Institute, 1999. http://newfederalism.urban.org/html/anf_31.html (accessed 14 February 2000).

Spain, Daphne, and Suzanne M. Bianchi. *Balancing Act: Motherhood, Marriage and Employment Among American Women*. New York: Russell Sage Foundation, 1996.

Spalter-Roth, Roberta M., Heidi I. Hartmann, and Linda M. Andrews. "Mothers, Children, and Low-Wage Work: The Ability to Earn a Family Wage." In *Sociology and the Public Agenda*, edited by William Julius Wilson, 316–38. London: Sage, 1993.

Stacey, Judith. "Dada-ism in the 1990s: Getting Past Baby Talk about Fatherlessness." In *Lost Fathers: The Politics of Fatherlessness in America*, edited by Cynthia R. Daniels. New York: St. Martin's Griffin, 1998.

———. "Gay and Lesbian Families: Queer Like Us." In *All Our Families: New Policies for a New Century*, edited by Mary Ann Mason, Arlene Skolnick, and Stephen D. Sugarman, 117–43. New York: Oxford University Press, 1998.

———. *In the Name of the Family*. Boston: Beacon Press, 1996.

———. "The New Family Values Crusaders." *The Nation* 259, no. 44 (1994): 119–22.

Stack, Carol. *All Our Kin*. New York: Harper and Row, 1975.

Staveteig, Sarah, and Alyssa Wigton. "Key Findings by Race and Ethnicity: Findings from the National Survey of Families." *Snapshots of America's Family II: 1999 Results*. Washington, D.C.: Urban Institute, 2002. http://newfederalism.urban.org/nsaf/race-ethnicity.html (accessed 28 January 2002).

Stone, Lawrence. *The Family, Sex, and Marriage in England, 1500–1800*. New York: Harper and Row, 1979.

Struening, Karen. "Feminist Challenges to the New Familialism: Lifestyle Experimentation and the Freedom of Intimate Association." *Hypatia* 11, no. 1 (Winter 1996): 135–54.

———. "Privacy and Sexuality in a Society Divided Over Moral Culture." *Political Research Quarterly* 49, no. 3 (1996): 505–23.

———. "Family Purposes: An Argument against the Promotion of Family Uniformity." *Policy Studies Journal* 27, no. 3 (1999): 477–493.

Sugarman, Stephen D. "Single-Parent Families." In *All Our Families*, edited by Mary Ann Mason, Arlene Skolnick, and Stephen D. Sugarman. Oxford: Oxford University Press, 1998.

Sugrue, Thomas J. "Poor Families in an Era of Urban Transformation: The 'Underclass' Family in Myth and Reality." In *American Families: A Multicultural Reader*, edited by Stephanie Coontz with Maya Parson and Gabrielle Raley. New York: Routledge, 1999.

Sunstein, Cass R., ed. *Feminism and Political Theory*. Chicago: Chicago University Press, 1990.

Taylor, Robert Joseph et al. "Recent Demographic Trends in African American Family Structure." In *Family Life in Black America*, edited by Robert Joseph Taylor, James S. Jackson, and Linda Chatters, 14–62. Thousand Oaks, Calif.: Sage, 1997.

Taylor, Robert Joseph, James S. Jackson, and Linda Chatters, eds. *Family Life in Black America*. Thousand Oaks, Calif.: Sage, 1997.

Thorne, Barrie, with Marilyn Yalom. *Rethinking the Family: Some Feminist Questions*. Boston: Northeastern University Press, 1992.

Tribe, Laurence H. *American Constitutional Law*. Mineola, N.Y.: Foundation Press, 1978.

Tronto, Joan C. *Moral Boundaries: A Political Argument for an Ethics of Care*. New York: Routledge, 1993.

Tucker, Belinda M., and Robert Joseph Taylor. "Gender, Age and Marital Status as Related to Romantic Involvement among African American Singles." In *Family Life in Black America*, edited by Robert Joseph Taylor, James S. Jackson, and Linda Chatters, 79–94. Thousand Oaks, Calif.: Sage, 1997.

Turetsky, Vicki. *Realistic Child Support Policies for Low Income Fathers*. Washington, D.C.: Center for Law and Social Policy, 2000. http://www.clasp.org/pubs/childrenforce/kellogg.htm (accessed 28 January 2002).

U.S. Bureau of the Census. *America's Families and Living Arrangements: Population Characteristics, 2000, P20-537*. U.S Department of Commerce, Economics and Statistics Administration. Washington, D.C., June 2001.

———. *Fertility of American Women: June 1998, P20-526*. U.S. Department of Commerce, Economics and Statistics Administration. Washington, D.C., 1998.

———. *Household and Family Characteristics: March 1998, P20-509*. U.S. Department of Commerce, Economics and Statistics Administration. Washington, D.C., 1998.

———. *Marital Status and Living Arrangements: March 1996, P20-496*. U.S. Department of Commerce, Economics and Statistics Administration. Washington, D.C., 1998.

———. *Statistical Abstract of the United States: 119th Edition*. Washington, D.C., 1999.

U.S. Department of Health and Human Services. *HHS Fact Sheet: Promoting Responsible Fatherhood, 2001*. Washington, D.C., 2001. http://www.hhs.gov/news/press/2001pres/01fsfatherhood.html (accessed 16 January 2002).

———. *HHS Fatherhood Initiative: Improving Opportunities for Low-Income Fathers*. Washington, D.C., 2000. http://fatherhood.hhs.gov/fi-prog.htm (accessed 28 January 2002).

Vandivere, Sharon, Kristin Anderson Moore, and Martha Zaslow. "Children's Family Environment: Findings from the National Survey of America's Families." *Snapshots of America's Families II: 1999*. Washington, D.C.: Urban Institute, 2000. http://newfederalism.urban.org/nsaf/family-environ.html (accessed 28 January 2002).

Wall Street Journal, January 1996.

Walsh, Froma, ed. *Normal Family Processes*. New York: Guilford Press, 1993.

Walzer, Michael. *Spheres of Justice*. New York: Basic Books, 1993.

Warren, Samuel, and Louis Brandeis, "The Right of Privacy," *Harvard Law Review* 4, no. 193 (1890).

Weiss, Penny, and Marilyn Friedman, eds. *Feminism and Community*. Philadelphia: Temple University Press, 1995.

Wertheimer, Richard, Justin Jager, and Kristin Anderson Moore. "State Policy Initiatives for Reducing Teen and Adult Nonmarital Childbearing: Family Planning to Family Caps." *New Federalism: Issues and Options for States*, Series A, no. A-43. Washington, D.C.: Urban Institute, 2000. http://newfederalism.urban.org (accessed 3 January 2000).

Weston, Kath. *Families We Choose: Lesbians, Gays, Kinship*. New York: Columbia University, 1991.

Whitehead, Barbara Dafoe. "Dan Quayle Was Right." *The Atlantic* 271, no. 4 (1993): 47–84.

———. *The Divorce Culture: Rethinking Our Commitments to Marriage and Family*. New York: Vintage, 1996.

———. "The Divorce Trap." *New York Times* (13 January 1997).

Wilson, James Q. *The Moral Sense*. New York: Free Press, 1993.

Wilson, William Julius. *The Transformation of Work*. Chicago: University of Chicago Press, 1987.

———. *When Work Disappears: The World of the New Urban Poor*. New York: Vintage Books, 1996.

Wilson, William Julius, ed. *Sociology and the Public Agenda*. London: Sage, 1993.

Wittig, Monique. "One is Not Born a Woman." In *The Second Wave*, edited by Linda Nicholson, 265–71. New York: Routledge, 1997.

Women's Committee of 100/Proposal 2002. *An Immodest Proposal: Rewarding Women's Work to End Poverty*. Copy on file with author.

Young, Iris Marion. "Making Single Motherhood Normal." *Dissent* 41, no. 1 (Winter 1994): 88–93.

———. "Mothers, Citizenship, and Independence: A Critique of Pure Family Values." *Ethics* 105 (April 1995): 535–56.

———. "Reflections on Families in the Age of Murphy Brown: On Gender, Justice, and Sexuality." In *Revisioning the Political: Feminist Reconstructions of Traditional Concepts in Western Political Thought,* edited by Nancy J. Hirshmann and Christine Di Stefano. Boulder, Colo.: Westview Press, 1996.

Index

About the Author

Karen Struening earned a Ph.D. in political science from Boston University. She taught in the Department of Political Science at Kalamazoo College from 1991 to 1998. Recently, she has taught political theory and feminist theory at Barnard College, Eugene Lang College at New School University, and Sarah Lawrence College. Her articles on the right of privacy and family policy have appeared in *Hypatia: A Journal of Feminist Philosophy*; *Women and Politics*; *Political Research Quarterly*; and *Policy Studies Journal*.